The Nanny Time Bomb

The Nanny Time Bomb

Navigating the Crisis in Child Care

Jacalyn S. Burke

Foreword by
Dr. Karen Kaufman, PhD, LCSW

 PRAEGER™

An Imprint of ABC-CLIO, LLC
Santa Barbara, California • Denver, Colorado

Library of Congress Cataloging-in-Publication Data

Burke, Jacalyn S., author.
   The nanny time bomb : navigating the crisis in child care / Jacalyn S. Burke; foreword by Dr. Karen Kaufman.
      pages cm
   Includes bibliographical references and index.
   ISBN 978-1-4408-3521-6 (alk. paper)—ISBN 978-1-4408-3522-3 (ebook) 1.   Nannies—United States. 2.   Child care—United States. 3.   Child welfare—United States. 4.   Discrimination against caregivers—United States. I. Title.
   HQ778.63B87 2016
   649'.10973—dc23   2015029443

ISBN: 978-1-4408-3521-6
EISBN: 978-1-4408-3522-3

20 19 18 17 16   1 2 3 4 5

This book is also available on the World Wide Web as an eBook.
Visit www.abc-clio.com for details.

Praeger
An Imprint of ABC-CLIO, LLC

ABC-CLIO, LLC
130 Cremona Drive, P.O. Box 1911
Santa Barbara, California 93116-1911

This book is printed on acid-free paper ∞
Manufactured in the United States of America

To all of the children currently experiencing nonparental child care and, in particular, to all of the children I have had the privilege of caring for.

Mission: This book is not a debate about whether mothers should go back to work or not. It is not a new thesis on child psychology. It is not an attack on nannies or working parents. *The Nanny Time Bomb* is a call for the universal reform of the U.S. child care industry. It exposes the failure of successive governments to protect working parents—the bedrock of our economy—and their children as well as our fellow citizens and nannies—the ones who enable parents to work—from potential abuse in an unlicensed industry.

Disclaimer: *The Nanny Time Bomb* is based entirely on the observations and interviews conducted by the author—a working nanny in Manhattan for over 10 years. Books and other publications quoted in this book do not necessarily reflect the opinion of the author. *The Nanny Time Bomb* does not contain or relate any incidents, facts, experiences, or personal information pertaining to the families with whom the author worked.

Contents

Foreword *by Dr. Karen Kaufman*   xi

Acknowledgments   xv

Introduction: My Story   xvii

Chapter 1. Why a Time Bomb? Risk Factors   1
    The Intrinsic Needs of Infants   2
    An Unlicensed Industry   8
    Conflicted Parents   16
    Frustrated Kids   19

Chapter 2. Nanny Archetypes: The Lottery of Trust   25
    The Good Nanny   25
    The Not-So-Good Nanny   30
    The Criminal Nanny   38

Chapter 3. The Work: Intimate Yet Invisible   47
    Hustling and Job Creep   47
    Denial and Sabotage   53
    Surrogates   62

Chapter 4. Child Care's Caste System: Stratification   67
    Mary Poppins: Myth and Fact   67
    Mammy: Slavery's Legacy   76
    Parallel Lives: Hidden Workers   83

Chapter 5. Hostage Takers: When the Time Bomb Goes Off   95
           When Nannies Become Killers: Shock, Collective
           Disassociation, and Aftermath   95
           Nanny Trapped: Guilt, Coercion, and Passive-Aggressive
           Behavior   100
           The 1 Percent: Privilege, Power, Pay   107

Chapter 6. Avoid a Time Bomb Now: Preventing the Unthinkable   115
           Prevention: Profiling Good Nannies, Deterring Bad
           Nannies   115
           Surveillance: Nanny Cams, Discovery, Action   128
           Management: Transforming Performance, Training,
           and Revisiting Day Care   135

Chapter 7. Child Care Reform: The Three Keys   151
           Wages and Taxes   151
           Immigration Reform   162
           Federal Reform   168
           A Proposal   172

Notes   177

Bibliography   185

Resources   189

Experts Interviewed for This Book   193

Index   195

Foreword

My first contact with Jacalyn was in 2006. She contacted me after reading an article I had written for *Big Apple Parent,* a free periodical that is circulated in New York City and the surrounding suburbs, on the subject of nannies and child care. In the article "Who's in Charge? Nanny's Not You," I wrote about my growing concerns about child care based on observations in my clinical work with children, parents, and adults who as children were left behind in their countries of origin by mothers who were employed as nannies in the United States.

I took great interest in Jacalyn's project because the subject is of critical importance in our society, and it was my impression that there could be no better person to document her observations and experiences than an intelligent, astute writer who was employed as a nanny.

She is an excellent reporter and covers many perspectives on the subject in a most comprehensive book: the state of child care in different parts of the country, parents' needs and expectations, nannies' backgrounds and emotional burdens they may bring to the job, and warning signs that parents should heed in hiring a nanny or continuing the employment of a nanny, along with the complexities of these relationships. This book is a must-read for prospective parents in addition to those already involved in the world of child care.

Jacalyn and I had lively conversations on the subject of what we identified as a child care crisis and shared many similar observations. Although our work is very different, we had both seen young children who suffered with anxiety because they had too much power in their households, despite appearing to relish the role of dictator; depressed children who felt abandoned by their parents, since it was the nanny who was present for school functions, medical visits, haircuts, playdates, and meals; and parents who overcompensated in the brief periods of time they shared with their children and could not parent effectively or consistently.

In addition, I worked with adults who were left behind as young children in the Caribbean or Central America when their mothers came to the United States for better employment opportunities. While they were aware that money was sent home to improve their lives, they missed being nurtured and raised by their own mothers, who were caring for the children of strangers. They struggled with depression and low self-esteem and had difficulty forming adult attachments.

For a country that values its children, the state of child care in the United States is dismal. On the spectrum, it may be inconsistent at best and dangerous at worst. The choices may appear plentiful, but whether it is day care, an in-home babysitter or nanny live-in or live-out, an au pair from another part of the country or the world with legal residency and reported wages or an undocumented worker who is paid cash, it all adds to the confusion about the best choice for a particular family. Jacalyn explores the views of experts in the field of child development and the possibilities for future regulations in the child care industry.

Well-meaning parents are typically unsuspecting of the risks confronting them when they introduce an employee into their homes. Jacalyn describes this beautifully and succinctly in the first few sentences of the introduction. But the simplicity of the description of how easily a caregiver gains access to every aspect of the home and the parents' personal lives in addition to the care of the children is chilling.

References may be called and background checks may be passed, but the nanny also brings her personal circumstances to work with her each day: sorrow over not being present to raise her own children, uncertainty as to when she will even see her children, loss of her own family supports, financial hardship, feeling marginalized and in the shadows in our society as an undocumented worker, or being mistreated or overworked by the employers who do not recognize that she needs time off for her own care and personal needs and see their own endless demands of her as just one more small favor. She may draw the children to her as if they are her own in the absence of her own children, thereby complicating the relationships with the parents. And soon enough as the children grow older, they will remind her that she is not their mother, adding to her sadness and grief.

While styles of child rearing and discipline have changed significantly in the past century, every school of thought in psychology and psychoanalysis emphasizes the quality of care in infancy and early childhood as the foundation upon which healthy adult relationships are built. This care must include consistency, attunement to the child's needs, physical and emotional availability, empathy, and the ability to soothe a child so that this becomes an internalized strength, giving the child the ability to regulate feelings and self-soothe when faced with distress. This is the foundation of healthy self-esteem and self-worth.

Jacalyn's observations are both heartening and terrifying at the same time. There are many devoted and loving nannies who care deeply for their charges. And there are many who should not be employed as caregivers. Parents are not always the best interviewers, since they are often under great pressure to return to work after a baby's birth or have had their child care arrangement interrupted. It is difficult to be objective when they desperately want to find the right caregiver, and so they may project many positive qualities onto the candidate with little or no documented information to support their hopes. Wishful thinking and projection should never be factors in hiring the person being put in charge of a baby or young child.

The Nanny Time Bomb is the beginning of a much-needed conversation on the subject of quality child care. It is a complex issue that varies with each family's personal needs and style, with no simple solutions; there is no one-size-fits-all remedy. But it is a critical conversation in which to participate. Nannies, mental health clinicians, pediatricians, and extended family often see the symptoms and consequences of poor matches with child care arrangements. Many parents sigh with great relief at the point in their children's development when they are less dependent on caregivers; the parents feel as if they have survived a long walk through a minefield. With all of the responsibilities, demands, and surprises inherent in parenthood, relieving the stress of child care uncertainties would replenish many parents and give them more energy and time to enjoy their children.

Dr. Karen Kaufman, PhD, LCSW

Acknowledgments

I'd like to thank my parents Martin and Dorothy Burke for always teaching me to do the right thing. I owe a huge debt of gratitude to my long-supportive partner, Kate Fitzgerald, for granting me the space, time, and resources to complete this book. I want to thank my almost to last employer CK for cheering me on to the finishing line. I wish to sincerely thank Karen Kaufman, a busy professional who believed in my book from day one and in numerous subtle ways made me dig deeper into the subject of child care. I owe much to my agent Maryann Karinch, a woman of vision who believed in the project from the beginning and saw it to a publishing contract; to my proposal's editor, JL, for her extraordinary skills with the pen; and finally to Hilary Claggett, my editor at Praeger, for her patience and focus.

Introduction

Within 24 hours I can have the keys to your home and access to your computer, your identity, your bank details, your car, and your child. I can accomplish all of this by providing ID and one or two references. I'm the nanny.

Despite the infamy of Mary Poppins, most British girls—indeed most little girls—don't dream of becoming a nanny when they grow up. I was no exception.

For as long as I could remember, the center of the world had always been New York. I watched *King Kong* and episodes of *Harold Lloyd* over and over again just to relish a glimpse of the city's skyline. It took me a long time to actually travel to New York, 26 years in fact, but eventually I did. The second I arrived, I knew that I had in some sense *come home.* I didn't find pavements glittering in diamonds, but I did end up working among New York's elite—and that was the next best thing.

Like most immigrants, I quickly had to find ways to make ends meet. Despite popular perception, there are few employment options in America if one doesn't have connections or a semblance of a profession. In my case writing was my passion, but I had no substantive publishing history. I was awful at waiting on tables and even more disastrous at mixing drinks. As luck would have it, opportunities arose with friends and friends of friends to, as Americans put it, *watch their children.*

Small children, like animals, can sense fear or fakes. In me, they detected a kindred spirit despite my "weird" accent. At night I instinctively closed closet doors and plugged in every nightlight because strange beasts might be lurking in the shadows. I skillfully engaged in spontaneous sword fights with five-year-old Knights Templars. I transported myself on the backs of dragons (in reality a sofa) into enchanted kingdoms. Above all else, I realized that I could still see what children saw. I didn't have a magic carpetbag. I didn't fly through the clouds singing "A Spoonful of Sugar." But somehow by the age of 40, I had become a sort of Mary Poppins.

One of the things I enjoyed doing with children was drawing cartoons. It's a useful nanny skill to have on rainy days. My artistic abilities also enabled me to pave a legitimate path to residency. I began to exhibit solo and group cartoon shows in New York. Before long, I had achieved enough exposure to apply for and be awarded an O-1 art visa. Contemporary cartoonists were generous in regard to my abilities, and before long I had acquired some worthy press clippings and a good reputation. In 2010, I petitioned for and was awarded permanent residency: a green card. I was deliriously happy.

Other nannies congratulated me and said, "Now you can be whatever you want in America. You don't have to be a nanny any more." Yet I continued to work on as a nanny, stuck in an intoxicating web of relationships and experiences. It was a rich subculture, and it fascinated me.

One neighborhood I first worked in was Tribeca. The average hourly rate among nannies was $10–12 per hour in 2005, and the nannies themselves were extremely diverse. They came from all over the world. Being gregarious, I quickly made friends.

Simone[1] was a naturalized U.S. citizen originally from Jamaica. Immigrants often gravitate to one another to share their experiences, and we instantly bonded. Simone earned $12 an hour looking after twin three-year-old boys. Her own children lived with her elderly mother in the Caribbean. Simone was committed to sending her mother as much money as possible and scrimped and saved every cent. She even shared a room with a cousin in Queens to make her money stretch further, despite their problematic relationship. In complete contrast, Simone's employers were Wall Street traders who enjoyed many luxuries, including living in a gorgeous penthouse and owning a beach house—not a crime in itself.

But Simone was deeply unhappy. She regretted her decision to move to America and leave her family behind, and she resented the wealth that her charges enjoyed compared to her own children. As a consequence, Simone referred to them as "spoiled" and expressed her displeasure in numerous unpleasant ways.

Simone's charges were still enjoying the stage of discovery, and they often left a trail of mess. At home, they'd turn their toy boxes upside down looking for a favorite truck. Outside, they'd search for puddles to jump in, mounds of dirty snow to climb over, and sodden leaves to kick up. They'd impulsively run into the apartment with muddy shoes to greet their pet dog.

The boys were not unusually naughty. They were typical three-year-olds. Simone, however, began to find their actions inexcusable. One day she told me that the cleaner had been let go. Allegedly, Simone's employers had wanted to tighten their belts in a depressed economy. It was felt that with a full-time nanny at home, a cleaner was superfluous. In Simone's eyes this was yet another example of how cheap her employers were. Thus, under a new invisible pressure to keep a large apartment clean, she hounded the boys and made their lives a misery. This—I marked—was her tipping point.

Simone had always appeared strict and fastidious with regard to rudimentary childhood things such as making messes and causing accidents, but as the months wore on she began to administer unnecessary and prolonged time-outs. One afternoon one of the children accidentally soiled himself with juice, and Simone exploded. "Why do you always do that? You just want to make work for me!" It felt like a storm that had come out of nowhere.

"It's no big deal," I countered. "Kids his age often have accidents. I'll change him." But Simone was insulted by my interference, and I was asked to leave. After that she wouldn't speak to me, although we frequently saw one another in the neighborhood. In Simone's eyes, I had crossed an invisible line of allegiance.

It was my first real brush with the more negative side of unlicensed child care, but unfortunately it wouldn't be my last.

During this time, child development books helped shape my theoretic outlook on child care. I quickly adopted Dr. Stanley Greenspan's child-centric perspective that encourages a calculated schedule of nurturance, floor time, downtime, and direct interaction. But I gained the most valuable insights by observing other nannies. One such nanny was Mercy, a woman in her 60s from the islands.

Mercy was like a grandmother to the younger nannies. She had skin as dark as an eggplant, and though religious, she never preached or judged others. She had spent over 30 years working as a housekeeper/nanny to various families in New York. A tender smile broke on her lips as she reminisced: "I done raised 18 children in this country." It was said in genuine pride.

On warm summer afternoons, I would seek out Mercy in her safe haven beneath a broad weathered oak tree in the local park. Her lips would often be moving, either in hymn or prayer. Her eyes lovingly tracked the child in her care, a gangly eight-year-old girl called Alice.

Alice was the only child of two middle-aged lawyers, a highly prized heir produced by countless fertility treatments. She was indulged by adoring parents and her nanny. To everyone in her life, Alice was a miracle child.

As Mercy liked to say over and over again, "When first me held that child, she was just this little pink bundle of crying. Boy, did she cry! But who can blame her? Her mommy she had to go back to work, you know; this country makes it hard to be a parent and successful. And the child, she sad. She cry, cry, cry all day long. I rocked that baby and I sing to her, you understand? I held her to my heart and I say, 'Mercy ain't going to leave you, sweet baby girl.' And she ate up all that loving. She settle down after a while."

Now a precocious third grader, Alice had become a fussy child. She would constantly demand things from Mercy and test her patience. "Why do you let her talk to you like that?" I asked. Mercy would just sigh. "It's not her fault. She has the whole world, and she has nothing. My own kids, they know who I am. I made sure when they was little, I was home. I worked at night. My husband he worked all day. We work it out. This little girl, she get everything she ask for but not what she wants. So she sad, real sad, and that make her angry. I know she hurting. She tell me every night, 'Don't go home Mercy, stay with me.' I know the child's heart. I pray for her."

One day Mercy went missing. I looked for her in all of our familiar haunts. It was a few weeks later when I spied Alice in the street, furiously charging ahead of a younger woman. I called over to them. The woman stopped and introduced herself. She was Alice's new tutor nanny, she informed me, emphasizing the word "tutor."

"Come on!" Alice ordered, roughly tugging the nanny's sleeve.

"Alice!" I interjected. "Wait a minute. Is Mercy sick?"

Alice's glazed eyes met mine. I watched her jaws clench. "Of course not!" She tossed her nanny a dirty look. "I got a new babysitter—her!" The young woman smiled weakly.

"I don't understand. Where's Mercy?" I asked.

Alice shrugged. "She had to go look after some baby. My mom told me. I'm too big for her now, so I got a new babysitter. She's American." With that, Alice tugged her apologetic caregiver down the street.

I called Mercy later that day after getting her number from a mutual friend. She was too upset to talk about it in detail, but she said, "Jackie, as God is my witness, they call me in early one day, while Alice is in school, and the mother, she tell me, 'Oh Mercy, you know, you just like family to us. But we feel Alice need someone more, you know, *academic*. It's nothing personal, just time to move on.' She just say it like that. She gives me an envelope with a week's pay and she tell me, 'You don't have to work this week. You can go. It's better that Alice don't see you no more. You understand, don't you?' And the husband, he looks to the ground. He don't say a word. I was shocked, Jackie. I didn't know what to say. I just leave. I feel like my heart is smashed to pieces. I don't understand these people."

I never saw Mercy again. I called her many months later, but the number was not in service. The last I heard, she had finally *gone back home* to retire in a small family house in the islands. As one island nanny put it, "You know Mercy, how hard she work, she just want to go back home and sit down a while in the sun."

Mercy brought many gifts to Alice's life, to my life, and to the lives of innumerable others. She taught me devotional child care—the kind that grants you the extra patience to attend to a child's every need, no matter how small. She showed me the enduring power of love in the face of challenging behavior. Mercy was a wise and loyal caregiver. Her nurturance was a warm and gentle river for Alice to swim down. But she was also Alice's anchor. In Alice's eyes, *she* was Mercy's baby. They had exchanged a silent promise thousands of times over in the quiet of Alice's nursery, and now that promise had been broken.

A conflict began to arise in me. I knew that the trust invested in some nannies by working parents was being violated. On a weekly basis I witnessed apathetic behavior by burned-out or resentful nannies. Yet I had also gained entry into a secret sisterhood of women who cared for other people's children for money. This gave me a window into the trials and tribulations that many nannies suffered in the course of their working lives. I became a confidante, privy to the innermost thoughts and beliefs, of a vast variety of caregivers: undocumented and documented, part-time and full-time, loving nannies and purposefully mean nannies.

I saw a clear correlation between a nanny's supposed grievances and the types of care she offered. I witnessed the most blatant acts of disrespect perpetrated against nannies by employers, and I observed the consequences. Gradually a bigger picture emerged: the child care industry is an outdated system based on depressed wages, unspoken grievances, and unfair demands. The consequences of this are dramatically visited upon our most vulnerable children.

Ultimately, I realized that there was a nanny hierarchy. Sometimes I had more in common with New York moms than I did with foreign nannies. I could hold my own at Hampton pool parties if I wore the right shoes. The simple fact that I was white and British opened doors to me, doors that seemed closed to other types of nannies and babysitters. I was also frequently mistaken as the mother of the child I took care of—*even if the* child belonged to a different racial group. Unlike women of color, I did not wear the job on my skin.

Despite society's best efforts, segregation along lines of race and class continues. It can be seen most clearly at events where people are indiscriminately thrown together such as a child's birthday party, where in the hustle and bustle of a celebration there will be two very distinct groups. At one end of the room, parents are socializing, drinking, and noisily catching up. At the other end of the room, nannies sit, often sullenly, counting time, looking bored or, even worse, invisible. Catering staff serving hors d'oeuvres might circle around them. Perhaps no one would offer to take their coats.

At times like these, I felt genuinely conflicted. Where should I sit? Who should I talk to? It was a more complex issue than simply one economic or racial group dominating another. For example, among the affluent parents there might be African Americans, Hispanics, or Asians present. Sometimes nannies self-segregated, making it awkward for others to interact with them. At other times it was clear that parents reinforced this segregation, albeit subconsciously. I walked from one group to the other as easily as I crossed the room, but each time I did, I imagined the other group's eyes on my back.

In 2009 I began a blog called The Nanny Time Bomb, penned under the alias of Nanny X. The blog became a constructive outlet for my observations as a nanny. Suddenly I had found a voice, but was it really mine? Nanny X did not clock off. Instead, she read Google news alerts about nannies and followed child care debates. Nanny X interviewed *New York Times* best-selling authors, and The Nanny Time Bomb began to rise in popularity. Over time, Nanny X's crusades became mine. Had I come here to become a child care advocate? What had happened to *my* American Dream?

Finally, when the Krim double homicide occurred, I knew that I could no longer remain silent. It was time to come out. It's one thing to blog about the problems inherent in the child care industry. It is quite another to remain silent over the mistreatment of children.

The Nanny Time Bomb: Navigating the Crisis in Child Care is an account not just of my personal descent but also of the psychological plunge that countless nannies, parents, and innocent children are taking in America everyday. Things in child care must change, because if they don't, I fear that the bombs will just keep on detonating.

Chapter 1

Why a Time Bomb? Risk Factors

Time bomb (noun): A process or procedure causing a problem that will eventually become dangerous if not addressed; an environmental time bomb.

Webster's Dictionary

Today I witnessed something that goes to the very heart of this book. I have seen this type of behavior often, to the point that it no longer seems extraordinary.

I watched a nanny enter a communal playroom with a toddler. Without looking at him or speaking a word, she methodically pulled him from his stroller and removed his jacket. A toy—a small teddy bear—was yanked from his hand and put away into the diaper bag. He immediately began to cry, reaching out desperately for his fluffy animal—probably something he took from his crib that morning. The nanny sat down and turned her chair away from him. She began to eat her egg muffin while texting on a phone. The boy fell to the floor and began to sob. Finally after a few minutes of whimpering he got up and approached his caregiver. He laid a hand on her lap, but she brushed it off.

"Go play!"

She gave her order without giving him a second glance. Dejected, the child wandered off and aimlessly picked up a book from the floor. Sadness was etched in his face and demonstrated in a slouched posture. Throughout the hour that followed, the nanny did not look up from her phone. In turn, while the little boy periodically looked in her direction, he did not gaze for long. He understood that his nanny was not available to him and that he was on his own. I estimate that he was around 24 months old. He's not alone in his experience.

Right now there are infants snacking on fast food to the backdrop of adult daytime TV; on the high street little babies are sitting mute for hours in a stroller as their nannies window shop, and in a myriad of New York City playgrounds toddlers are pottering about aimlessly as their nannies check their e-mail.

These unfortunate though often affluent children may never enjoy a tender moment or read a book with their nanny. In fact, they may rarely get to play a game or cuddle with her. Their most consistent interaction with this type of caregiver will be one of gruff commands, of rough handling, of profound emotional neglect.

Most hardworking parents *trust* that they've chosen the right nanny. But what if that nanny is consistently neglecting or mistreating their children? How can parents tell? What are the intrinsic needs of infants, and why is child care's so-called good enough care possibly failing them? Conversely, can parents contribute to an environment of poor performance? How can this affect a nanny's caregiving abilities? Are nannies being overworked, underpaid, and generally unprotected as employees? Are families being rendered powerless to efficiently protect their children from criminals or mentally unstable persons? In my 10 years of working as a nanny, I have come to believe that both are so.

THE INTRINSIC NEEDS OF INFANTS

According to Daniel Goleman, "The first three or four years in life are a period when the toddler's brain grows about two-thirds its full size and evolves in complexity at a greater rate than it ever will again. During this period key kinds of learning take place more readily than later in life—emotional learning foremost among them."[1]

Our newborn infants enter the world with unparalleled physical and emotional vulnerability. New parents are often overwhelmed and exhausted, concerned with the essentials: Is my baby thriving, is he eating enough, is she normal? Hidden from sight is the baby's raw emotional body, a rich network of neurons and nerves all firing simultaneously. It is in this fragile exposed state that our children are often passed, in as little as a few weeks, to a relative stranger for care.

Our baby cannot comprehend that the periods of time spent with his mother and his caregiver are regulated, that there is an undercurrent of stability and routine. He lives moment to moment gripped by a primal concern for survival. If his caregiver is a kind, attentive, loving person, our infant will respond to her soothing and settle down to a schedule. If our nanny is an impulsive, disengaged, negative, or perfunctory caregiver, our infant will feel threatened to the point of possible disassociation.

We understand that our babies are helpless, unable to feed themselves or keep themselves clean. What is often overlooked is that our infants are equally unable to self-soothe and regulate their emotions. Our baby has no sense of self, and her only model is the attachment she shares with her primary caregivers: parents, nanny, or day care worker. If that attachment figure is not available or is unpredictable or negative, our infant will fail to develop a healthy sense of self. All of these hidden developmental stages are regulatory processes learned from others, and its currency is emotional intelligence.

Scientists now understand that emotional intelligence, or EQ, can only be taught human to human. EQ is imparted through attunement, that is, by being in sync with an infant's emotions. Being in tune means letting a baby/ child know that her or his emotional state has been understood, comprehended, and acknowledged by the caregiver. It is demonstrated in a hug, a soft word, a lullaby, a smile, a gentle kiss, a warmed bottle of milk, or an invitation to play. These are the natural actions of loving parents. It is what babies need in order to thrive.

With repeated attunement, an infant discovers that those around him or her can understand his or her feelings. At around eight months old infants recognize that they are separate from their parents/caregiver, and this recognition continues to evolve through intimate relationships with others, such as siblings, relatives, friends, and associates. This is the seed of self-consciousness—the intrinsic idea of self.

What does this require from a nanny? According to T. Berry Brazelton and Stanley I. Greenspan's *The Irreducible Needs of Children,* it involves

one or two primary caregivers who remain in a steady, intimate relationship with that child. . . . There should be no time, other than when they are sleeping, that they [children] are out of sight of caregivers. No more than one-third of infants', toddlers', and preschoolers' time should be spent in fully independent activities [playing by themselves]. . . . The other two-thirds or longer time should be spent between two types of activities: those in which the caregivers facilitate interactions with the environment and direct interaction, such as cuddling, holding, shared pretend play, and funny face games. Infants and toddlers need at least four or more 20-minute or longer periods of direct interactive time. Preschoolers need at least three of these direct interactive play opportunities. . . . In the first three years, no more than one half hour per day should be spent watching TV.[2]

In 2005, *Newsweek* magazine ran an article titled "Your Baby's Brain." It featured the groundbreaking research of leading scientists and psychologists, including Dr. Stanley I. Greenspan. Findings around emotional intelligence and its role in early childhood development were illuminating.

Andrew Meltzoff, a professor of psychology at the University of Washington, noted that "gaze-following" in children as young as 10 months old was not only a precursor for emotional and social intelligence but also a good predictor of potential language skills. For example, research showed that language develops more slowly in blind children and the children of depressed mothers where there is *little eye-to-eye, facial interaction.* It is not a stretch to substitute here a depressed or apathetic nanny.[3]

I have observed hopeful infants time and again peering up into the face of their caregiver. The looks are nonverbal, but what is being communicated is a plea to engage. "Look at me—I am here!" If a nanny is either too preoccupied to notice or make eye contact or is simply disinterested—indeed, some nannies are bothered by an infant's needs and will actively turn the stroller away or will move their own body away from the child—the opportunity to interact is broken, lost. It is heartbreaking to then see the face of the infant change. The child will have a sad, frozen expression or will slump and stare blankly out at the world. What has been profoundly communicated is that the child is not worthy of a caregiver's time. And over time the infant becomes compliant—or transforms into *an easy child*—a human being who does not attempt to get its needs met.

Parents who believe that stimulating bedroom materials, such as CDs and books, or activity classes will compensate for regular human engagement should be aware of a study that Patricia Kuhl, professor of speech and hearing at the University of Washington, conducted. Dr. Kuhl's original research over a decade earlier proved that very small babies have the unique ability to learn foreign languages. But time proved that playing tapes over the crib did not inspire millions of babies to pick up, say, Japanese or Russian. Why?

Dr. Kuhl discovered that infants needed emotional context, that is, a connection to another person who spoke Japanese or Russian. Tapes of another language were simply filtered out by the infants as "background noise." Dr. Kuhl concluded that "people—at least babies—need people to learn."[4]

Dr. Michael Goldstein, a psychologist at Cornell University, conducted a study involving two sets of babies and parents. One set of parents was instructed to give praise and encouragement randomly as their infants babbled. The other group was asked to specifically reward infants' language attempts with smiles and physical touch. The second group of infants was recorded as advancing faster than those who did not receive specific encouragement. Goldstein's research demonstrates that loving confirmation of a sound, mimicking a baby's gibberish, and correctly responding to a baby word empower an infant to try harder.[5]

Failure to attune successfully with an infant impedes that child's emotional and intellectual development. When a parent or nanny fails to show empathy with an infant's range of emotions (sadness, pain, joy) and respond appropriately (hugs, kisses, acts of elation), the infant will begin to avoid expressing those emotional states entirely. The consequence of this withdrawal isn't just experienced between the infant and the parent/nanny. It can be experienced in all intimate relationships and throughout a child's life. As Sue Gerhardt, a prominent British psychoanalyst and psychotherapist, asserts,

If we continue to insist on the primacy of production drawing all adults, including the parents of young children relentlessly into the pursuit of material goals and careers, then we may have to bear the emotional fall-out. Without attentive adults to protect their developing nervous systems, enabling children to develop into emotionally robust adults capable of meeting challenges and sustaining relationships, there is a price to pay.[6]

EQ is also an emotional evaluation of the exterior world—our social environment—resulting in an appropriate response to it. Key components appear to be self-control, endurance, objectivity, and motivation to make and maintain meaningful relationships. EQ enables humans to exercise empathy, an emotional state that generates altruism. This in turn leads to peaceful coexistence and tolerance.

EQ tools enable our children to make the best use of whatever genetic intelligence they inherit, like premium oil in a machine. Perhaps more vitally, it enables our children to have the ability to read other people's emotions correctly and to react or act in an appropriate manner. EQ cannot be downloaded like software. It is learned human behavior that processes over time. The importance of EQ during our babies' early years is crucial for their overall development.

In today's depressed child care climate, nannies can show up too tired or unmotivated to perform even the basics of what is required of them to impart regular, consistent emotional care and stimulation. The most common examples of dysfunctional, emotional relating are

- Ignoring (consistent failure to respond to the child's need for stimulation, nurturance, encouragement and protection or failure to acknowledge the child's presence);
- Rejecting (actively refusing to respond to the child's needs—e.g., refusing to show affection);
- Verbally assaulting (constant belittling, name calling, or threatening);
- Isolating (preventing the child from having normal social contacts with other children and adults);

- Terrorizing (threatening the child with extreme punishment or creating a climate of terror by playing on childhood fears); and
- Corrupting or exploiting (encouraging the child to engage in destructive, illegal, or antisocial behavior).[7]

There are times perhaps when many parents and nannies exhibit one or two of the above responses. However, in general, most of us strive to impart powerful lessons in empathy, self-control, and resolution when our children are upset. When parents are absent, it is vital that nannies step in to assist these children in verbalizing and analyzing what is disturbing them in order to help them reach a satisfying yet fair resolution. In addition, the manner in which a nanny resolves conflict can set a powerful example for a child. These are nonnegotiable skills that nannies should have. But conflict resolution and soothing are not the only needs infants have. There is a day-in, day-out, moment by moment interaction that must be felt consistently for a baby to develop normally—nay, to thrive.

In Sue Gerhardt's book *Why Love Matters,* the author explains that "according to Allan Schore, looking at faces has an even more powerful role to play in human life. Especially in infancy, these looks and smiles actually help the brain to grow. How does this work? Schore suggests that it is positive looks which are the most vital stimulus to the growth of the social, emotionally intelligent, brain."[8]

Gerhardt goes on to explore how exposure to a constant negative feed of angry, disinterested, or sad expressions is also stored in our baby's brain. This produces a biochemical response in the form of the stress hormone cortisol. Simultaneously, stress shuts down the production of endorphins and dopamine, hormones that help an infant feel safe and happy. Babies are totally reliant upon the adults in their life, and on a primitive level the infant brain equates negative interactions with a threatened survival.

One can only imagine the anxiety felt by a baby who senses that her caregiver resents her or blatantly fails to attend to her basic calls for help and comfort. Perhaps even more confusing is the daily switch over of care—the handover back for a few hours a day to those familiar loving people (the parents) at night.

Karen Kaufman, PhD, LCSW, has worked in the field of mental health for over 25 years. She currently works in a private practice with children and adults in Manhattan and Westchester County, New York. Kaufman has been a major contributor to this book and is an authority on the subject of child care, having been published in the *Clinical Social Work Journal,* the *Big Apple Parent,* and *Westchester Parent.* She has much to say about inconsistent caregiving:

When a nanny is employed during the mother's absences, it is critical that her style be as close to the mother's parenting style as possible. If the mother is loving and attuned to her baby's needs but the nanny is cold, distant, under great stress in her own life or simply disagrees with the mother's style, she will communicate differently with the baby, both in her physical handling and emotional responsiveness.[9]

Examples of a markedly different style of care given from a nanny would be

- Leaving a baby alone too long for periods of time when the baby is hungry, thirsty, and uncomfortable in soiled diapers.
- Withholding attention such as hugs, soothing, singing lullabies, or holding when a toddler or infant is in need of comfort.
- Using media to entertain or distract a toddler instead of interacting.
- Keeping a baby or toddler confined for long periods of time in a stroller with little to no interaction.
- Being preoccupied with her own (the nanny's) thoughts and personal life to the point that the infant's demands are viewed as an intrusion or an annoyance.

There are many reasons why a nanny might not give our infant what she or he needs. A nanny might be depressed, stressed, or resentful. She may not understand how complex a young child's needs are. We will explore some of the possible reasons for this in more detail later in this book. For now, it's important to understand that these types of behavior by a nanny now can have long-term effects.

Unlike intellectual pursuits or sporting activities, emotional caregiving never stops. It is a constant need as important to a baby as breathing. Our infant's emotional development isn't just dependent upon us as parents. It involves every person our child comes into contact with. Most important, it involves our child's nanny. This is why it is vital for parents to ensure that their child's nanny comprehends and displays emotional intelligence, that she is emotionally solvent and happy in her job—that she loves our baby. In other words, if our nanny is stressed out, overworked, or unhappy in her job, our baby will soak those feelings up like a sponge. As Sue Gerhardt states,

Parents [here we can substitute "nannies"] who are reluctant, stressed, hostile, absent or indifferent to their children won't be able to provide the kind of environment a baby needs for optimum development of his underlying emotional equipment. Their babies may be well fed and meet all their developmental milestones, they may even be cognitively "bright" if they receive other kinds of stimulation, but they may nevertheless develop poorly in an emotional sense.[10]

Are private in-home caregivers meeting the intrinsic needs of our infants? I think in truth a percentage are not. But it's important here to make *some distinctions* between nannies when we speak of nannies as a general group. Organizations such as the International Nanny Association (INA) as well as the better agencies and colleges do much to connect prospective parents to professional American nannies nationwide. Indeed, there is a great deal of pride among INA members and graduates as to what constitutes good child care. These nannies do not professionally identify with other groups of child care workers such as undocumented domestic workers. Nevertheless, many parents do not hire American child care professionals who are graduates, some holding master's degrees in early childhood development.

If the percentage of child care workers who were bad at their job nationally was as low as 1 percent it would be unacceptable, but I suspect that it is much higher and especially in large cities such as New York, where most parents do not seek or employ professional child care graduates—that is, nannies who specifically studied and attained undergraduate or graduate degrees in early childhood development. This is a fundamental flaw in modern child care practice. Unfortunately, there are others.

AN UNLICENSED INDUSTRY

A U.S. industry exists that generates possibly millions of dollars a year. It underreports taxes but is never audited by the Internal Revenue Service. The child care industry employs an estimated 1 million people a year, a substantial percentage of whom are undocumented foreign workers; however, neither the U.S. Citizenship and Immigration Services or/nor the Department of Homeland Security has a definitive idea of how many. This industry's primary service involves American children as young as newborn, but governmental child protective services are not concerned with screening the individuals charged with children's day-to-day care. Successive administrations have shown no desire in regulating this industry, and yet it functions at the very core of our society.

That industry is private in-home child care.

Statistics on private child care are impossible to come by precisely because it is an unlicensed market. According to the International Nanny Association, there are no concrete statistics for nannies in the United States. The Department of Labor can provide figures encompassing all domestic care workers, but the figures are not dissected into types of domestic care, such as senior caregivers, cleaners, housekeepers, gardeners, and nannies.

Au pairs, who are foreign-born young graduates, do have a governing agency—the Bureau of Educational and Cultural Affairs of the Department of State—in contrast to nannies as a whole, so we do actually have some statistics on them. There are approximately 12,000 au pairs working in the United States.

Here's what we know about nannies in general. According to the Bureau of Labor Statistics, the median annual wage for all 1,312,700 child care workers in May 2012 was $19,510. The projected percent change in employment from 2012 to 2022 for all child care workers' occupations is 14 percent.[11]

One of the top organizations to offer parents a comprehensive approach to good child care choices is the International Nanny Association. Here is its mission statement:

The International Nanny Association (INA), a nonprofit organization, serves as the umbrella organization for the in-home child care industry. INA members include nannies, nanny employers, nanny agencies, educators, and industry service providers. Since 1985, INA has worked to professionalize the industry by setting high standards for industry professionals and nanny agencies. INA leverages the expertise of industry professionals from around the globe to help increase awareness about the industry, to develop the professional skills of nannies, and to educate parents about the benefits of hiring a qualified nanny to care for their children.[12]

Every year the INA conducts a survey among its members and associates on subjects such as salary and benefits. In 2011 the INA polled a total of 817 workers.

Nanny Profile

- Responses were mostly split between Nannies (52%) and Nanny/ Household managers (42%); 5.3% were Specialty Nannies
- 70% of nannies work full-time
- 90% of nannies live outside their employer's home
- 71% of nannies have more than 5 years experience
- 85% of nannies have at least some college education
- 46% of those with college degrees majored in a child-related field
- Less than 7% of nannies have taken either of The Nanny Credential Exam (6.8%) or the INA Basic Skills Exam (6.6%)
- 6% of nannies have attended a Nanny school for nanny training
- 87% of nannies have CPR certification

- 80% of nannies have first aid certification
- 48% of nannies have maintained their INA membership

Nanny Pay

- 55% of nannies get paid hourly, 34% get paid weekly
- Based on stated and computed hourly rates, the average hourly rate for nannies is $17.44. The median rate is $16.
- 38% of nannies had a salary increase in 2011
- 53% of nannies received a year-end bonus in 2011
- 36% of nannies are not compensated for overtime
- 51% of the those compensated for overtime receive time and half pay
- 74% of those than travel as part of their job are compensated through coverage of all their expenses while traveling
- There were quite a few differences in the hourly rate based on particular nanny profile, but few were surprising
- Certain types of specialty nannies get paid more
- More tenure, more experience, and advanced degrees are associated with higher pay
- Couples where at least one doesn't work pay more for nanny care

Nanny Benefits

- 66% of nannies get paid holidays
- 64% of nannies get paid vacation (89% get 2 or more weeks)
- 47% of nannies get paid sick days
- 13% of nannies get full health insurance premium contribution
- 13% of nannies receive no benefits

Aspects of Nanny Job

- 88% of nannies do not provide overnight care
- 72% of nannies get paid when employer does not need them
- 74% of nannies do temporary assignments outside of their regular job
- 35% of nannies found their job using a local nanny placement agency
- 30% of nannies found their job using an online recruiting service
- 77% of nannies care for one (30%) or two (47%) children
- Even distribution across child age from infant through 12 years; the percent caring for preteens and teens is lower
- 15% of nannies care for multiples
- 11% of nannies care for special needs children

- 35% of nannies have children of their own
- Approximately 10% of nannies with children bring their child to work with them
- 76% of nannies have been with their current employer for less than three years; 43% less than one year
- More nannies with a job through an agency have written work agreements (78%) than those not placed by an agency (51%)
- 79% of nannies work for couples where both parents work
- 66% of employers withhold federal taxes from nanny pay
- 31% of nannies are paid through a payroll service
- 66% of nannies said they earn more than they did in 2008
- 13% of nannies said they earn less than they did in 2008

Ed Halteman, "2013 INA Salary and Benefits Survey," International Nanny Association, http://www.nanny.org/wp-content/uploads/2013/12/2013-INA-Salary-and-Benefits-Survey.pdf. Used by permission.

Some of the most interesting features of this survey are that the nannies themselves self-represent as *career nannies*. This indicates that they have chosen this vocation because they enjoy it, not because they couldn't find any other type of work. As a consequence, they typically attend seminars or conferences and take extra classes to supplement their knowledge base.[13]

These nannies have higher salaries as a group than other nannies, such as new immigrants and undocumented workers, especially if they develop skill sets that make them more attractive as employees in the child care market. Peak hourly rates tend to be paid to nannies who demonstrate job loyalty, although rates begin to dive after a nanny has been employed between 10 and 15 years, perhaps denoting fewer hours or different chores such as housekeeping. It's also worth noting that agency-placed nannies generally work under a negotiated contract or agreement and as such enjoy more worker benefits.

Aside from excellent organizations such as the INA, there is no federal central body governing nannies. There are a plethora of nanny organizations, agencies, and associations should one wish to join, but there is no obligation or mandate. None of these organizations provide universal protection of children other than advising parents to voluntarily engage with them in the organizations' programs.

The child care industry has also spawned a canon of self-help books by experienced working parents and nannies alike. These books prove very useful on a personal level, but none call for the industry to be regulated and nationally reformed.

Another Look at Child Care

Nannies are not all self-determined American professionals. Some nannies are students looking to make an extra buck or two in between studies. Others are transient workers, people who do not identify themselves professionally as nannies but who do the job temporarily to pay the bills. Then there are migrant workers, a percentage of whom are undocumented—they are often termed "domestic workers" because their actual work can run the gamut from child care to housework.

A definitive study of the industry by the National Domestic Workers Alliance (NDWA) taken from June 2011 to February 2012, polling some 2,086 domestic workers in 14 metropolitan areas, remains a fairly faithful snapshot of child care to date and its workers today.[14] Here are the NDWA's findings:

Pay

- Twenty-three percent of workers surveyed are paid below the state minimum wage.
- Seventy percent are paid less than $13 an hour.
- Sixty-seven percent of live-in workers are paid below the state minimum wage, and the median hourly wage of these workers is $6.15.
- Using a conservative measure of income adequacy, 48 percent of workers are paid an hourly wage in their primary job, which is below the level needed to adequately support a family.

Employment Benefits

- Fewer than 2 percent receive retirement or pension benefits form their primary employer.
- Fewer than 9 percent work for employers who pay into social security.
- Sixty-five percent do not have health insurance, and only 4 percent receive employer-provided insurance.

Financial Hardships

- Sixty percent spend more than half of their income on rent or mortgage payments.
- Thirty-seven percent of workers paid their rent or mortgage late during the year prior to being interviewed.
- Forty percent paid some of their essential bills late during the same time period.

- Twenty percent report that there were times in the previous month when there was no food to eat in their homes.

Labor Conditions

- Key provisions in standard employment agreements are often absent for domestic workers.
- Thirty-five percent of domestic workers report that they worked long hours without breaks in the prior 12 months.
- Twenty-five percent of live-in workers had responsibilities that prevented them from getting at least five hours of uninterrupted sleep at night during the week prior to being interviewed.
- Thirty percent of workers who have a written contract or other agreement report that their employers disregarded at least one of the provisions in the prior 12 months.
- Among workers who are fired from a domestic work job, 23 percent are fired for complaining about working conditions, and 18 percent are fired for protesting violations of their contract or agreement.

Disrespect and Abuse in the Workplace

Interviews with domestic workers reveal that they often endure verbal, psychological, and physical abuse on the job—without recourse. Domestic workers, who are unprotected by contracts and laws available to other workers, fear employer retaliation.

- Ninety-one percent of workers who encountered problems with their working conditions in the prior 12 months did not complain because they were afraid they would lose their job.
- Eighty-five percent of undocumented immigrants who encountered problems with their working conditions in the prior 12 months did not complain because they feared that their immigration status would be used against them.

The two studies by the INA and the NDWA, respectively, offer us a polarized view of the child care industry. On the one hand, professional American nannies appear to enjoy higher hourly rates, attend conferences, specialize their skill sets, and receive employment benefits. On the other hand, another group of child care workers complains of low wages and poor treatment. The overall picture of child care offered through studies such as these is therefore confusing. It is no wonder, then, that parents are bewildered when left to navigate child care solutions on their own and often when they are most vulnerable—when their first child is born. In her book *It Takes a Village,* Hillary Clinton observes that

The variety of arrangements these children are left in is dizzying. Neighbors trade child-care duty with each other, or relatives are called in to help. When those options do not exist, parents must turn to a marketplace that is complex, confusing, costly, and extremely uneven in quality. Their choices include family day care homes in which one adult takes care of several children from the neighborhood; day care centers that run the gamut from very good to very bad; preschools attached to religious institutions and universities; nannies, au pairs, relatives, and full- and part-time baby-sitters.[15]

It Takes a Village astutely frames the argument for the federal regulation of child care so that parents might more safely and easily navigate a path to a good nanny. But some might ask why child care should be regulated or licensed. Perhaps we should explore why other U.S. professions require a license.

According to the online resource University Language Services, "In the U.S., licensure is intended to ensure the public that a person is competent to practice in that profession."[16]

Licenses are safeguards, operating like a firewall to protect the public from incompetent or fraudulent practitioners. In general, professionals become licensed through training or by passing an exam. In many fields, the person seeking U.S. licensure must obtain an advanced degree before becoming eligible for the license. The license is often provided by an established authority with a history of excellence in that particular field. More important, according to *It Takes a Village,* there is compelling evidence that introducing licensing in day care centers motivates providers to raise their standards:

A study of Florida's child care centers measured the quality of care children received before and after state regulations went into effect. These laws put more adults in charge of fewer children and required that at every licensed center at least one staff person have a Child Development Associate credential or its equivalent for every twenty children served. Researchers observed that the day care workers were more responsive and positive in dealing with the children after regulations went into effect. The children themselves exhibited greater language and social development, and the number of behavior problems went down.[17]

The following professions require U.S. licensure before a person is legally allowed to practice:

- Accounting
- Architecture

- Dentistry
- Education/teaching
- Engineering
- Law
- Medicine
- Nursing
- Pharmacy
- Psychology
- Veterinary medicine

In New York state there are 125 professions that require a license, including librarian, therapist, midwife, social worker, and nurse—all people who come into regular contact with children. There is no category for in-home child care workers.

How does licensing an industry work? According to labor.ny.gov, industry regulation comes in two forms, licensing and registration:

Licensing is the most restrictive method of regulation.

It requires any person wishing to earn a living in a licensed occupation to obtain permission (license) from a specific government agency, designated by law to issue this license. To receive a license, the applicant usually completes the following requirements:

- Graduate from an approved training program and/or complete a certain amount of work-related experience.
- Pass a qualifying written, verbal, and/or practical examination.
- Qualify on certain personal prerequisites, such as age, citizenship, or bonding.
- Meet comparable standards set by some other state (reciprocation).
- Pay a prescribed initial and renewal license fee.
- Certification.

Registration is the least restrictive method of regulation.

Those wishing to engage in registered occupations must submit an application to be placed on an official roster maintained by the appropriate organization or agency. The requirements for registration are usually minimal. Individuals may be asked to produce documentation for qualification, character reference, and bonding.[18]

Libertarians might argue that agencies and individual parents in effect self-regulate the industry on their child's behalf by screening for suitable caregivers, and thus there is no need to license the child care industry as a whole. But recent abuse cases by nannies involving even accredited online agencies powerfully demonstrate that background checks alone are not enough to weed out potential offenders or low-performance nannies.

In other words, even if an individual nanny has a glowing resume and a stellar educational background or has equivalent experience in caring for children, there is still no absolute guarantee that she or he will provide a high standard of care consistently. Also, when nannies are let go by employers for failing to provide adequate child care, there is no official procedure for recording grievances or concerns. This leaves the general public ignorant to substandard caregivers and can keep those same nannies in circulation for decades.

It's important to remember that police background checks are there to flag *convicted* criminals. Nannies who are simply bad at their job or are serial abusers on a smaller scale can easily operate under the radar if they are never caught and reported.

On a more positive note, if the child care industry were properly regulated, it could more closely resemble organizations such as the INA. It could facilitate significant progress for families and nannies alike in terms of promoting basic mandatory training such as CPR and could offer online courses on early childhood development, stage conferences, and provide nutritional awareness, on-the-job mentoring, and opportunities to add college credentials to a nanny's resume, thus leading to higher earnings. All of the above systemic changes would inject an enormous amount of vocational motivation among child care workers: the desire to provide the best possible care and to stay with a family for longer and remain a human asset within the child care sector.

In summary, modern child care has a second flaw: it is an unregulated industry. It virtually stands alone in terms of being a profession that engages small children on a regular and intimate basis and does not require even a basic registration of practitioners. Up until this point we have focused on the needs of infants and on the unlicensed industry of child care. Next we will examine how modern work practices have impacted families and their choices in child care.

CONFLICTED PARENTS

Sue Gerhardt in her book *The Selfish Society* asks "How *can* parents meet the emotional needs of their children if they're working long hours? How can mothers breastfeed their babies if they are at work, and how can either parent be sensitive and attuned to a baby—or an older child for that matter—if they only see them at the end of a long, busy day?

If governments are confused, so are the parents, who are equally torn between the pull of their financial needs and the pull of their baby's emotional needs."[19]

Most working parents are run ragged from pillar to post. They work long hours and organize child care, playdates, and meals. They shop, pay bills, and go to school fund-raisers. They ferry children to games and classes on weekends, and after all that they attempt to have social lives and healthy marriages. Most of the time their marriages, careers, and children survive intact, but are they thriving?

As Arlie Russell Hoschild, professor emerita of sociology at the University of California, Berkeley, astutely points out, we are essentially asking questions about *mothers* when we speak about "parents" or ask "how is the family doing?" For the most part the role and activities of fathers have changed very little since the women's liberation movement in the 1960s. What are the statistics on working mothers?

2013
- 69.9 percent of all mothers with children under age 18 were working or actively looking for work
- 63.9 percent of mothers with children under 6 years old were working or actively seeking work
- 57.3 percent of mothers with an infant under a year old were working or actively seeking[20]

According to a study by the Pew Institute, public opinion about working mothers hasn't changed much since the 1970s: "Americans also continue to think that having a mother (or parent) at home is best for a child . . . 60% of respondents said children are better off when a parent stays home to focus on the family, compared with 35% who said children are just as well off with working parents."[21]

It should be noted that almost 79 percent of those polled did not believe that women should cease working outside the home and return to their traditional roles as homemakers. Clearly, then, the public is conflicted over the individual rights of mothers to work and the long-term benefits of at-home nurturance for small children.[22]

In the media even prominent businesswomen such as Nicola Horlick, a mother of six children, says that "today's generation of mothers can't have it all." What do women such as Horlick mean by "having it all"? Generally, it is the idea that working mothers can enjoy a rewarding professional career and an equally rewarding home life—just as men do as working fathers.

Horlick was the poster child for working mothers in the 1990s. At age 32 she was managing director of the Morgan Grenfell Asset Management in the United Kingdom. In her 40s, she set up her own business and started an investment house, Bramdean Asset Management. In 2012 Horlick formed Rockpool, a private equity business. In among all of this she was raising six children. How was she able to juggle motherhood and a successful career? "Childcare is a major issue. I was very lucky, because I was very senior very fast and was able to afford a nanny. We had the same nanny for the first ten years, plus I had back up and support from my mother and my husband. I was also lucky to have children who ate a lot and sleep well, so from ten weeks they were flat out all night." She says that a nanny is now impossibly expensive for most people. "With all the costs of employment it costs around £40,000 to employ a nanny for a year—which you need to earn £80,000 to pay for."[23]

In other words, Horlick had a strong network of a good nanny, a supportive husband, and an extended family, plus she maintained a very strict work and home schedule that allowed her to stay a daily loving presence in her children's lives. Due to Horlick's extraordinary early business success, she was able to afford the type of long-term in-home caregiver growing children require. But as the cost of good child care continues to rise, new mothers attempt other solutions such as taking a career break for three to five years or using cheaper day care centers. Horlick contends that mothers still pay a price for taking a maternity break in the corporate world and that day care only works when a child is healthy. Mothers more than fathers will take a work absence to care for their sick children—a habit that is duly noted by employers.

More than ever, today's mothers are responding to the economic need to return to work quickly after their children are born. Mothers continue to receive no federal support in sourcing child care or by corporate America as a whole, and as such they have to turn to the market for their needs.

It is small wonder, then, that when it comes to sourcing a good nanny, the stakes have never been higher or more costly. Children today respond to the absence of both parents during the week in different ways depending on the level of substitute care they receive.

Universally, however, there comes a time when children figure out the fundamental difference between parents (those people who come and go but are related to them) versus caregivers (those people who come and go but receive a wage and are unrelated to them), and their behavior can change overnight. Little angels may morph into despots actively resisting a caregiver's authority. This process can be a testing time for loving working parents and for the nannies they employ.

FRUSTRATED KIDS

One nanny to another, overheard:

He's just begun to figure out that I'm hired help—me—the person who raised him from birth while his mom and dad worked day and night in their law firm. He's getting fresh always answering back when I try to correct him. He's already started referring to me as "my sitter" to his friends at school and on playdates. He constantly questions my authority, and his parents they don't back me up. It's not just me; he's the same to the cleaner, to the doorman. He's just plain arrogant.

During this process, parents may sometimes feel powerless to address the consequences of their children missing them. They may attempt to justify rebellious behavior by dismissing their children as spirited or by saying that their children are merely going through *that stage*. What is often overlooked, however, is the internal and the collective process. A child's awareness of the parents' continual absence over time can be deeply painful. In turn, parents burdened by economic or career constraints can feel equally saddened when a small child clings to their legs and begs them not to leave for work in the morning.

Coupled with that joint grief is a sudden awareness in the child that the nanny who has loved them from birth or early infancy actually receives a paycheck for doing so. It's almost as if an age of innocence has passed, and the reality of a child's home life sets in.

When a child's loss is not acknowledged, the grief can be overwhelming. It can take the form of resistance to a nanny's presence and her role in the home. Conflicted parents may feel helpless to fix their child's sudden disdain for a nanny. They might even wonder if she is truly caring for their children.

The child's anger and resentment are easy to understand. On Monday mornings when the parental honeymoon ends, the nanny's mere arrival can be a terrible source of angst. Even the most beloved of nannies has experienced this. Hence, when a nanny attempts to enforce the rules of the household, she may find herself engaged in a bitter power struggle. Children who feel helpless or angry about their parents' absence can easily project their anger onto their nanny in an effort to gain control of the situation. This can be a challenging time for working parents.

A child's sense of loss may be expressed in sporadic acts of defiance, disrespect, temper tantrums, rage, and even depression. Parents may find themselves compensating for their absence and their child's poor behavior with indulgences such as lax rules on the weekends, toys, media, and a general lack of discipline. In reality, children need clear, strong boundaries to feel safe. So, a child's attempts to resist the nanny's authority can actually, if successful, create greater tension for the child.

Occasionally children are simply picking up patronizing or ambivalent attitudes toward caregivers from their parents. In other words, how children observe their parents and their parents' social peers treating nannies in general can intensify their own behavior.

I have seen a nanny's authority being undermined by parents in front of their children. For example, if a general household rule is no TV in the afternoon or no candy during the day, this rule should be enforced by both the parents and the nanny. It is confusing for a parent to ignore the rules that they set up because they didn't want the bother or because they want to wield some temporary influence. What children learn from this is that with extra whining they will always get their own way. Most important, the child in question might come to understand that the nanny has no real authority in the home. The child realizes that *he or she has the authority*.

How can this situation affect a child over time? I asked Karen Kaufman, PhD, LCSW, for her professional opinion, and we discussed a few anonymous scenarios where the children of working parents might require therapy. Out of these dialogues I created a case study that I simply called "Family B." Names, occupations, and genders are fictional, but the dynamics are based on a series of sample cases.[24]

Family B: Deborah, Richard, and Their Two Daughters, Mara and Joanna

Deborah was employed in a major New York City law firm, and Richard worked in investment banking. As a result of their long work hours and travel, they were required to relinquish most of their parenting to their live-in nanny, with detrimental effects on their children, ages five and seven.

The work-obsessed cultures of the couple's employers lacked any flexibility for them as parents, in particular for Deborah. She felt that any indication of her work slipping or unavailability for travel would quickly put her on the "mommy track," which would never lead to higher rungs of success in the firm; that is, she would never become a partner. Richard, developing his career in banking, was required to travel to Europe at least twice each month and was not yet at a senior enough level whereby he had any choices other than to accept the new assignments that were given to him.

Joanna, age 5, and Mara, age seven, were completely dependent on the care of their nanny, Anna. While she was a devoted employee and caregiver, living in the home since soon after Joanna's birth, in the children's eyes she lacked authority and was not to be taken seriously in their parents' absence. This led to a gradual disregard of Anna's efforts with discipline and limit setting, finally escalating to a situation in which the older child, Mara, was tyrannical and oppositional and whose overall behavior in the home was angry and increasingly out of control. Joanna observed her sister's behavior and reacted to this by developing a style of being too well behaved and voicing a minimal amount of her own needs.

Anna arrived in the United States from a culture in which families are very close-knit, and when child care needs arose these were typically met by the extended family. She was therefore bewildered by the amount of parenting and authority her employers expected from her. In addition, she tended to overcompensate for Mara's behavior by being overly subservient with the girls, thereby enabling the bad behaviors: she allowed Mara to speak to her disrespectfully, did not report being hit by Mara on several occasions, and was left to clean up messes of toys, clothing, and food despite the parents' efforts to teach the girls to participate in the cleanup. As a result, the parents' efforts with limits and consistency were undermined, leaving them feeling more frustrated and powerless.

The parents were so depleted from the demands of their jobs that Mara's unhappiness and provocative behavior proved to be another drain on them. Mara was therefore fulfilling her own prophecy and was pushed further out of her parents' lives. Joanna's agreeable and compliant behavior made it easier for the parents to spend more time with her, as she presented few demands on them. It was also easy for them to ignore the obvious fact that Joanna was developing a false exterior by behaving in a manner too mature for her age. She had learned to adapt in this environment and at a young age saw which behaviors would be rewarded and what would isolate her further, like her sister.

After a few family therapy sessions, the problem as perceived by Mara was a simple one: Anna was not mom or dad. The grief and loneliness that resulted from the continual parental absence and Mara's resulting unmet needs had gradually turned into feelings of rage and powerlessness; she felt neglected and in need of real hands-on parenting. She desperately needed her parents to take more of an interest in her life, to show enthusiasm about her and involvement in her school and other activities, along with their supervision, guidance, teaching, and limits. Anna the nanny could not provide all that was necessary for the children in these circumstances.

Any suggestions to repair the family's home life had to be realistic and manageable, given the reality that the parents' occupational demands and stresses were not changing. Ideas were discussed, such as one parent going to work a little later whenever possible and the other coming home somewhat earlier, thereby allowing each to participate in some morning, dinner, and evening routines; weekend time spent as a family, with Anna given much-needed days off; and each parent spending individual time with the girls, allowing each child to choose a special activity to enjoy with her mother or father. These activities can be as simple as having breakfast out, going to the market for ingredients to prepare dinner together, going to a movie, or taking a trip to the local playground. Another important element in the family time was the understanding that work could not intrude; calls, e-mails, and any outstanding work had to be tended to either before or after family activities to ensure the parents' full attention on their daughters.

What we can learn from this case study is that ideally, parents must try to take time from busy work schedules to be available to their children even if that time is limited. When children feel important to their parents, as evidenced by their care and positive regard for them, this is the foundation of self-esteem, which affects their feelings about themselves and how they can expect to be treated by others. When early and age-appropriate dependency needs are chronically unmet by parents, some children may learn to adapt, as Joanna did with a false exterior, or display feelings and behaviors that add to the child's isolation, as in Mara's case, but there is a high emotional price to be paid in terms of self-esteem, future attachment styles, mature relationships, and adult commitments.

While most families (with two working parents) will not face such a dramatic home situation, some will have children who are clearly angry and periodically act out.

The fundamental challenge for two wage earners is to create a home life of consistent care for their children. In the above-mentioned case study, the nanny did not feel in charge and thus could not provide a stable domestic experience for the children. It is essential that working parents not only find a person who closely resembles their child-rearing practices but also that they *always* follow through with the same rules and standards that a nanny enforces during the week.

A confused domestic regime will ultimately create two sets of bad guys in the child's eyes. A nanny will be seen as a tyrant associated with school and a person who inflicts strict rules. The parents will be seen as the rescuers, the ones who liberate the children from their weekly hell. Yet the rescuers also disappear every Monday morning, and this can make a younger child absolutely livid.

The cost of modern living often places an enormous financial burden on both parents to work long hours. A prolonged daily absence from the home can create a deep sense of grief for both the parents and their children. In those circumstances it is vital that parents find ways to collectively and individually spend time with their children in activities that engage both parties, as in the following schedules.

Monday–Friday

Parents rotate their schedules so that Parent 1 leaves later one to five mornings a week and serves the children breakfast and takes them to school; Parent 2 arranges to leave work earlier one to five afternoons a week and gets to eat with or serve dinner to the children, bathe them, and tuck them in bed. Parents can rotate these schedules so that both parents experience a morning and evening ritual with their children.

Parents can make phone calls home throughout the day if a child is very small or even make Skype calls; parents can make a daily phone call to older children after school ends. Phone calls from a parent can make an enormous difference to a child experiencing sadness or anxiety. The soothing sound of a parent's voice helps children feel connected to their parents during the day despite their physical absence.

Weekends and Holidays

Enrichment, sports, and entertainment classes can be fun over the weekends, but if scheduled excessively they can also act as a barrier to intimacy between parents and their children—especially if parents use these times to catch up on their phone calls or social media. Alternatively, parents can use the weekends to spend quality time together as a family enjoying simple things such as taking a hike or having brunch together. Parents can also schedule individual time with their children, playing board games, going grocery shopping and preparing family meals together, walking the family dog about the neighborhood, jogging down by the river, or riding bikes— all of these activities convey to children that they are seen by their parents and loved. It also demonstrates that a nanny is a loving supplement to their caregiving.

Vacation times too are a golden opportunity for parents to leave their jobs behind for two weeks or more and concentrate on their children. Leaving one's work behind truly does mean switching off gadgets and being present for our children—or at least it does to children. Holidays are also an excellent time for children to take a break from their nannies and hectic weekly routines in order to directly source their needs via their parents. These periods of intimate engagements will forge powerful bonds of mutual trust between parents and their children. It can be tempting to bring along a nanny on vacation, particularly if working parent are exhausted from a year of demanding employment, but consider using her services sparingly so that you and your family get alone time.

For new parents looking for child care, it's important that they *look for and employ a nanny who most closely follows them in their child-rearing methods.* If parents and nannies are diametrically opposed on such issues as discipline, napping schedules, nutrition, spirituality, creativity, sleeping, and academic enrichment, the child in question will experience a polarity of caregiving in the formative years. As important, such differences could lead to power struggles and disagreements between parents and their nanny.

In the event of children acting out against a nanny, parents can discuss their children's sadness or anger with them and sympathetically support them in the process. They can also schedule a monthly meeting with their nanny to stay attuned to the flow of their children's home life.

Later in this book we will explore ways in which the government, corporations, and even the market can work together to create more family-friendly practices. In the meantime, let us move on to child care's actual workers themselves: nannies.

Chapter 2

Nanny Archetypes: The Lottery of Trust

THE GOOD NANNY

To understand why poor child care occurs, one must examine the sectors of the workforce itself and the treatment of that workforce by employers and by society in general.

Arlie Russell Hochschild most accurately labels nannies as "emotional laborers," for there is no better way to define what nannies actually do. Emotional labor is a service that involves an intimate offering of time and dedication. Love is the currency exchanged for a wage, and the caring attentive adult is a temporary substitute for the parents' actual presence, not a surrogate.[1]

In generic terms, nannies tend to fall into these basic categories:

- *Nanny.* This is a consummate caregiver, a person who considers her vocation as a professional choice. A nanny will often take on all of the day-to-day duties associated with child care such as enrichment, intellectual growth, nutrition, and health.
- *Caregiver.* This the more politically correct title for a person who approaches child care as an opportunity to enrich a child's life. Many of the duties and ideologies of a caregiver are the same as that of a nanny.
- *Babysitter or sitter.* This often applies to an individual who offers caregiving services on a more casual basis, generally during evenings or

weekends, or someone who acts as a fill-in when a parent or nanny is not available. Sitters are often students or graduates—younger American people who are transient workers in child care, using it as a means to pay college fees or bills.

- *Manny*. This is a male who offers his child care services as either a nanny or a babysitter.
- *Housekeeper*. A person who takes care of the house, including the cleaning and running of a private home. This role can spill over into a small amount of babysitting or cooking for a family.
- *Au pair*. This is normally a younger foreign female who trades her child care services for a cultural experience and study in the United States. Generally, au pairs live with a family and are given a weekly salary.
- *Newborn care specialist*. This is a specialist caregiver who exclusively works with newborns and infants usually for two to six weeks. Her role is to help facilitate breast-feeding, sleep routines, bathing, umbilical care, and nail cutting and to help regulate an infant's bowel movements.

Our exploration of what it means to be a good nanny refers not to an intrinsic moral character or the economic value of a child care worker. It is used to denote the level and quality of care that nannies are able to provide. It's like a simple rating system: good = high-end caregiving, and not-so-good = unsatisfactory to chronically poor caregiving. A nanny's performance spans the spectrum of race, class, educational background, and immigration status.

In a country such as America, however, there is a core group of professionals who define themselves as nannies. They diligently study up on early childhood development and apply what they learn in their careers. Often they are members of the International Nanny Association (INA)—some have been nominated as Nanny of the Year for their excellence. In this section I have turned to two such nannies—Michelle LaRowe and Marni Kent—for their insight into what qualifies a good nanny.

Michelle

Michelle LaRowe was the INA Nanny of the Year in 2004. In many respects, Michelle exemplifies the highest ideals in child care:

You don't choose to be a nanny, *it chooses you*. Every good nanny I have ever encountered has echoed that sentiment using one phrase or the other. When I read *A Spoonful of Sugar*, the story of Barbara Ashland, a long retired Norland Nanny, and she echoed the same thing, it cemented in me the belief that regardless of your age, where you are from, or the type of families you serve; this is a universal nanny truth.

I had always cared for children. My mother had cared for children. As far back as I can remember, I was helping her in the church nursery, then serving there on my own. That grew into babysitting for church families, which grew into babysitting for my schoolteacher's children. This grew into becoming a summer nanny through my high school years that grew into my full-time job as I put myself through college.

I received my bachelor of science degree in chemistry on a Sunday and started work caring for newborn twin boys on that Monday morning. I was with that family for nearly seven years. Early in my career I became involved with the International Nanny Association. I went to my first nanny conference and felt at home with others who shared my daily joys and struggles and really understood what it meant to be more than a babysitter. I was recruited to be on the board of directors, and I diligently served in many positions over the years.

It was at the 2004 INA Annual Conference that was held in Boston, where I received the Nanny of the Year award. After having children of my own and caring for the children of others, I can honestly say that when I said to parents "I will love and care for your children like they are my own," I meant it. It seems like only my best friend who adopted her children truly gets this. When you are charged with caring for someone else's children 40, 50, 60 hours per week, to do the job right you have to be fully in love, fully invested.

Is being a mom different? When it comes to caring for the kids, *not really*. I love them and care for them just as I did with the kids I once cared for, and in some ways that's a huge relief. It confirms that I did my best with those children I was entrusted to care for.

A good nanny knows that part of her job is to support the parents and to foster the parent-child relationship. This is key in reinforcing the nanny's role as family supporter.

Open and honest communication also helps prevent issues. Every day for seven years I called my boss at 1 p.m. Even if I just left a message, I checked in. It was our touch point during the day that allowed us to connect. We also talked often and didn't wait for things to blow up before addressing them, most of the time anyway.

That's where work agreements come into place. Relationships get sabotaged when expectations aren't clear. Families and nannies should always have written work agreements that outline the terms of the employment relationships and the expectations of each party. This prevents job creep and unclear expectations and ensures that everyone is on the same page of the same parenting book.

When you are hiring a nanny or being a nanny you have to understand, it's rarely the kids who cause the issues in the relationship. It's issues among the adults. To be successful you have to invest the time and energy in building the relationship. There are going to be bumps in the road, as with any relationship. There's going to be battles that are better left unpicked and things you're prepared to go to war over. Being committed to navigating the relationship together is what guides you through. Your commitment to work together, in the good and the bad, is what drives lasting nanny and family relationships.[2]

The key point that stands out for me in Michelle's testimony is her insistence on nannies and parents working as a team. She also clarifies that love is not an exclusive commodity—it is the currency used in child care to nurture childhood development. It's also worthy to note that not all good nannies are career nannies. Michelle is now a mother and a child care consultant with her own website.

Marni

Marni Kent currently works in San Francisco, California. In 2002, the INA honored her as Nanny of the Year. She has 28 years of experience. Over the years Marni has been both a friend and a mentor as I wrote this book, providing me with an invaluable American perspective on the child care experience:

When you're a nanny, you never know what surprises each day will bring—like an impromptu biology lesson and stand-up comedy act. A few years ago, I took fourth-grader Sammy [her charge] to Hobby Lobby to pick up all the raw materials for her class project on the human ear: papier mâché head, Silly Putty for the outer ear, and pipe cleaners for the inner ear. During her presentation, Sammy meticulously explained each part of the ear and how it contributes to processing sound and sending signals to the brain. With a deadpan delivery, she showed her classmates where the brain was located. It was represented by a pea—as in "pea brain"—a gag inspired by her brother.

I was sitting with Sammy's parents and siblings, and the crowd went wild with laughter. At that moment, I was so proud of not only how she used all those big words but also that she had put so much work into this project and was able to entertain and explain this in front of a large crowd.[3]

It's natural for nannies to experience parenting-like moments such as these. Although the public often assumes that a nanny is merely a full-time babysitter, the truth is that nannies are constantly switching roles as trusted guardian, teacher, and friend. Marni explains:

Some people see the career of a nanny as simply unchallenging, yet where else can one take credit in playing an integral part in the way a young person will become an adult among society? We get to mold the content of a child's character face to face and see the results first hand.

I've learned that you can't learn how to be a professional nanny from a book. Each family has a specific blueprint of needs and expectations. The nanny has to be able to morph into those needs, be flexible and accept different parenting styles, temperament and personalities. Child development is about playing and modeling, exploring the world around them. And a little praise means a lot to a child—it helps with building independence and self-worth.

Last year two Stanford University professors hired Marni for a brief stint as an overnight nanny. The mother, feeling overcommitted at work, felt conflicted about sleeping through her newborn's cries. But she also knew that she needed to be fully awake during the day.

"Marni changed our lives by supporting and nurturing our whole family unit at a very trying time," the professor recalls. "She has a deep humane interest in people, young or old, novice or experienced, and helping them to craft their best lives. She is imaginative, inquisitive, professional, and dynamic in everything she does. I felt immediately at ease with her. Having the right nanny means that our baby is happy, healthy, and thriving because of the great support Marni provides, and we are able to spend more high quality time focused on our baby and enjoying our time as a family. Marni is wonderful with our daughter—she is upbeat, engaging, affectionate, and focused on helping the baby develop and thrive. She takes the time to observe and ask about our preferences, and she honors those preferences. She has established a strong connection with our daughter and at the same time has completely reinforced and supported our primary roles as the baby's parents," the mother adds.

According to Marni, "Parents come from a heart-centered place, and nannies use their heart with logic. When the two combine, it makes for a great relationship and excellent child development. Children have such a profound effect on you whether you realize it or not," she says. "When you get down on their level, you are forced to think and learn about patience. Your tone of voice can affect a child so greatly, and most important, children teach you how to be happier and more positive about yourself when you are the one who is supposed to be teaching them."

Marni's Tips

1. Every nanny should think of herself as a "wife to the wife." The parent-nanny relationship is about discipline, development, and rearing that will allow for long-lasting relationships.
2. Growing with a family requires great commitment, dedication, and desire—even when things get rough.
3. Nanny resources and support are key for self-care, personal growth, and creating new opportunities to advance further in this career.

Nannies such as Michelle LaRowe and Marni Kent offer us the highest examples of what child care as an industry can offer new parents. For dedicated professionals such as Michelle and Marni, the vocation they have chosen deserves to be both embraced and supported by our society as a whole. The industry has many such professionals and at the same time also has workers who are not American or are not members of the INA.

Migrant nannies such as Mercy did not go to college to study child care in their home countries. Most of the nannies I interviewed for this book would not describe themselves as career nannies. Nevertheless, they were all excellent nannies. What unites them all is the understanding that their brief or lifelong venture into child care was a definitive opportunity to enrich the lives of the children they cared for. Therefore, a 100 percent commitment by a nanny albeit for a few years is golden. A good nanny might be an undocumented migrant worker, a part-time college babysitter, a professional career nanny, or a newborn care specialist. (However, the not-so-good nanny and the bad nanny can also come from any of these ranks.)

THE NOT-SO-GOOD NANNY

The aim of this book is not to cast doubt on nannies en masse. This book is primarily concerned with the regulation of the child care industry. Despite long hours, modest to low wages, and a lack of job security, nannies from all walks of life attempt to be present for and loving to the children in their care, but that should not make us complacent *right now*.

According to FBI statistics analyzed by James Alan Fox, a criminologist at Northeastern University, the number of infants younger than 12 months killed by a nanny hasn't significantly risen since 1976. It hovers at approximately 18 deaths a year. Babysitters who do harm the children they are hired to protect are more likely to commit sexual assault than murder.[4]

The likelihood of your infant being murdered by her or his babysitter is statistically low but frightening nonetheless—it is the equivalent of boarding a plane and knowing how unlikely the risk of a crash is. The point is that none of us wants to be on the plane that does crash. And no parent wants to come home to a dead, dying, or badly injured baby. Today almost 70 percent of mothers with children under the age of 18 are working or looking for work. Now more than ever, parents who return to employment want to protect their new babies.

There are many factors that contribute to underperformance. It is a testament to the human spirit, for example, that I observed the vast majority of undocumented nannies whom I knew working with integrity. Generally, however, low morale within the workplace caused by low wages, long hours, and a lack of respectful communication can easily create conditions of apathy. Nannies who underperform for whatever reason can be detected and helped to become better at their job. In the next section we will examine some types of nannies—or nannies in some types of situations—who *can* potentially underperform, with negative results for the children in their care.

The Apathetic Nanny

It's a sunny afternoon. A crowded park swarms with children. Swings are being swung on, slides are getting slid down, and the sandpit resembles a toddler's construction site. Hovering beneath the play equipment are concerned relatives and nannies. Some are merely there to enjoy their child's every triumph; others remain close to prevent an accident. Small groups of adults stand farther back and monitor their older child's actions without being overbearing. On the benches sit grandparents, pregnant moms, and, unmistakably, another group: apathetic nannies. Apathetic nannies are easily detected by these observable traits:

- They constantly use their cell phones.
- They often sit *away* from their charges in playgrounds.
- They cook or buy foods that require little preparation.
- They complain about the elements: it's either too cold or too wet or too hot for them to be outside.
- They have no interest in play and other forms of enrichment.
- They arrange playdates with other nannies (who are their friends) for personal stimulation and to pass the time.
- They feel overwhelmed by the normal energetic behavior of their charges.
- They keep infants strapped in strollers, preventing valuable exploration, to avoid work.

Apathetic nannies will not help infants navigate their milestones. The apathetic nanny might fail to guide and monitor social interactions between groups of children, therefore missing invaluable opportunities to instill socialization empathy and emotional intelligence. More important, she might be too distracted to prevent serious accidents. As a result, your toddler might fall on her face, your infant might eat dirty sand, and your overwrapped or underwrapped newborn might wail unnoticed in the stroller.

If you think that the behavior of the apathetic nanny is exaggerated, unfortunately it isn't. Nannies like this exist. Apathetic nannies don't just confine their chronic lethargy to their employers' homes. They act the same way in the bookstore, at the playgroup, in the park, and in fact anywhere. Beyond an apathetic nanny's general lack of motivation can hide a more serious problem. There can be a chronic absence of meaningful interaction between her and the children in her care. As we have previously discussed, children—especially newborns, infants, and toddlers—need daily stimulating interaction with their caregivers in order to develop emotional intelligence. In her book *The Other Secret: How to Recover from Emotional*

Abuse and Live the Life You've Always Wanted, Jennifer Quaggin offers this definition of "child mistreatment":

Adults [or caregivers] who have had few of their emotional needs met are often unable to respond to the needs of their children. They may not show attachment to the child or provide nurturance. They may show no interest in the child, express affection or even recognize the child's presence. Many times the parent [or caregiver] is physically there but emotionally unavailable.[5]

The apathetic nannies I observed demonstrated little interest in the emotional and intellectual well-being of their charges. They were preoccupied by their own personal dramas. Without major adjustments in their attitudes and daily life experiences, such nannies may continue to coast through one of your infant's most formative periods of life—on your dime but at a true cost to your child.

Burned-Out Nannies

Other nannies who were once excellent in their job have over the years slowly fallen into another category: burned-out nannies.

Burned-out nannies, for one reason or another, have been drained to the point of emotional exhaustion by their work. Low pay, an undocumented status, a constant hustling for jobs, a decades-long separation from loved ones, long working hours repeating monotonous chores, and a low social status eventually take their toll.

It's good to bear in mind that being a nanny is one of the few jobs where the longer one has been in the position, the less time one has in that position. A typical job can last anywhere between 2 and 10 years. Once children are in full-time education, most nannies are expected to either reduce their hours, take on housekeeping duties, or leave. A nanny often leaves a position with little more than a reference. That alone is a chronic ever-present stress.

Such was the case with Brenda. At 63 years of age, Brenda had worked paycheck to paycheck for over 40 years. She had been worn down by a hard life, and although a loving person, she is now too tired to be a good nanny. She naps on the job but feels bad about it. Brenda's arthritic body is too slow to play with the toddlers in her care, but she can't quit. If she retired she would have no income. Brenda has successfully "raised 12 children" during her long child care career. Yet her career path is invisible and, perhaps most important, comes without health insurance or a pension.[6]

The two children in her care, a toddler and a pre-K child, fortunately have never been placed in direct danger, but they have both adapted to accommodate their nanny's limited abilities. They often amuse themselves at home and do not make many demands for stimulation. Occasionally they even wander around their apartment as their caregiver dozes. It's important to ponder the factors that may contribute to a nanny's burnout.

The emotional fortitude that is required to leave children behind when a position ends and to work with a new family can take its toll on the best nanny. I personally suffered a dose of this during the months of my last permanent job. It's almost as if you suddenly hit a glass ceiling where you realize that the job has reached its own natural conclusion and that you will have to descend, disconnect, and begin all over again with another family.

Nannies rarely indulge in downtime or recuperative therapies. Being paid $12 an hour or less often does not allow for such luxuries. Weekends and evenings can be taken up with second and third babysitting jobs just to make ends meet or to send money back home overseas.

Some nannies have to work when the families they work for go away because they usually do not get paid holidays or vacation time. Their ever-present financial demands do not allow for downtime. In some extreme examples, I have witnessed a nanny emotionally shut down on a child in their care. The more this happens, the more needy the child becomes, and a love-guilt-resentment sequence unfolds. It can be bewildering to a child when all of a sudden a once mild-mannered nanny becomes impatient or when an enthusiastic nanny seems depressed. And the child always notices. *Always.*

To remedy the burnout syndrome, I recommend that employers offer at least one paid vacation per year and a living wage for their nannies. In and of itself, having more money to live on will reduce the need for nannies to moonlight during their spare time. I also believe that the burnout stage is nature's way of making a nanny take stock. Perhaps there comes a time when a nanny needs to take a different direction in career terms even if that means switching from being a one-on-one nanny to day care management or consultancy work.

Ultimately nannies are adults and must bear the responsibility of taking care of themselves so that they can provide decent care for their charges. If they do not, burned-out nannies may find themselves on the proverbial scrap heap looking for a job. Parents are fairly shrewd when it comes to the signs of a burned-out nanny and soon replace them—as they should. Having a consistently lethargic caregiver is bad for children. Whether apathy or lethargy, it all amounts to the same thing for growing, developing children. However, parents must recognize that they have some responsibility in working a nanny to her career death.

Brenda, our burned-out nanny, is essentially a loving person, but other nannies who are burned out can develop behavior that is more damaging to your children, such as snapping at them or administering excessive punishments. It is at this point that such a nanny if left unchecked can transform into a type of nanny who can be lethal to a child's sense of self-esteem and long-term happiness.

Resentful Nannies

A nanny was waiting for a bus—the bus approached. In the stroller to her right sat a very quiet, sad-looking two-year-old boy with red curly hair and large blue eyes. The nanny held three heavy shopping bags, and with the stroller, it proved difficult for them to board the bus. Without looking down at her charge, the nanny pulled him up by one arm at an angle so that his legs became entwined in the stroller's safety buckle. Frustrated, the nanny jerked him up a couple of times. But she couldn't get on the bus. The driver wouldn't wait, and the bus pulled away. "You made me lose my bus!" the nanny yelled, slumping back down at the bus stop. What would become of that sad little boy. Is this your son?[7]

The resentful nanny is perhaps the most damaged caregiver a child can have aside from a criminal one. The above excerpt is not a one-off example.

In the course of their job experience, most nannies have personally witnessed small children being yelled at, having affection withheld from them, or having their crying ignored—by a resentful nanny. The terrible part of it all is that the children involved cannot advocate for themselves. They are truly helpless. Parents should not naturally assume that they'd notice a child's suffering early on.

"Emotional abuse can be very hard to diagnose or even to define. In some instances, an emotionally abused child will show no signs of abuse. For this reason, emotional abuse is the most difficult form of child maltreatment to identify and stop."[8]

Resentful nannies wield enormous emotional power. They are generally with children all week long. If a child so much as squeaks its protestations, a resentful nanny has an arsenal of emotional weapons at her disposal. A child would lose every time. Emotional neglect is serious business. It may not cut or bruise, but it attacks a child where he or she is most vulnerable.

According to Jennifer Quaggin,

emotional abuse . . . is commonly defined as the systematic tearing down of another human being. It is considered a pattern of behavior that can seriously interfere with a child's positive development. Emotional abuse is probably the least understood of all child abuse, yet it is the most prevalent, and can be the cruelest and most destructive of all types of abuse. Because emotional abuse attacks the child's psyche and self-concept, the victim comes to see him or herself as unworthy of love and affection. Children who are constantly shamed, humiliated, terrorized or rejected suffer at least as much, if not more, than if they had been physically assaulted.[9]

The roots of a nanny's anger may go deep; however, a resentful nanny with unresolved issues does not seek a legitimate redress. Instead, she takes her frustrations out on the children in her care.

I can talk about resentful nannies because I have seen and heard them engaging in a form of talk that is pure venom. This type of resentful nanny may taunt, tease, and ridicule your child in front of his friends or her peers. Resentful nannies with grudges against their employers will make derogatory comments about them to her peers. You cannot assume that your child is off playing, oblivious to the slander that is spewing out all around the child. A resentful nanny often speaks when a child is within earshot.

If a resentful nanny speaks little English, again do not assume that her charges escape the thrust of her angst. Tone, facial expressions, and gestures communicate the subject of a nanny's tirade. Constant slander is deeply humiliating to a child's sense of esteem, but it can go further. Malicious gossip in public is a betrayal of your family's trust.

It's important to detect a resentful nanny as soon as you can, and in Chapter 6, I will give you some signs to watch out for and the tools to deal with a resentful nanny.

Some nannies are not apathetic, burned out, or resentful. In fact, they may present the illusion that all is well. They keep their charges neat and nourished while following a strict cleaning schedule. But that doesn't necessarily mean that they are good nannies. This type of nanny I refer to as the perfunctory nanny.

Perfunctory Nannies

Perfunctory (adj.). Used to describe something that is done without energy or enthusiasm because of habit or because it is expected.

Webster's Dictionary

Some of my observations of nannies included persons who were well intentioned but not necessarily *good* caregivers. Out of these I have created a fictional construct we shall call Celeste.[10] Celeste is a typical perfunctory nanny. She is a U.S. citizen, married with five grown children. Her employers are restaurateurs, and both parents work long hours. Celeste works more than 50 hours a week and is paid $12 an hour for taking care of Luke, a three-year-old boy. She is happy with her job.

Celeste considers herself to be an excellent housekeeper—that is, her employer's home is her top priority. As a consequence, she follows a strict cleaning regime. She speaks little English but does not regard that as an impediment to her work. While Celeste maintains a spotless house and is always visible to Luke, she does not feel moved to interact with him beyond rudimentary caregiving.

There is no malice involved here. Celeste is a wonderful housekeeper, but she is also a perfunctory nanny. On the surface, the home gleams and Luke appears well fed and mild-mannered. Behind the scenes, however, there is an unspoken absence of emotional stimulation and socialization occurring. As a direct consequence, from an early age Luke has learned not to ask for attention from his caregiver. He also rarely makes emotional demands on the other adults in his life.

My point with this story is to demonstrate that different people bring different gifts to a home. But if you are hiring someone to take care of your children, ensure that you have not simply hired a cleaner who happens to keep an eye on your child. That's not to say that a nanny is not expected to tidy up but rather that her main attribute is her devotion to your children.

Perhaps your nanny is one of those vibrant college babysitters or cultured au pairs. That's great, but what if she also likes to pole dance and post her exploits on YouTube?

Immature Babysitters

College babysitters and au pairs can bring zest, enthusiasm, and a sparkle to your household. A younger babysitter bridges the generation canyon between you and your child. Baffling gadgets, cryptic computer games, and certain tattooed singers on *American Idol* can be sources of bonding between a college babysitter and her charges. Immaturity, however, can rear its head when it comes to establishing clear child-adult boundaries. It can also interfere with maintaining schedules that govern mundane daily events such as homework, bathing, and feeding.

In a major urban area such as Manhattan, younger nannies socialize and network outside of college and child care. But the temptations of city life can impact a younger babysitter's child care performance. The following is an excerpt from *Page Six,* the *New York Post* weekend magazine:

"I'm a great nanny and I absolutely adore the kids I care for, but to be honest, when I'm not working, I'm out of control," says Hannah, a 25-year-old Canadian import who's been working three days a week for her family for over two years. "One day,

I started drinking at 4 p.m., and stayed up until 5 in the morning partying. Then I lost my phone, so I had to get up at 9 to track it down and be at work at noon, and then I worked from noon to 9." That day, Hannah took the kids to an event at Chelsea Piers and spent two of her working hours in a room filled with screeching children . . . and there are times, she admits, when she's gone straight to work after partying, without sleeping at all.[11]

Some parents might pass this behavior off as what comes with the territory in hiring younger nannies. Yet parents should be vigilant against actions that might spill over into their children's primary care. Here's another example from *Page Six:*

A 23-year-old nanny did drugs—not to get her mind off work, but in order to focus on work. She worked for an Upper East Side family with a boy and a girl, both under age 5, and would smoke pot every morning before she went to work at 7:30. . . . They [her employers] just thought she was chilled out.[12]

Other babysitters, particularly au pairs away from home can feel overwhelmed by their new responsibilities. European au pair Marjorie[13] came to Manhattan at age 19 to study film. Once placed with a host family including two small boys, she felt put upon by the parents and worn out by the children in her care. Subsequently, Marjorie reverted to immature behavior herself. She became apathetic and at times even mean to her charges—often resembling a disgruntled older sister more than a caregiver.

One day Marjorie jaywalked across a busy road while talking on her phone. Trailing unseen behind Marjorie, the youngest boy was almost hit by a car. Fortunately, a neighbor witnessed the event and reported Marjorie to her hosts. When confronted, Marjorie whined and blamed the child in question for not keeping up. She also stated that she felt alone and was unable to make any friends due to a language barrier. This, Marjorie insisted, had made her depressed. Marjorie was sent back home, but the family concerned was left with a bitter memory.

If your nanny is an au pair away from her country and family for the first time, watch out for signs of reckless, juvenile, or depressive behavior. Being young and fancy-free does not excuse poor behavior. While it's good to be supportive, you didn't pay to have another child on board.

When hiring a younger babysitter, whether she is a college babysitter or an au pair, be aware of her ability to be present for the task at hand. Taking perfunctory care of young children can be really easy. Some college babysitters choose to babysit because it can be easier to perform than waiting tables, walking dogs, or cleaning houses. Employers who suspect that their younger babysitter is hung over, high, or sleep deprived might feel awkward asking whether this is the case. But they should ask anyway, especially if their babysitter drives their children about the neighborhood or swims with them in a pool.

Up until now we have explored the different types of caregivers that can inhabit the world of child care. Some are excellent examples of emotional intelligence, others are works in progress, and yet others are worth looking out for and avoiding altogether.

In the next section we will explore a final group of nannies—the very worst kind of nannies—criminal nannies.

THE CRIMINAL NANNY

It's difficult to imagine that the sanctuary of our home might potentially harbor a criminal. We like to believe that the people we meet in everyday life are good and honest and what they seem to be. Children are less naive. They will pull their tiny bodies back from a grown-up who gives them the creeps while we anxiously attempt to coax them into a smile. Small children believe in monsters. They instinctively search for them as the lights dim before bedtime. We trail children, following their instructions to tightly shut closet doors and shutter down windows—with patronizing smiles. But maybe it's we who are wrong.

No matter how well we check a nanny's references, at some point we must trust that she is a good person. There's a point where a parent must let go and walk away—to work, run an errand, make an appointment, or enjoy a date night. In those unknowable gaps of trust, certain types of people can do terrible things. In this section I call to your attention three kinds of criminal behavior that can occur within child care: theft, sexual assault, and other forms of physical violence. We will look at three cases and explore prevention.

Thieves

Abigail Pogrebin recounted a personal story of betrayal by a nanny in her article "Nanny Scam" for *New York Magazine:*

A number of close friends imparted stories of being robbed or duped by babysitters, housekeepers, or workmen, stories they'd never shared before. It was a strange torrent, these tales of trickery, and they actually made me feel worse. Implicit in them was that awful cliché: "You can't trust the help," a line that made me shudder. I didn't want to be part of such a cynical chorus. I hated the lessons that this situation seemed to teach: that you have to be suspect [*sic*] of anyone you pay, that just because a nanny is loving toward your kids doesn't mean she loves you, that if you're going to hire a stranger to help raise your kids, you get what you deserve.[14]

Pogrebin described how she discovered that her children's nanny, Maria, had been stealing money directly from her bank account. The sum was in excess of $1,600. Pogrebin uses the term "cautionary tale" when describing a chain of events that led to a flagrant abuse of trust. It goes something like this: a nice open, friendly couple who have been burned a few times by some not-so-great nannies finally find what and who they considered to be a good nanny. By all accounts, on that score they were right.

Over time as the trust between them grew, Maria's employers gave her access to their bank card and pin number. She would run errands for them and, handy for them, could withdraw sums of money at the ATM on their behalf. Allegedly at some point the temptation to withdraw extra cash without permission occurred to Maria. Later the Pogrebins discovered that their nanny had begun to arouse suspicions among her nanny peers. Lavish purchases had been made, and naturally the Pogrebins concluded that their nanny had been using their cash to buy some of these items.

The point of this cautionary tale is that the Pogrebins were good people. They would never steal what did not belong to them, and they expected the same moral behavior from their nanny. It's a sad tale, but unfortunately it isn't a rare one. As a nanny myself, it feels particularly hurtful that decent people are taken advantage of and by the one person they are forced to trust the most. As Abigail Pogrebin soon began to realize, other parents had had a similar experience—betrayal and dishonesty by a nanny. This knowledge has left an otherwise optimistic person with a jaded opinion of nannies.

"I have a wonderful new nanny who I tell people is a godsend—creative, kind, and trustworthy. But now I always add a caveat: 'At least as far as I know.'"[15]

How can we protect ourselves from dishonest nannies? In hindsight, many of us who have experienced a theft in our homes were perhaps too cavalier about personal security in the first place. We might have tossed bunches of money onto side tables or left our bank statements or credit cards lying around—actions we wouldn't do in our own workplace or in a public space. It's as though we magically believe that within *our* four walls no badness can penetrate.

The reality is that theft in the workplace is a common occurrence. More revenue is lost annually in retail via employee theft than by shoplifters. Our home is a workplace if we hire and employ strangers to work within them. Background checks might not flag petty or casual theft, especially if it has previously gone unnoticed. A nanny might have pocketed a few dollars a week in petty cash or, as in the Pogrebins' case, many hundreds of dollars from her employer's bank accounts.

How can we protect our financial assets in our homes?

- Never allow an employee to use your bank card or conduct any banking business for you, including paying bills or mailing checks.
- Keep your personal financial details somewhere private, preferably locked away in an undisclosed location in your home.
- If you have a petty cash drawer, keep that under lock and key and withdraw a set daily limit of cash for a nanny's expenses.
- Always ask for a receipt. There may be times when a nanny buys your child an ice cream or an item that does not come with a receipt. Simply ask her to make a note of the cost. Check costs against losses.
- Don't make your nanny feel like a criminal. Be upfront with her, and tell her that you value her honesty but that you like to keep track of personal spending. Thank her periodically for her honesty.
- Keep precious items locked away and out of sight.
- Keep track of other workers who come and go.
- Retain house keys, and keep a ledger when you loan a key out.
- Use a nanny cam in any area that you feel needs extra surveillance.
- When reviewing receipts, be aware that a nanny may have tipped the pizza guy or the grocery guy a couple of dollars, which is standard behavior.

The second violation that can occur in child care is sexual abuse. It's the one that holds a peculiar fear for any parent—as well it should.

Predators

Pedophiles often look for positions where they can be in close unsupervised contact with children. It isn't rocket science to presume otherwise. The law as it currently stands does little to protect parents from hiring nonconvicted sexual offenders. Even online nanny agencies and high-street boutiques cannot detect pedophiles unless they have been convicted as adults. Nor can they track pedophiles who use aliases or have committed a crime in another state. Parents cannot prevent a caregiver from taking obscene photographs or filming their children and sharing them online. Therefore, unlicensed child care as it currently exists can be a natural magnet for pedophiles.

Unfortunately, it is difficult to get definitive statistics on any type of aberrant behavior that occurs behind the closed doors of unlicensed child care. When public cases arise, however, we can tease out the flaws that led to a child's exposure to abuse.

In 2009 on the Champlain Islands, a nanny by the name of Douglas Shepherd, age 23, was accused of child molestation. Upon further investigation, he was discovered to be a pedophile. The child in his care was a 10-year-old boy, someone Shepherd had been grooming for sexual advances and whom he had described as a "lover."

Shepherd had managed to get through multiple nets that are supposed to protect our children. He had been hired through a well-known online nanny service. Furthermore, he had deliberately used false names, including Jon and Parker Wilder, and worked with children in other jobs, including boys' summer camps. He had also been approved to be a substitute teacher in Grand Isle County. He also possessed vast amounts of child porn. This all indicates that Shepherd was *intent* upon gaining access to children for sexual purposes.[16]

Shepherd had found his way into the private lives of vulnerable children. That is what parents need to remember. How can we protect our children from predators? In the first instance, we can be strong, present, and loving hands-on parents. Pedophiles like to exploit any perceived adult gap in a child's life.

- Is your child old enough to understand what pedophiles do and who they are? Does he or she understand that (a) it is more likely to be someone (90 percent) they know and (b) can be a man or a woman?
- Most child molesters are male. Why have you decided to hire a man? If you believe that your son or daughter could use a positive male influence, are there other candidates for this role: your brothers, cousins, close male friends? How do you know the candidate? Did he come recommended? Did you check all of his references? Did he approach you?
- Most child molesters prefer talking to a child in the room or on a playground rather than an adult. They feel more comfortable with children and will often talk to a child as one would an adult. Is your caregiver just a Peter Pan, or is he someone who overly identifies with children for other reasons?
- Is he too nice to be true? Pedophiles will groom an entire family using excessive charm just to gain access to one particular child.
- Is his display of affection appropriate? How does your child respond to him or his embrace? Pedophiles will use innocent displays of affection in public to manipulate a child. Later on and in private, he will make sexual advances to a child as though that were a natural progression of mutual affection. This is known as *grooming*.
- Does he offer to stay extra for no pay or run errands for free, or does he ask to take junior on special outings? He may be simply trying to isolate your child so he can perform a sexual act.
- Do you use a nanny cam?
- Did you check your nanny's name on the Department of Justice National Sex Offender Database (www.nsopw.gov/en-US)? Have you checked to see if sex offenders live in your zip code?

- Are you a single parent or on a low income? Pedophiles seek vulnerable families because they view them as easy targets.
- Has your nanny signed a document stating that he or she will never photograph or film your child without your consent? Have you checked your nanny's social media accounts? Has he posted images or reproduced images of children on his websites?
- Has your child changed in any way since you hired a new nanny? Is your child acting out sexually? Has the child become withdrawn?

A pedophile can be anyone: the coach, a piano teacher, a tutor, a teacher substitute, a summer camp leader. Our children should never be left alone with adult men in particular, nor should we allow small children to use a public male toilet by themselves. It is unfortunate that a few sick men and women spoil it for the rest, but when it comes to pedophiles we must remain hypervigilant.

Another criminal type that can lurk hidden within child care is the violent nanny. Any routine search online for "nanny cam horror" will pull up scores of videos showing caregivers slapping, hitting, or knocking children over or shaking them. Using a nanny cam from day one will help to prevent such abuse, especially if you notify a candidate during the interview that you intend to use one. Why do some seemingly nice people suddenly snap and assault a child?

Physical Abuse

Most of the advice that is given with regard to violent nannies is what to look out for *after the act*. In other words, our children will begin to demonstrate some common signs of distress:

- Our child is *consistently* not happy to see the nanny. The child does not want to be left alone with her.
- A child has bruises or marks that cannot be accounted for or that are simply brushed off as "accidents" by a nanny.
- Our child has begun to act out in violent ways: pushing and shoving other children, hitting or kicking them. The child has begun to pull toys apart and destroy them. The child has begun to hit dolls or teddy bears. The child may begin to act violently toward the family pet.
- Our child has begun to regress by bed-wetting and/or thumb sucking, actions that are not age appropriate.
- Our child has begun to automatically flinch when you raise a hand too quickly.
- Our child has become too obedient to the point of being overly submissive.

- The child exhibits vacant staring. Our infant avoids our eyes. She seems to be lost in a world of her own. This could be a sign of a child seeking to avoid confrontation. Children who do this might be afraid of provoking a violent confrontation from the adults around them.
- Our toddler constantly craves attention when we are home. He is clingy and irritable with you but passive as soon as his nanny walks in.
- Our child has begun to draw violent images or scenes involving blood and injury. The child uses black and red over all other colors. The faces of the child characters they draw are angry, sad, or extremely small compared to the adult figures. The figures they depict are often hurting one another or animals.[17]

Prevention

Prevention is trickier, in part because violent, mentally ill, emotionally unbalanced, or disgruntled caregivers can be superb manipulators. They can give you the illusion that everything's fine. Later in this book I will offer more ways to weed out potentially bad candidates. At this stage and in terms of prevention, it's important that you always listen to your gut. If you meet a prospective nanny and there is something about her that just doesn't sit right, then 100 percent go with that feeling. Even if a nanny appears wonderful, a thorough background check is your first port of call.

Screening

You will want to establish a candidate's *full legal name*. That might require a candidate producing multiple identifying papers, such as a passport, a driver's license, a work permit, bank cards, etc. Then you will want to check a *combination* of a candidate's legal name. So, if you have seen legal documents with the name Mary Ann Jones, try searching under Ann Jones, Mary Jones, Mary Ann Jones, and Ann Mary Jones. You should request proof of a maiden name if the candidate is married or divorced. You should then search under that name too.

When conducting background checks on candidates, include a search for any incidents related to domestic violence, public disorder, driving under the influence of alcohol and/or an illegal substance, and any notices to do with child protective services. Some caregivers may have had turbulent lives that can cause them to spiral out of control from time to time. They may have been arrested for being drunk and disorderly. This could indicate a propensity toward addiction or poor anger management or impulse control issues. You will also want to look for signs of financial insolvency. Search a candidate's credit history. Any red flags concerning credit card defaults or recent bankruptcy notices could indicate a person who is in dire economic straits or who engages in risky spending. While this is not a judgment on a nanny's moral character, it could suggest that she is already under chronic emotional stress—not a good starting point for your baby.

If your candidate is an immigrant, you will want to consider how long she has lived in the United States, that will reflect on how far back you can accurately screen her background. If your candidate has moved around a lot, you will need to conduct background checks in every state she has ever lived in. In the long run it might be more economical to outsource this type of screening to a third party, such as a security agency.

Profile

When you first encounter someone, your entire body will be focused on first impressions. It's at this point that a parent's radar is sharpest. Look for these signs:

- Does the candidate seem hyper or nervous?
- Does she maintain eye contact with you?
- Did she greet you with a smile that felt genuine?
- Does she seem glum or too serious?
- Is she lackluster one moment and then superanimated the next?
- What does she talk about when you first meet? Are her interests unusual?
- Did she look healthy? How was she dressed?

Follow-up

As indicated elsewhere in this book, you absolutely *must* check every single reference provided by a nanny. Talk to all references, and listen closely to what they say and how they say it. There are questions specifically provided in Chapter 6 for you to sample. Arrange to meet face-to-face with a nanny's former employer in the employer's neighborhood. If at all possible, talk to the reference's children. Your nanny should have provided *at least* two local recent references. Your nanny should also come with *at least* two years of direct experience working with children in your geographical area.

Risk Factors

Rarely does a nanny wake up one morning intending to deliberately harm the child in her care. In terms of statistics, a child is more likely to be injured by a complete stranger or a relative, such as a parent, than a nanny. When harm is done to a child by a nanny, several factors come into play:

- *The age of the child.* Newborns, premature infants, multiples, infants with disabilities, and small children are more likely to be physically abused by a nanny than are older children.
- *The age of the caregiver.* Some nannies and babysitters lack the emotional maturity or experience to weather normal infant behavior, such as excessive crying, regular diaper changing, erratic feeding, erratic napping, vomiting, spitting up, and general fussiness.
- *Candidates with a previous history of child abuse.* Candidates who perpetrated abuse on children or experienced abuse in their own childhoods are more likely to offend.
- *Stress in a caregiver's personal life.* Chronic stress can lead to insomnia, depression, and extreme anxiety. In these states a child can more easily tax a caregiver's patience.
- *Unrealistic expectations of the child, of caregiving, and about child development.* The caregiver expects the child to fulfill her needs and as such can become furious when her needs are not met or are subservient to the child's needs.
- *The caregiver has unresolved emotional issues.* The caregiver's intrinsic needs were not met in her own early childhood. Thus, such a person can be triggered into feelings of rage and anger when the healthy demands of an infant in her care are expressed.
- *The caregiver is resentful and envious of her employers.* She expresses her resentment against their child.

This last risk factor should not be overlooked in terms of importance. Nannies today are feeling more stressed and challenged by a lack of real benefits available to them within an unlicensed industry. Some struggle daily just to pay their rent and bills. Others are the sole breadwinners in their families. Chronic stress and fatigue create conditions whereby a caregiver's last nerve is stretched, and she snaps.

Having watched numerous nanny cam abuse videos, I have noticed a few common themes:

- The abusive caregiver—once caught—expresses extreme remorse and attempts to blame her actions as a one-off stress response. She will cite personal stress as a factor. She will suggest that the child himself was to blame or that in some way the parents contributed to her behavior.
- In nanny cam footage, an abusive caregiver will often be seen picking up or rocking the traumatized child immediately after an attack sequence.

(I use the word "sequence" here to indicate that an abusive nanny will appear to rotate back on a wailing child and attack him again until it appears that she is sated.) This is one of the most disturbing aspects of viewing nanny abuse caught on camera.

This action perhaps suggests that an instantaneous split or temporary psychosis has occurred—a profound schism within the individual's psyche. By comforting the traumatized infant, is the nanny merely expressing guilt at what she has just violently perpetrated on an innocent, vulnerable baby? Or does it signal a more serious indication that her schism has deeper, subconscious roots? By her action of seemingly comforting the traumatized infant, is the nanny on some primal level attempting to soothe her own unresolved infancy-based pain? Has the traumatized baby therefore merely become an object of a nanny's fragmentation?

For the child concerned, it must be a terrifying and confusing experience to be beaten and then held or attended to, over and over again. If left unchecked, this type of abuse can produce the same types of behavior later on in life. It is therefore essential to screen for bad nannies *and* to use nanny cams.

While we can never excuse or condone the abuse of children by nannies, it behooves us to explore some of the risk factors behind their acts of violence. Poverty and a lack of long-term benefits rank high on the list. The constant financial hardship experienced by many nannies both in the present and in their perception of a bleak future necessitates an action that comes with sourcing child care income: *the hustle.*

Chapter 3

The Work: Intimate Yet Invisible

HUSTLING AND JOB CREEP

Hustle (v.): force (someone) to move hurriedly or unceremoniously in a specified direction; "they hustled him into the back of a horse-drawn wagon."

Webster's Dictionary

The single most powerful characteristic of a certain class of child care workers is the need to *hustle*. Hustling is not an autonomous action. As the definition above states, a hustle is an active external force that is exerted upon an individual *unceremoniously*.

Hustling is easily confused with the act of speculation—but it's not the same thing at all. To speculate is to take a risk and to gamble on positions or other ventures in the hope of long-term gain, albeit with attendant risk. This is the alchemy of the American Dream. Child care workers who hustle can exist in a nightmare world of ever-diminishing opportunities. The primary cause of their situation is their status as undocumented workers, for without papers there is little hope of being placed by a nanny agency. But it can also arise because the industry of child care itself fails to provide universal benefits for its members, American or otherwise. In the long-term the hustle can become a slow and exhausting dance with poverty and one that often ends before the proverbial music stops.

I spoke with two undocumented workers in order to fully comprehend the mental and emotional mechanics of hustling. One is a new immigrant—a

Caucasian Russian woman I'll call Sasha—and the other is an older Afro-Caribbean woman named Marge.[1]

Sasha

I met Sasha a little over a year ago. I was with my then two charges in a local playground when I first spotted her. She was blond, slender, and outwardly beautiful, but her sadness was palpable. It seemed to radiate out of Sasha like a blinding fog, and at every opportunity she pulled up the toddler in her care and hugged him. The child—a frail little boy as thin as a wooden puppet—dropped limply in her arms with a fixed smile. His eyes shut tight as he swooned in her desperate affection.

Something is not right with this picture, I thought, *that woman looks depressed.* Patiently I circled her until we locked eyes.

"Hello" I said, "you look like *you* need a hug."

Sasha beamed me one of her characteristic smiles and then began to cry. I suddenly found myself comforting a stranger. The little boy glanced fearfully up at us. *Had I hurt her?* Perhaps, he wondered. Sasha immediately reached down and clutched him up in one arm—with me in the other. Other playground attendees began to stare. I offered her a tissue. I felt awkward.

"I'm sorry, forgive me," Sasha blubbered, sensing my unease and pulling away.

"No, no. Honestly, it's fine. I could just tell you were having a bad day," I recanted, edging back closer.

"Sasha is okay, baby," she gently whispered to the boy in her arms. Satisfied he wriggled back down to his toy truck.

I introduced myself, and once Sasha knew that I was a nanny, she told me her story. It blew out of her like a fierce tsunami, and once done she plopped down onto a nearby bench—exhausted.

Sasha is my friend to this day. I love her like a sister. I suppose that in some way she is. One of the most precious things I own is a necklace of colored pearls that Sasha gave me the second time we met. It was the only thing of value she owned. She told me her story:

I used to work in Russia for very big bank. My job was important. I made very good money. I am highly educated. I have a masters in international business. I lived very well [in St. Petersburg]. I had a big apartment and a cleaner, and I could do whatever I wanted. One day the bank it went bankrupt. Overnight I have no job, no compensation. I support my elderly mother. She is invalid. In Russia you must bribe people to get good medicine and care. Without me she would die.

I had no choice but to leave Russia and come to the United States. My brother, he told me to go. I came here with an address for a cousin. She lives in Queens. I stayed with her one week. She took me to an agency that places Russians without papers. The jobs are all bad. They are live-in jobs, and my cousin told me, "You can't stay here anymore; you must take a live-in job."

The first family, they are Russian Americans. I work seven days a week all day and all night with three children. I sleep on the floor. I am not allowed to stop and eat, so I eat from the scraps of the children. The father is very angry all the time, and he yells at me "clean this, move that." He drinks all the time. I think the children are afraid of him. The oldest child, he bullies the youngest children. He yells at me like the father.

The mother, she watches everything I do. She follows me around, and she tells me, "This is not clean, clean this again"; even if the plate is clean, I must clean it again to her satisfaction. I must prepare all the meals, and I must clean the apartment. I must wash the clothes. I receive $200 a week, but they keep $50 and pay for me to stay in a cheap hotel one night a week so they can practice their religion. Every day I must leave the apartment with the children even if it is cold or raining. The parents do not care if we are cold. I must always get out of the apartment so the father can work.

One day I was sick. I had something from the children. I could not leave the bathroom. The next day the mother, she asked me to leave. She did not give me reference, and the agency was very angry with me. They told me, "You cannot be sick and miss work ever again."

The next job was even worse than the last job if you can believe it, but as I had nowhere to live I took it. The family had five children and a dog. Again I sleep on a mattress on the floor with a baby in the same room. I must clean and cook and walk the dog. The parents are crazy, and everyone yells at everyone. The children were very rude to me. They say to me that I cannot speak English, that I am stupid. They drop their food on the floor and laugh because they understand that I must pick these things up. I cry every night. I wonder, "Am I being punished by God for once being rich?" I learn very quickly that I have no choice but to be strong. Without me my mother will die.

I have no papers. I have nothing to tell that I am a smart, hardworking person. Here I am nothing, just a pair of hands. I send back money so my mother has medication. I buy cheap coffee with lots of sugar so I don't feel hungry. I buy cheap clothes from market. I smoke cheap cigarettes.

I buy a cheap phone. I look for ways to find a job. I ask other nannies, "How can you find a good job in America?" I tell some of them about my situation. One girl, she feels very bad for me, and she tells me she will help to find me a job. She is from Mexico, and she asks some people. I find this job [the current one] through her. But straight away I know the family [former one] would not be happy. I knew that the agency would be very angry. It was a big gamble, but I was so tired and the work was too hard, and I was getting skinny, and I could see in my face [she was 45 in 2014] that I am becoming an old woman.

I had no choice; I must leave. I met with the new family [current one]. They are very nice, and they have one child. I work 12 hours [a day] including one night that is late, and I earn $300 a week. I cook and clean for them. They are good people, but they do not have much money. But the situation is not good because I cannot live in. I must now pay to share a room with another lady in a bad neighborhood. This means I must travel a long way to my job. The lady [her roommate] is very clean and we are polite, but I do not know how long she will stay. The other people who share the apartment is a family. They have a big bathroom and a kitchen. The mother [lease holder], she does not like us [boarders] to use the kitchen or the big bathroom, so we eat our meals outside, and we use the small bathroom. It is just a sink and a toilet. It is not acceptable, but the rent is cheap.

I must clean for other people on Saturday. I have two jobs I work for extra money. On Sunday I go to church, then I wash my clothes. Most of the time I must sleep. I love culture, and I like to look at beautiful things. In Russia I used to go to the opera. I was a person who went to fancy restaurants. I liked to read good books and watch movies. On Sundays I try to remember that I am the same person. I sometimes take a little walk. I sometimes pretend I am on a date. It helps to keep me strong.

This family is mostly very good, but I do not know how long the job will last. The child is going to school maybe soon? I do not know. So I must always look and ask for jobs. I love this little boy so much. He is allergy [allergic] to so many things. Oh my God, he cannot eat this, he cannot touch this. I tremble when we go out; I must to watch him like a hawk in case he takes a snack from someone. His parents work very long hours, and they work very hard. They are kind, and they cannot pay much. But they let me eat food from their house, and the mother she gives me a coat or shoes sometimes.

Without this child [her charge] I think I would die. I know he loves me. Every day when I am sad he does funny things to make me laugh. It's like he understands. I don't know what comes next. One day maybe I have no room. They [the family who sublet their apartment to Sasha] might change their mind. I have no papers. I have no proof that I pay them. I have no bank account. I have nothing. One day the parents [whom she works for] maybe they lose their job? Again I have nothing. I must always look. I feel like an animal in the ground. Every day I must to go out and look for food. I must go and find a warm place. Always I am afraid.

I asked Sasha what one thing would change her life.

It is simple. It is this—to have papers. I want to come and say to the authorities that I will do anything to have papers. If I have papers I can find a good job. I can rent an apartment. I can pay my bills, and I can pay my tax. If I have papers people they cannot exploit me. I know that people [some Americans] know I have no papers. I do not have to say it. They can see that I am desperate. Sometimes I think they prefer people without papers so they pay less, so they can treat us badly. I do not want to ask for anything. I have proud [pride]. It is important that America understands that to give papers is to make more money for everyone. We are already here. We already make job. We are human beings. I think that is it. We must have papers.[2]

Marge

I call Marge "aunty" because she reminds me of the many older Caribbean women I grew up knowing back in England. Aunty Marge is now in her late 60s, although no one is supposed to know that. Her story is typical of many undocumented domestic workers. In the mid-1990s the World Bank loaned the island of Trinidad millions and in return dictated a series of harsh economic measures, wiping out entire public service industries and forcing locals—mostly women—to migrate to Europe or America for work.

Aunty Marge had two small daughters, and when she lost her job at the national telecom company she had no choice but to say goodbye to them, to take a plane and join a cousin in New York City. Her first job was as a live-in domestic worker and involved walking a dog at 6 a.m. in the morning. In her own words:

It was in Long Island, and back then it cost $15 round trip. It was my first job, and I got it through my cousin. That's how we do it. We don't come to America unless we have something—you understand? After I walk the dog I have to take the child to school, then housekeep. Every damn thing they have in that house was white: white floors, white walls, white sofa. You know how hard that is to keep clean? I sleep in a tiny room in the basement, just a bed. They pay me $175 per week. I work from Monday 6 a.m. until they want to go to sleep. If they have a dinner party, guess what? It's Marge that has to clean everything up. Some nights I get to my bed at 1:00 in the morning. On Saturday night after they come home I must go home to my cousin's that same night. I often reached home to Brooklyn on a Sunday morning at 2 a.m.! I just sleep on the sofa, and then Sunday evening I must return back to Long Island.

So out of the $175 I send $100 back to my mother who is raising my children. I pay my cousin $20 for one night to sleep and a little food. Then I have to pay to go to Long Island. Then I must save a little. I lived on coffee, rolls, and 99-cent soup. The employers they asked me if I knew what toothpaste was? They thought I came from a cave. I was crying in my bed every night. I woke up on the step looking to go home. It's not easy.

Then I came in to work with these other people in Long Island; they had a dog and were just to have a baby. They were nice people. They pay me the same money but I do less. I work Monday to Friday, and I was able to go to school on Saturday to do a Certified Nurse's Aide [CAN] course. Then on Sunday I took a little cleaning job. I felt very good. I didn't want to be a cleaner no more. I wanted to make a future for myself here.

I got my certification and I was able to get a job working in a hospital. I got $700 a week looking after mostly the elderly. The work was hard, but I felt good. I was able to send more money home and to take a small apartment. I said to myself "Margie, things is looking up for you now, girl."

Well now let me get to the point of my story. Fifteen years ago I met a rich, rich lady in the hospital, and she say, "Come and work for me. Take care of my father, and I will pay you good money." You see, that's how she work. She set you up high. Then slowly she break you down. She suckerd me in. She had me take care of her father, who was an invalid. It was the biggest mistake of my life. But I was loyal. I stayed too long. I let my CAN [certification] run out. I begged her to let me get certified through her MD because she could have done that, and the woman she just keep fobbing me off—making excuses.

I don't know why I stayed. It was a mistake. I felt trapped. The money was good to start, but when my certification expire the woman began to nickel and dime me. She say she had to make cuts. She know I'm trapped. Then the father, he moved away into assisted living in Florida. So she say, "Marge I can't manage without you. Stay and clean for me." She was married, and she have children. So I worked for her and I cleaned. I worked seven days a week for $500. Then she wear me down to $350, and I work 10 hours a day Monday through Saturday. Some days the regular babysitter she can't work, so the woman she ask me to stay late. Sometimes she ask me to clean on the weekend if she has a party. I get $350 a week just the same, but I'm trapped, you see? Because I'm old and if I leave, she won't give me a reference. How can I go to another job without a reference for 15 years? They think I stole something?

Now she pick on me. She figures that if I stay on another year or two she must give me a pension or something. She want rid of me. Everything I do she picks me up on it.

You see times is bad right now, and no one happy. No one can take a little break and find someone to fill their job like they used to because this woman, your friend, she might steal your job. That's how rough it is—and everything it going up. It's a hustle. People like me who don't have the paperwork in order, we got nowhere to go. People they look for workers like us. So they can squeeze us.

I got nothing back home—no pension. When I go back home all I have is what I saved, and I'm old. My children, they trying to make it for themselves. They can't help me out, and my mother she now pass. I send my money bit by bit back home, and I trust the bank that it don't go out of business because I will live on the streets. And it make me think maybe I come to America for nothing? I didn't raise my kids. I didn't care for my mother before she pass. Me just clean. These things can weigh heavy—you understand?

You know how much trouble people is in right now? You have no idea. There is a lot of anger out there. People is working two days a week and treated like s**t! My friend she has her papers, and she still can't get something steady. It's the economy, it's this [points to her skin], and people is getting angry. As far as "we" are concerned things is not right. We can't get wages or medical help, and we do all the work? If I had enough money in my bank account I would just walk away and have peace.[3]

Sasha and Marge represent a hidden underbelly of domestic workers, and like the base of a gigantic iceberg they remain submerged in a frozen sea of invisibility. Yet the work they do is vital to our economy and to the way America runs. Despite what one popular advertisement states, America doesn't run on doughnuts. Its economy depends in part on the work done by unrepresented labor and undocumented workers. Organizations such as the National Domestic Workers Alliance endeavor to help these workers with solutions such as matching workers to fair-wage positions. Its director, Ai-jen Poo, states:

We're working on developing some resources and services to help match domestic workers with good, fair employers. It's a challenge, because not every employer will pay a living wage, but we're actively looking for those job opportunities for our members because we absolutely agree, at the end of the day, finding work is key to our survival and it's not easy.[4]

Getting the word out to undocumented workers is the biggest challenge, because so many of them work indoors and out of sight. Therefore, the typical experience of an undocumented worker can be one of grinding poverty, of living on meager cash payments, of daily interaction with indifferent or rude employers, and of working with angry or frustrated children. These conditions are bound to produce chronic resentment and apathy in the workplace—a child's home.

In turn this glut of cheap labor undercuts the median wages of trained American or documented child care workers. This undocumented and low-paid group also has a quick turnover rate. Immigrants look for better jobs once their English improves or references build up. Equally true is the scenario of employers dumping a new immigrant on a whim, as though the immigrant were a used toy. The rapid change of nannies within families affects the children deeply.

In summary, we have seen that the labor of undocumented domestic workers who serve as nannies often involves a great deal of hustling—that is, the constant search for work and of living on meager wages—and that these workers often operate in depressing conditions without protection of the law. But low wages, long hours, and the absence of voting rights are not the only impediments to the workforce. Another one lurks, and it can be as corrosive as a low hourly rate to a nanny's performance in your home.

DENIAL AND SABOTAGE

Denial. Psychology: a condition in which someone will not admit that something sad, painful, etc., is true or real.

Webster's Dictionary

A New York mother of two whom I know has successfully used the services of a nanny, but she has also witnessed the darker side of child care. I will call her Mariah.[5] One day, Mariah observed a nanny slapping a little boy (her charge) in a playground. She determined to follow the nanny home, observing the nanny pulling the child en route. The child was clearly in a state of distress. Once at the apartment building, Mariah asked the doorman for the telephone number of the child's mother. Later that evening she called the mother and informed her of the nanny's poor behavior. The mother dismissed Mariah's eyewitness account as a mistake, stating that "My nanny would never do that. You must have the wrong person." The telephone conversation promptly ended with the woman hanging up.[6]

Why would a mother refuse to acknowledge her child's potential mistreatment? Has the answer got to with conflicted feelings that some parents have toward child care?

"When a parent must leave a small child in less than optimal child care, that parent is bound to grieve," according to T. Berry Brazleton and Stanley I. Greenspan. "The grieving can take many forms: denial, detachment from the child, and anger and/or depression at the workplace that demands the separation."[7]

The mother in question might also have felt a little ambushed by Mariah's—a stranger's—comments and intrusion into her daily life, and perhaps upon reflection she reevaluated her child care situation. Still, denial can be a common first response to something negative that a nanny does to a child.

There are other ways that parents can react to a nanny's performance, especially and ironically if it's good. It's called *sabotage*.

Sabotage

Sabotage. The act of destroying or damaging something deliberately so that it does not work correctly.

Webster's Dictionary

Sabotage is not always a conscious weapon of war in the power struggle between mothers and nannies, but it can be an effective one. At other times it is all too apparent that a nanny's work is being hampered deliberately, and when a nanny feels that she is not being supported in her role this can almost destroy her professional identity.

What are the ways in which sabotage can play out? I have identified six main ways:

- Micromanaging (not allowing a nanny to make basic decisions)

- Nitpicking (criticizing every action or choice made by a nanny)
- Being sent on a fool's errands (being sent out to find stuff that's almost impossible to get or is entirely superfluous)
- Leaving out pertinent information (so that the nanny makes obvious mistakes) on specific duties
- Not respecting professional boundaries (being late, demanding more hours)
- Bait and switch (changing duties or tasks at the last second, creating confusion)

I asked three nannies about job sabotage and what it can lead to in the workplace: Anna, an undocumented Polish woman now returned to the European Union; Lisa, an American graduate since turned professional actress; and Carly, an Ivy League graduate.[8]

Anna became a nanny because she needed money to travel around the United States. Lisa wasn't sure why. It just happened to be the first job she found when she moved to New York City. Carly became a nanny to pay her rent and to pursue her art career. Anna claimed to have no child care qualifications. Lisa felt that she was only qualified by the mother's standards. Carly had a master's degree but not in early childhood development.

Anna

I left my country over four years ago. Back then I did not have any idea that I am going to stay so long and be taking care of kids. I have never visited my country since I left. Babysitting is an amazing experience. First of all, I found out a lot about myself. I did not even realize how much patience and how much I could possibly endured. This is extremely hard work sometimes. In terms of emotional and intellectual stimulation, I found out myself as someone who is showing the world to somebody who do not know anything. This is very serious position that we are in. We are carrying such responsible for that little person, we simply cannot make any mistake. I'm paid $12 per hour. Normally I was shown what my duties are. That usually last no longer than two hours. I usually work with two working parents, middle class.

Generally they [employers] were nice people; however, there were situations, which I felt that they don't really care about me. It is dependable on the situation that I was in. I would say that was the broken promise. Being told a holiday would be paid and then it was not. . . . This situation is really fresh only from yesterday. I was asked to babysit in the evening. Before I agreed I asked about the transportation back to my home. So we [nanny and parents] agreed that after 9:30 p.m. I will be sent [home] in the taxi. What happened they come back at 9:50 p.m. and decided that they could not afford the money for a taxi. I have to mention that if I knew in advance I would not agreed to babysit that late because I do not live next door in Manhattan but all the way down in Queens. The trip back to my place took me about 1.5 hours.

I asked Anna how an employer's behavior could affect the way in which she treated their children.

Well, there is nothing [physically] harmful that I could possibly do to the child. Anyway, the fact is that the poor behavior of my boss affect the way I treat their children. It is sort of lack of patience. I begin to see in the child kind of little enemy that I have to fight with. When situation with parents gets back to normal I start to treat the child the way I used to.

I wanted to know if Anna believed that bad nannies were wholly to blame for their actions? And if not, who else was?

That might be several reasons like terrible relationship with parents of the child or extremely difficult child. The other thing is just simply not everyone was born to be a nanny.

Anna recently went back to the European Union and has since returned to a career in the civil service. She still has much to say about her time as a nanny and the lack of general oversight that the child care industry has in the United States. But I thought it important to dialogue with an American-born nanny to see if she felt the same way as Anna.[9]

Lisa

Babysitting taught me the importance of boundaries: very important, but almost impossible to achieve. My schedule was nonexistent. I felt my personal time was ignored because you have to put the child's needs first—how can you argue with that? At times when I was asked to work later into the evenings I knew I would be there after midnight and had to be because if I wasn't there, who would be? They [the parents] couldn't leave her [the child] with anyone else because she screamed and cried the entire night. I became the only person they trusted with this job—and because I cared about the child, I stayed.

They [the parents] assumed I could be available Monday to Friday 9 a.m. to 9 p.m. or noon to dinnertime, depending on when they wanted me. I should have set good rules for availability, but I trusted them and hoped my weekly salary was worth it (the hours worked). I was paid the same amount every week regardless of how many hours I worked. I was paid $500 per week.

From the first day on the job I was alone with the child for almost eight hours! I don't know how I survived. Her mother sent us to a class, then to get pizza, then we spent hours at her mother's office reading, playing pretend, making cookies, or taking imaginary trips to her imaginary beach house. I remember thinking "How can I be doing this?" They were two working parents, wealthy types both very self-absorbed in their careers.

From the beginning I was treated like a nanny, a personal assistant, a house-keeper, a teacher, a marriage guidance counselor, and occasionally as a shrink. They treated me as if I should love doing whatever they felt like asking me to do—because they knew I loved the child so they took advantage of that. They asked me to fold laundry and wash dishes, quite a lot of menial tasks—things they could easily have done—like wash their own dirty plates or move a coffee cup from a table to their own dishwasher. I was also expected to come to their parties as a friend, but I would end up taking care of the child so they [the parents] could socialize.

I had to do a lot of different stuff like family laundry that was not just the child's. I had to pick out gifts for her child's friends or family, grocery shop, being in her apartment when workmen were there.

I asked Lisa how her employers' behavior would affect the way she treated their child.

They made me feel constantly guilty for not being more available when I was already giving up my entire Monday to Friday for them. They made comments and made me feel bad for trying to have my own life. At times I would get so angry, and I think I took it out on the poor child. I was very impatient when I was angry.

I mostly got angry with [the mother] when she would keep me past the time I needed to leave to go for a class or a dinner date or whatever—you know, my own life. . . . It wasn't the child's fault. But my anger would result in me distancing myself from the child. She could always tell when I was distant and tried to get me to play with her. I usually did snap out of it. I never yelled at her or made her cry—but I think she got nervous when I was distant, and that made me sad to think I could make her feel uneasy. Children are so intuitive.

I asked Lisa what she would say to her employer if she didn't care about losing her job.

I would say that nannies need to be treated like real people. They need overtime pay, vacations paid, living wages, health benefits, and above all else just simple respect. They [nannies] are some of the most important employees in this country. Why should they be treated any different than your child's teacher or doctor? They [nannies] are the voice of reason for your child 40+ hours a week.

Parents need to really think about that before they invest in a caretaker—if they [parents] want quality, then they should be prepared to pay for it. Otherwise your $11 an hour simply buys you a whole lot of neglect. I saw a lot of nannies who didn't get treated well by their employers take it out on the kids. . . . Children deserve more than that.

Yes. I think the parents are ultimately responsible for the treatment of their children. They [parents] have to take the time to find a good nanny through interviews, references, and personal taste. If they are taking their time to find someone they can truly communicate with, then there is hope that the child will also be communicated with in a healthy way.

Do the research. Have guidelines. Ask other parents or teachers. Don't base your decision on money. Introduce them [nannies] to your children to see if there is a connection—that is the most important thing—so you know your child will listen to that person and love them.[10]

I really wanted to drill down further and explore the impact of sabotage on a working relationship. I was introduced to a nanny who had borne the full brunt of it. When I listened to her story, I couldn't help thinking of those lines from *The Nanny Diaries* and how true they had become:

Looking back, it was a set-up to begin with. They want you. You want the job. But to do it well is to lose it.[11]

Carly

If there were one woman who had impressed me to the point of adulation in child care, it was Carly. Carly never missed an opportunity to shower love and attention on the three girls in her care. She was a smart American— someone who viewed her temporary sojourn into child care as an important opportunity to enrich lives. She was my nanny hero—my nanny crush.

It sounds gushy, but observing the delicacy with which Carly navigated her work and the time she took to care for each child, despite the fact that the children concerned clearly had some issues, was inspiring. But Carly's boss did not see her in the same light. In fact, she not only resented Carly for being an amazing nanny but actively sabotaged her. The 12 months Carly spent with the family were grueling and almost drove her to the point of total burnout.

To be honest I would say from the first week it was like a slow buildup—a feeling of being gently bullied, but you can't quite put your finger on it? I think I had one day without any criticism. Maybe she had a migraine that shut down her jaws or something. I don't know. It was the shortest honeymoon of my life. But then—oh boy—it started.

So it was like constant nitpicking. I would get blamed for things that no parent in the world would ever blame themselves for. Like the kids had not put their homework away perfectly or that the dog had gone behind the sofa and peed. I mean stuff happens. She [the mother] would then go over in absolute minutia how she wanted everything to be done. She'd talk to me like I was the dumbest person she had ever met, like with wide eyes, emphasizing every word, talking slowly, then she would say "Do you even understand what I am trying to explain to you right now?"

I wanted to tell her so many times, "Yes, I'm working a job, sure, taking care of your kids but I don't feel inferior to you." I had the same amount of education—in fact in this case I had more education than her. And there she was making a point of treating me like a complete moron in front of the kids. It was totally humiliating.

Especially when I would put in my all—literally everything they asked of me— not just performing but trying to do it well. You know how it is. I would buy the girls little toys out of my own money or buy them special snacks that I knew they loved. I'd do extra stuff around the apartment—stuff I was never required to do. But you just get beaten down enough, and when everything I did was wrong in some way I stopped caring about how well I did it. I began to switch off. Like when you're not even trying or caring anymore, you're just doing. I mean where did caring get you? And the girls would be extra clingy, but I just kind of vanished—and the kids felt it. I know they did.

Here's the real kicker—there were days where I just managed to pull off every one of her stupid nitpicking requests, and it totally pissed her off. She'd be hunting around for anything to be wrong and it wasn't. Did I get a thank-you or a smile? Nope. So, like if the kids had done their homework, had a great time with me, had eaten their dinner, blah-blah-blah, she'd just sort of have this look on her face. Then I'd know there'd be more nitpicking—more blame.

I became the queen of useless tasks—more lists, more hunting around for honestly useless crap. Like the classic fool's errand—like "Find me 15 organic silk lilac hair bows?" So I'd have to schlep around getting a bunch of crap, and it sort of communicated to me "I don't value your time. See how I can use it?"

And such awful double standards like she'd buy them pizza and candy while I had to serve tofu and fruit. I couldn't let them use media. She'd let them do media. I was the bad cop, she was the good cop. And, look, I get when you work 8 to 10 hours a day you want to spoil your kids, but I'm talking about when I was there. She would pop in and change the rules, then leave. And the kids thought that was hilarious. So in the end—guess what—I didn't insist on no media or them eating every single last veggie up. I mean, why should I follow her rules? She didn't.

The other thing was that my needs were completely irrelevant to her. She would say stuff like "My big CEO boss is coming tomorrow, and I need you to do XYZ. I have to fly to Beijing Monday; I need you to live in all week." It's not that I'm inflexible. It's just that I was always the *last* person to find out. She would know days in advance. The cleaner would know. The kids would know. The doorman would even know. I would be told the day before or a few hours before. Like she enjoyed dangling me on a string.

For people like her, I think it's way easier to have an undocumented worker as a nanny. They [the parents] can automatically feel somewhat superior. My boss would get rattled by my knowledge or ideas, like when I was helping the kids with their homework, so there was this double intimidation. She hated the fact that I went to an Ivy League school. She'd say stuff like "I guess you just know everything." So I made myself smaller. I just hit a wall. The nitpicking gradually became incessant—voice mails, texts, long e-mails, post-it notes—always pointing out what she thought I'd messed up—and to intimate that I did anything to hurt those kids in some way was just cruel.

There were times I thought she hated her life or her job or her role as a mother, and she'd start in on me. It's a great way to take out on someone not related to you something you hate about your family. You know what I mean? We're a scapegoat. Parents get to dump all their shit and guilt and jealousy onto us.

Are moms in general patronizing toward nannies? I think they try not to be, but there's always this "mom's club, nanny club" kind of deal. It's how women treat women. Even stay-at-home moms can be bitchy or preachy or judgmental. It's because they have conflicted feelings about having someone else around coraising their children. Or they have weird guilt about not working full-time and living in their gym wear 24–7. I mean, I get it—so, yeah, there's a lot of them versus us. As if somehow they got first prize, and we're like the handmaidens—the runners-up.

Nanny jobs are considered less important. So you must be kind of less intelligent to want to do them. But I actually think that's just BS, and deep down nannies threaten moms on a very primal level. Think about it—what does it mean if the nanny totally succeeds? Have they outdone, outperformed, outsourced the parents? That's a horrific thought for mothers. Most women still totally define themselves primarily as a mother no matter what they do. I'm telling you, nannies get nervous when the children prefer them. When that happened to me it made me so uncomfortable, because I just knew there'd be fallout.

My advice to a nanny: know your worth and don't let anyone take it away from you. My advice to a parent employing a nanny: know your nanny's worth. Treat nannies the same way you treat your super, or the person who cuts your hair, or your child's teacher. No, treat them better—because they do one of the greatest jobs on earth.[12]

Carly's story is fortunately a rare one. Most parents get the connection between how they treat their nanny and how their nanny will treat their children. It's kind of like child care's version of instant karma. But less discussed is the jealousy that working parents experience intensely from time to time. Jealousy is a natural parental emotion that is associated with effectively sharing our children with others. It can rear its ugly head in any moment. For instance, a nanny talking about her fantastic day with our toddler can provoke intense feelings—and often conflicted ones. In the one instance the parents are happy to hear that their child is being expertly cared for. In another they may feel as though they are missing out on precious moments. As Karen Kaufman, PhD, LCSW, puts it:

Nanny jealousy, while not a diagnosable condition, is real and problematic and can adversely impact the nanny/parent/child relationships. Seeing one's child become attached to the nanny can threaten the new mother and her developing sense of herself in this role. This can lead to passive aggressive behaviors on both sides as the tension mounts.[13]

I spoke to numerous parents, mostly working mothers, who spoke of the sadness they feel when they try to cram in a few intense hours of together-ness with their children on the weekend only to know that come Monday morning, they must hug their children goodbye for huge chunks of time. If we add to that those awkward times when small children suddenly cling to their nannies at the end of the day, it's easy to see how the dynamic of emotional tug and pull occurs.

How can parents manage eruptions of nanny jealousy? Annabelle Corke, president at Hey Day Nannies, offers these tips on coping:

1. *Open up.* Encourage a dialogue between you and your nanny that is ongoing.
2. *Be patient.* Like any relationship it takes time, maturity, and trust to develop. Not making the time to get to know your nanny and vice versa can be detrimental in the long run.
3. *Be confident.* Encourage your child to show affection to others and encourage your nanny to show affection to your children, but know that your unique bond with your child is not being threatened.
4. *Be creative.* Look at your nanny as part of your team, not just as an employee, and mold her role to make the most of her best qualities.
5. *Listen to yourself.* Know what kind of nanny you want. Do you want more of a housekeeper who watches the kids, or do you want an interac-tive teacher type whose presence and influence are more strongly felt? Knowing what you need from your nanny and being able to communi-cate this is key to a thriving relationship.

Employers who are able to acknowledge their feelings—no matter how up-setting—while managing how they respond to employees can navigate jealousy effectively and make a long-term success of their child care arrangements.[14]

Someone else must plug the gap between when parents are home and when they are not, and that person should be exceptional. Her gentle hands will be needed to soothe away tears of separation anxiety or mold the gingerbread dough for festive cookies. She will be the one to tuck your children in bed on nights you have to work late. Your infant will fall asleep to her lullabies. If parents can open their hearts to this type of love and understand that it does not replace them, they can transform the power of child care into a deeply moving experience.

As with all things concerned with child care, there are times when a line gets crossed. It can be one that a nanny chooses to cross. It's the difference between being a temporary substitute for a parent or in becoming a *surrogate*.

SURROGATES

From the Latin *surrogatus:* A surrogate is a substitute or deputy for another person in a specific role.

Webster's Dictionary

For many nannies, the role and work goes far deeper than simply providing care. As one nanny expressed it to me:

I find comfort in knowing that . . . I become somewhat of a surrogate mother to her. I get to keep all of her memories, the memory of my teaching her how to wash herself. I get the memory of wrapping her up in a towel after the bath and seeing her cherubic little face. I get comfort for the painful process [of eventually leaving] by giving away all my love to her, so that I don't have guilt later when I leave that I didn't give her everything I could, because I did. Whatever present I wrap each day with her, on love and manners, ways of the world, childhood silliness, it becomes unwrapped each night after I leave, and she's left with her own family. The great part of it, while egotistical, is knowing that I was a safe, bright, loving spot in her day every day.[15]

The act of surrogacy on the part of a nanny is ultimately an act of unconditional love. Like the surrogate mother who offers her womb to carry a child for another couple, surrogacy involves personal sacrifice—the offering of something deeply personal to another or others for their future happiness with no long-term gain. For the children concerned, surrogacy does not feel like a violation on parenthood. It is what it is—love. I interviewed two nannies on their roles as parent surrogates to determine what conditions arose to evoke the phenomenon.

Eve[16] was a nanny who took over the entire live-in role of parenting a young female child. The parents concerned were hands-off from the get-go. Eve began her position when the little girl was two years of age. The child's room was adjacent to her room, and to ensure that the parents didn't lose any sleep, the baby monitor was also in her room. Eve literally managed every single facet of this little girl's daily life. Prior to Eve beginning the position, the child had been cared for by an equally full-time baby nurse. Eve accepted the position the same day the baby nurse had her last day. Eve felt an immediate connection to the little girl.

When the parents told me they were hiring me, I burst into tears of joy, and I cooed to this sweet little girl, "I get to be your nanny!" I have never connected with any other child the way I connected with this child.

The circumstances have been so different in every other family I'd ever worked for. They all had mothers who were very hands-on. These were women who cherished that close attachment with their children and as such would never allow this type of bond to develop with the nanny. The other parents were also much more hands-on. In addition to the loving presence of one or both parents, these previous families were also 9–5 positions. Here, with this family, I woke the child up in the morning, I made her breakfast, got her dressed, planned her play classes, coordinated with her pediatrician—all the things most parents are handling. I was present through sleep training, through potty training, and other developmental stages. I bathed her, made and ate dinner with her. I did the bedtime routine. And when she cried at night, I got up with her to get her back to sleep. I was there for the critical time when most parents would be bonding and attaching. I've never had that kind of position before. I can't help but be in love with this little person I am raising.

I asked Eve if there were any awkward moments for the parents and herself. She responded, "Yes—plenty."

One that she vividly remembered was on the child's fourth birthday. All of the family—including the child's extended family—was present, and as the cake was being cut, the child announced to Eve, "I want you to sit next to me, because I'm your child and you're my momma." Eve continues:

And I looked at the parents, hoping they'd say something as they were cutting up and serving cake awkwardly, but they said nothing. So that night as we were doing her bedtime routine, I said to her "Honey, you know that I'm not your mom, right? And even though I'm not your mom, you know that I still love you, but it just means that you didn't come from my belly." So she confidently says, "I know that!" but I don't really know what she's thinking. I mean I wish I did.

Then, one day we're making cute mother's day cards, and I was having her answer some fun questions about her mommy. One such question was, what is mommy really, really good at? Sadly, her response was "working on her computer"—because whenever she's around she's not actively engaged with her child. So out of curiosity I asked, "Well, what am I good at?" To which she replied, "You're really good at taking care of me and playing good games." Even though I was honored, I also felt sad that she felt that way about me and not her own mother.

Lately it seems as if she feels really angry, deep down, that her parents aren't present for her. For example, I take her to school every day and to summer camp, so it's really not uncommon for them [the parents] not to see her until the end of the day. Recently they have begun to periodically come home earlier, and when they approach her, instead of running to them and saying "I missed you today," she gets really angry and says, "Go away!" or "you're in a time-out. I don't want to play with you!" So I feel like she's angry at them for not being around.

Then last December she had her end-of-year ballet recital for the holidays, and all the other little girls were happy and singing their parts and were cute and adorable. First I walked in, and then her parents walked in a few minutes after me. She saw me and smiled and waved. She saw them and folded her arms and frowned. So her instructor asked her, "What's the matter?" And she replies, "My parents aren't here." And her instructor said, "They're right here, look." And her parents were looking right at her and waving and smiling. She simply insisted, "No, they're not here." Throughout the whole performance she looked disturbingly angry. After the show, the parents went up to her and asked her why she was so upset, and she responded, "I thought you weren't here."

What I took from that was that somehow, on some level, she felt like they were trespassing. That all year they were just not around and then at a special event, when all the other parents are around, they show up. And she was pissed. I will never forget her facial expression; it was so disturbing and just made me feel sad for her.[17]

I shared with Eve the stories I had heard from other nannies about surrogacy and how sometimes surrogacy can turn sour. It goes something like this. One day children fully comprehend that their parents are just not around for them, but rather than process the pain of that loss, the children choose—in order to emotionally survive—to identify with and align with the dominant party—the wealthy but remote parents—while creating a safe scapegoat, their nanny. They may push the nanny away in an attempt to cry out to their parents for the attention and affection they are missing. Some might see this identification with parents as healthy, but underneath this action is an active denial of the years a child grieved for the parents' absence. It can also lead to the dissolution of an otherwise healthy attachment to a major consistent caregiver.

Another way that surrogate attachment can be broken is when the parents—threatened by an enduring bond between their children and the nanny they employ—abruptly dismiss her. Unfortunately, this is not an uncommon way for emotionally distant parents to prevent their children from bonding with other emotionally solvent caregivers. Paradoxically, in the process these children might be unable to learn how to properly attach in a healthy, stable way. There is often more than one casualty. An abruptly dismissed nanny can be deeply scarred by the experience.

Leah

Leah[18] was brought in by a single mother to care for her three-month-old baby boy full-time when she went back to work. The woman's long hours demanded that Leah spend every waking hour with the child. On weekends he sometimes even stayed with Leah in her home. A natural bond not only developed between the nanny and the child but also with the nanny and the mother. They were extremely supportive of one another. The mother not only viewed Leah as part of the parenting team but also encouraged it. She would often say, "The more people that love my baby, the better."

When the boy turned two, his mother got married after a whirlwind romance. The new partner was an overbearing, insecure person who did not care for the deep connection between Leah and his wife. He convinced his wife that Leah's relationship with the child would prove to be confusing and that he needed to know that they were his only parents. Within a few months he had persuaded his wife to let Leah go. Leah was devastated. Not only was she forbidden to see the little boy ever again, she was asked not to contact him at all.

So no birthday cards—no Christmas presents—no phone calls. I cannot tell you how painful it was to think that I wouldn't have this little boy in my life. But it was even more painful to know that they probably didn't tell him the truth as to why I wasn't there anymore. In his mind, I had just disappeared. What does that do to a child? Someone that he loved just left—abandoned him. I'm an adult, and the situation was very difficult for me to accept, but what about him, how could he possibly understand? It just killed me. One day a couple of years later as I was out walking in Central Park, I saw him playing ball with some friends. My heart stopped. I just froze in place, torn about what to do. Did I dare approach him? But my decision was made for me—at some point he saw me. He stopped what he was doing, came running toward me, and jumped into my arms sobbing. I will never forget the look on his face. It was like he had seen a ghost. He clung to me as if he would never let me go again. We held one another for a long while until the adult he was with began to pull him away. The child was crying and begging for me to come see him.

He was a mess. I was a mess. It was awful. That same day I got a horrible e-mail from his "father" telling me that if I ever went near his son again he would take out a restraining order against me. He implied that I was some kind of pervert that was stalking his child, but in fact it was only a chance meeting. I always held that boy's best interests at heart and still do. I'd never do anything to harm him or *confuse* him. To this day I wonder what they told him. If I had my way, I would have always stayed connected to him somehow. Yes, for my sake but also for him. I'm angry to think that he might believe that people who love you just disappear out of your life when in truth I never would have left him.[19]

The two women's testimonies were moving for sure, but I felt equally compelled to pose a final question to Eve and Leah about the issue of possibly overattaching to a child: "Do you feel that sometimes you overstepped a boundary and that in fact you should have left more emotional room for the parents?"

Eve replied first:

Um, yes, of course, and I really feel torn about that. I feel like the longer I stay, the worse it will be for her ultimately. But deep down I know what kind of people they are, so rather than the alternative that is a gap, I'd rather be the person who provides the consistent love. I understand that I'm choosing a role that isn't ethically mine, but I feel that she needs somebody. She needs to feel safe. And her parents are not the safe grown-ups in her life, and I'm too aware to allow her to suffer because of them. So, yes, I actively seek a role that isn't mine.

Leah responded next:

In my case I think the role was left open for me. I would have been irresponsible as a human being not to have filled it. I have no regrets for loving him the way he needed to be loved.

Before we judge nannies who step into roles not intended for them, let us remember that a surrogate is a deputy for another person in a specific role. There is often no long-term gain for these caregivers; in fact, as we have seen in Leah's story, it can sometimes end in heartache. The act of surrogacy is a selfless act.

A nanny who takes on this position in a child's life is not paid any more or perhaps even valued more. Rather, she walks into a situation that demands that level of attachment because a child's sense of worth is on the line. Surrogacy as a practice in child care is a noble sacrifice, but ultimately it is not the true replacement of parenthood. Our children naturally yearn for their parents, not their nannies—as much as they might cherish them. If you employ a nanny, be sure to be the omnipotent presence in your child's life—the sun to your nanny's moon—for that is the true order of things.

Chapter 4

Child Care's Caste System: Stratification

MARY POPPINS: MYTH AND FACT

Child care is a stratified industry. In the long history of nonparental care, certain types of caregiver have occupied different positions in terms of prestige and pay. Like India's rigid caste system of old, some of the positions held within child care can be based purely on race, nationality, and class as well as other credentials such as higher education, immigration status, and personal experience.

Educated professional nannies occupy the top of child care's caste system in a city such as New York. They are likely to be paid more than migrant nannies or nannies without a graduate degree and are generally expected to do less manual work but more academic work with their charges. Associates of this top tier might also be European, South American, or Australian au pairs. The expectations projected onto these nannies when race is not a factor can tell us much about attitudes toward service and class.

This privileged caste comes with its own archetype, a figure closely aligned to fictional characters such as Mary Poppins, Maria Von Trapp, and more recently Annie Braddock, the protagonist of *The Nanny Diaries*. Are educated nannies in debt to Mary Poppins and similar protagonists, or do they owe more to an older child care archetype: the English nanny?

Annabelle Corke, owner of Hey Day Nannies in Manhattan, and I discussed the appeal of Mary Poppins and Maria Von Trapp as ideal stereotypes for parents seeking nannies:

When parents say to me "I'm looking for Mary Poppins," Annabelle explains, I will ask them, "Are you really looking for someone who will proactively take control in the raising of your children? Do you want to give a nanny that kind of role?" I mean, Mary Poppins had some pretty fixed ideas on how children ought to behave. So, in theory, that can sound like a relief to new parents, especially with someone going back to work, maybe a new mom who doesn't want to worry about how their home is being run. In practice, however, I'm sure most parents don't want that kind of control handed over. Parents today don't really believe anymore that children should be molded.

Mary Poppins also came to a family that was already pretty fragmented. She basically asks the father to take more of an interest in his family. That's an interesting point. Mary Poppins brought them together, which is what the Banks family actually needed and not so much her. The role of the nanny in both characters—Mary Poppins, Maria Von Trapp—was actually to facilitate and strengthen the connection between child and parent, not to take over for the parent.

The Julie Andrews archetype continues as Maria Von Trapp, who was the original creative nanny. I mean, you couldn't ignore her energy and enthusiasm, right? She invented wonderful games and played instruments. She made the children clothes. She had a fun, nurturing role, whereas Mary Poppins was much more about adhering to the rules. Mary Poppins also had a weird magical quality about her, of course, almost like an alchemical role in transforming people within the family unit. And again, I think that appeals to the unconscious childish ideas we have about adults, that in some way they are superhuman.

There are strong themes in both *Mary Poppins* and *The Sound of Music* that have to do with children connecting with their parents. In *Mary Poppins* the children's mother is distracted with a cause, and their father is a remote authority figure. In *The Sound of Music* the children's real mother is dead, and a potential stepmother is not that into the kids. Georg Von Trapp, again, is a distant, strict man who has kept his children at arm's length. Maria completes the family unit once she marries Georg.

So when people seek that kind of archetype in childcare, I think subconsciously they are looking for a person who understands that their role is less to raise the children but more to support and encourage the parents to raise the children so that they can connect with them and have lasting relationships with them even after they've grown up and left the house. This is the profound role of parents. And that this person won't worry if the children make a mess or head off singing to the hills so long as they are learning something bigger. There's an automatic trust element being conveyed. The children will be helped to feel connected to their parents, their caregiver, and their world.

It's also very important that this type of nanny both sees herself as an equal and is seen as an equal and that in that role she is able to bring harmony to the family without usurping her position. People want a nanny who is self-assured because they know where they stand. Most of what a nanny does is about being an expert in human relationships. Professional nannies are sought because they are able to navigate the children's complex day-to-day life as well as knowing when to delegate as necessary to the parents. Working parents want that kind of simplicity.[1]

After speaking with Annabelle, I wondered *was it that simple*? Could a few books and two movies really convey all of that about professional nannies to new parents? Or did a true archetype come first, inspiring the creators of *Mary Poppins* and *The Sound of Music*? It was a chicken or egg kind of question. I turned to Geraldine Youcha's book *Minding the Children* for some answers:

We not only had two parents of whom we were extremely fond, but also that strange English institution, a perfect nanny—Ruth Plant, Nanny and I.[2]

With the above quote Youcha opens her section on nannies in the Gilded Age. For America's rich and the upwardly mobile, argues Youcha, the hiring of an English nanny brought the veneer of aristocracy upon a family. The nanny in question could just have easily been a fishmonger's widow from London's East End or a middle-class Parson's daughter who had fallen onto hard times. It mattered not. Being an English nanny evidently did.

It was imagined at the time that an English nanny mysteriously preserved within her calling all of the appropriate qualities and traits that a new ruling elite would require. After all, if England's kings were trusted to be molded within their nurseries, why shouldn't Americans follow suit? English nannies were known for their strict regimens and rules about manners, training that many felt helped to shape a good character. For the nouveau riche, employing an English nanny was the first step toward prying open the establishment's door. In other words, it was an attempt to mimic the customs of the blue bloods, the old money in America.

Just as English nannies paraded their charges in London's fashionable Hyde Park in the 1860s, New York's high-society nannies would exercise their children in the newly created Central Park, at that time still surrounded by mansions. Pushing glistening perambulators, the nannies of the rich would meet and brag about the wealth of their employers. The park was also a good place to gossip and find friends, a fact that is not lost on today's New York nannies.

Other non-English caregivers who were highly sought after for the nursery were French mademoiselles and German frauleins. These women would be hired to teach both the language and the culture of their respective countries to young Americans—hence, once again, the notion of European superiority in child care was a popular one.

The classic nanny was hired to care exclusively for the children, not to help the mother. She was to the children what the lady's maid was to the mother of the house. Other women were brought in as household help, including the new immigrants, mostly Irish and German women of certain backgrounds, and of course in some homes African American women.

Nanny versus the Help

During the Gilded Age when so many of America's values were being developed, the idea that a nanny was different than a domestic worker in rank was pretty universal. The nanny's social position was a unique one. She hovered above the servants and floated a few steps beneath her employers. She was also in total control of the nursery, and if she was a loving person the children would adore her. This helped to preserve her position within a wealthy family long after the children had been sent off to finishing school.

The household's maid, on the other hand, was viewed much more as a person who mostly cleaned and sometimes helped with nursery duties, generally under the supervision of the nanny. The help was not encouraged to forge deep or long-lasting connections to the family she served. Often she was a transient worker who could be dismissed on a whim. She would be a person of a markedly different race, nationality, or class than her employers. Most of her time in the household would be preoccupied by relentless and repetitive hard labor, such as scrubbing floors and cleaning fireplaces.

The characters Mary Poppins and Maria Von Trapp therefore continue to promote the idea of European nannies or their educated American counterparts as being the crème de la crème of child care. These nannies in turn embody ideas about class and wealth that they then project onto their employers like a talisman.

Mary Poppins and Maria Von Trapp also represent the distinction within domestic service, that of nannies versus the help. And again, that distinction reflects upon the families that hire nannies exclusively as opposed to domestic workers or in addition to hiring domestic workers. It suggests that the employer is wealthy enough to hire different people for different roles.

This concept of European cultural superiority, though vastly outdated, is both powerful and persistent. For example, the developers of a new children's app tested an assortment of accents out on 600 families with children as young as 18 months old. It was discovered that the children responded and listened more attentively to an English voice on the app, compared to any other accent:

The study found that 95 per cent of the children in the UK responded better to an English accent and surprisingly, 70 per cent of children in the US did too. Kevin Croombs, chief executive of Little Clever, said: "We made sure any words which are pronounced differently in the US were correct, but even the parents in America preferred the English accent, believing it sounded more *authoritative*."[3]

This most recent research and its findings seem to suggest that in terms of cultural authority, many Americans turn back to Europe in general and to England in particular for values of excellence. Anthropologists might challenge the legitimacy of this claim, so I will add this caveat: *perhaps only Americans of European ethnic descent do this,* in which case it makes more sense.

Annie Braddock represents a modern take on the English nanny archetype. She, like her predecessors, also confers a whiff of privilege onto her employer's family because of her educational status. In Annie Braddock, however, we have a subtle American inversion of the original archetype. Deep down Americans are both bewitched and repulsed by extreme wealth and ideas of inherent cultural superiority. The lack of virtue that Mrs. X demonstrates in her penny-pinching and in her unnatural behavior toward her child places her on a collision course with wholesome middle-class American values.

Annie Braddock can therefore represent the archetype of the revolutionary who challenges the moral corruption of a ruling elite. As a social champion she ultimately escapes her servitude in *The Nanny Diaries*. This is a universally accepted fact offered by novels with downtrodden *white* protagonists. Despite her suffering, Annie Braddock remains heroic and unsullied by her ordeal in service, not defined by it.

Educated American nannies therefore symbolically communicate that social aspiration and hard work pay off. Upwardly mobile parents hope that this notion rubs off on their own children—if they hire her. For these liberal types, the idea of hiring an expensive English nanny is a distasteful one. They also may struggle politically with employing migrant women of color. Annie Braddock fits their lifestyle.

So, what does it actually feel like to be an Annie Braddock today, some 10 years after *The Nanny Diaries*? Is Mary Poppins alive and well in child care? I asked an Ivy league graduate called Elizabeth.[4]

Elizabeth

When I think of Mary Poppins today, I think of Nanny 911, of Jo Frost. She's no-nonsense. The parents listen to her whereas Annie Braddock is just that girl from next door. Mary Poppins just controls everything. So, like if a child was not listening, I or Annie Braddock could say something like "knock it off" but it's just me saying it, but when an English nanny says it—it feels more proper. I think parents respond to the accent or the tone. I don't know which. I was raised on *Mary Poppins* as a child. When I would think of a nanny, she's what comes to mind and she's British. She takes charge. I don't know if Americans feel or project that sense of power. I think kids pick up on that. So maybe it's a cultural thing?

I asked Elizabeth who Annie Braddock is today.

Me. I'm Annie Braddock. I loved *The Nanny Diaries* and I totally identify with the way in which Annie, the protagonist, gets treated. I have numerous girlfriends who have had that experience also.

I asked how class affect a nanny's work when race is not a factor.

There are definitely, well, I would say, specific challenges inherent with white people hiring white people. I feel like some middle-class parents don't know how to be around employees per se—like what are the rules here? They were not raised with nannies or housekeepers. So they can go one or two ways. They are either super casual or super managing. I've worked with a couple of families who were super casual.

Like I immediately hit it off with the mother of family #1 and she would hang out with me half the time. She began to tell me everything. Then she began telling me stuff about her husband, how he was a bully and how he would get really drunk and use drugs. I felt that was unfair of her. I mean, he was my boss. He paid me.

It was weird, like, what was I supposed to do? I know she needed to vent but I'm not a shrink. So, through her I got to know her friends. I became a part of her social circle. Then the dad quit his job. They were trust fund hippies. Here I am being paid to hang out at home with them. It was three adults and two kids, so a lot of the time I felt like they hired me to be a friend.

Then they got pregnant. Oh, yeah, and in the holidays they invited my visiting parents over for dinner. So they actively encouraged me to feel just like a member of their family. Long story short, one day the mom asked me if I had been talking about them at the school. I had not. The reason being, she said, was that people at the school wanted to know if her husband had lost his job. I told her I hadn't heard that or even talked about it to anyone.

After that it got seriously weird. They cut my hours in half and then one afternoon I get a text from a nanny friend asking me for directions to their apartment because she was helping them with one of the kids' birthday parties. I was floored. They had not mentioned anything to me at all. And I had been in that child's life from since he was born. It really felt awful. So fast-forward to the day when they just sent me an e-mail telling me that they no longer needed me. The day before I had been with the kids just hanging out, and if I had known it was to be my last day I would have planned something really special. It was like the guillotine. I cried for a whole week.

It's like one moment you're a deep part of their private life, then wham you're gone. It felt like a really bad affair, you know, when one goes really deep, but the other person doesn't tell you why it ends? Here's a weird part too. So one year later this mom just suddenly appears on my Facebook page. She starts making comments and liking my posts, and so I wrote back asking if we could have coffee just to get some closure, but I never heard back from her. From the beginning they were just so happy with me, but ultimately I feel like the mom realized that she had to save her marriage and that she'd told me too much—*so I had to go*. Which on some level I get. But I never ever asked her personal questions. She would just let it all out. What I don't get is how it hurts the kids. I have a nanny friend with a kid in one of "my" kid's class and he still asks about me. It's supersad.

I also feel that when you're in a group setting like helping out at a birthday party with white parents and they don't know where to put you or how to interact with you—it's so awkward. There's this schism, and it can make employers go the other way too, like trying to completely control you. I had that experience with the third family I worked for.

So basically the parents hired me to be the educator in their children's lives—but the kids were like two and three and a half. But I was cool with that. I thought of some really fun games we could play to help them learn their numbers, colors, and, you know, letters. But when I told the parents, they went ape-shit. They told me to stick to these really advanced workbooks that the kids hated. Anyway, they [the parents] began to grill me everyday on what I was teaching the kids. The dad would yell at the kids too and ask them to recite stuff from the day's lessons. It was awful. They became so completely overbearing that I actually quit—and I've never just walked out on a job before—on the spot.

The tipping point was when the mom asked me why their four-year-old child couldn't read yet. The pressure to be some kind of teacher stopped me being a good nanny, and that pissed me off. I definitely think college grads are expected to perform educational miracles for $20 an hour especially if the kids are maybe academically challenged. And don't get me started on the families who don't acknowledge that their kids have a major issue like ADHD or Asperger's or mild autism. They just expect you to turn their kids into some highly functioning genius. Plus, every graduate will tell you this: your own time, be it academic or your social life or maybe you're interning a couple of days a week, rarely gets taken into consideration. They completely think you're just whooping it up in New York City getting drunk or high or something else lame, so you'd be better off working for them whenever they ask you. I can't tell you how many writing interviews I've lost because the parents got home late. It sucks.

I actively avoid getting outed as the nanny. Often other moms will approach me in the playground or in the community center and ask me about my son [the child she currently works with] even though he is Korean and I am white and have red hair. Go figure. And I kind of shrug away because I know as soon as I tell them I'm his nanny they will have that look on their face that says "Oh, right. Got it." It's like instant disappointment. And it's shaming, and you feel like a complete loser and you hear yourself trying to justify why you babysit while you work toward your intended career.

Another time I was hired just to wait at a kids' birthday party. There were around 10 parents just sipping cocktails and completely ignoring me. So when I arrived the mom hands me a bag and tells me to clean up in front of everyone. The kids had made a mess, and there was wrapping paper all over the floor. I was so humiliated. I will never ever do that again.

It's weird, because like I said parents either want to make you a friend because they feel so conflicted about employing a white person or they totally feel like they have to emphasize their position over you. So you get a ton of micromanaging. I think that when you culturally and ethnically and maybe even economically match a family, you present more of a threat to their power or sense of identity.

I feel that most white nannies employed in the city are really young, and I'm 35. So right there people wonder why I'm a nanny and not halfway up my career ladder or married with kids of my own. Also, I'm the same age as most of the moms I work for. That creates either conflict or a weird immediate intimacy. I don't think it's appropriate, for instance, to ask if I'm in a relationship. Like my private life has nothing to do with your family. But it's just assumed I will girl-talk with the mom. I also don't want to be paid to hang out with a mom and her kids. What's that about?

I do feel that the job is a brain drain or a time-suck even though I get paid more than most other nannies. It's also tiring looking after little kids. That actual labor, if you will, and managing the parents is exhausting. You have to have the skills of a diplomat to manage everyone—honestly. Ultimately I'm not a career nanny, so navigating this type of work often leaves me with a sense of shame amongst my white peers. In some sense I guess I'm always reminded of where I am by the fact that I work for these white people, and aside from their incomes there's no difference between us.

There are a lot of positives. I have never had to ask for a higher than average rate because they just automatically pay me one. I think black nannies have it much harder. They get paid less and they usually have a few more kids to look after. People with no papers get it the worst. I think the hourly rate difference has more to do with the parents' assumption that you will bring more educational value to a job than the fact that you're white. I mean, some white nannies are from Eastern Europe and Russia and they don't get paid much either. Some educated American nannies are not white and they get paid well. So it's more to do with your educational level and national status, I think.

I've also never had to look for work. I'm always in demand. I also have no problem saying no when parents try to add to my work. And they back right down and apologize. It's like I know they would totally pull that shit on some poor, and I don't mean economically poor, lady from Mexico and have her take on more kids for a huge playdate—you know like carpooling the nanny? Or like when the employer calls up their nanny and just tells her to collect someone else's kids and watch them—like they own that woman's labor? No way—you ask me first, and if I agree you get to pay me an additional hourly rate on top of what I'm earning. I've said no to picking up and dropping off laundry and doing the parents' laundry or tidying their bedroom. I've told employers I won't walk their dogs. So that's what I would define as white privilege. It's just knowing that you could and should say no to stuff and that they [employers] just get it.

As an American I also don't ever get asked to work public holidays, and those days get paid. I think that's because of the law and that I know the law and, more importantly, they know I know the law. So it doesn't have to be said.[5]

What white nannies can teach us through their experiences is that class is still an insidious marker in America. Social death can be instant once a nanny's true class identity is known. Nannies are routinely looked down upon across the board—white, black, or otherwise. Years ago white nannies wore uniforms that advertised their position in service. Black women will tell you that their skin color does the same thing today. Either way, class plays an enormous role in American life.

Can white nannies ever understand or experience racism in child care? Probably not, but that doesn't mean it never happens. One British nanny I know had a bizarre experience working for a Middle Eastern family in Dubai:

If we're talking about race, though, I have one experience where class kind of tipped the racial status quo on its head. The family I once worked for were fabulously wealthy Middle Easterners. The staff was all white, mostly imported English people. They had deliberately reconstructed an entire upper-class household with a butler, serving staff, maids, and two nannies. The husband had gone to Eton in England, so he had this weird complex about being proper. It was like working in an Arab version of *Downtown Abbey*. And we were all made to feel like second-class citizens. They barked orders at us. We were never allowed to eat anywhere else other than the kitchen. We couldn't look them in the eye. That really brought home how degrading racism could be. Were the employers racist? Maybe, maybe not; they could have just been assholes, however, having that express itself in terms of race kind of added an extra layer of humiliation. I can only imagine how awful racism must feel year in year out.[6]

The white nanny's experience of the child care industry can give us an invaluable peer into America's class system. At once ethnically and sometimes educationally close to their employers yet still operating as employees, white nannies often walk a fine line between confidante and servant. Sometimes white employers overextend their authority through passive-aggressive behavior or despotic micromanaging and even active on-the-job sabotage, as we have already seen. At other times, employers might overidentify with their nannies either through enforced friendships or even romantic gestures.

In conclusion, while readers might not shed too many tears for the trials of child care's elite nannies, it is worth contemplating how class often affects their working relationships and, as important, how the distinction of class still divides this country.

Child care, like all institutions, has a hierarchy. At the top we find the educated, mostly but not exclusively, white English or professional American nannies, then European au pairs and a few nannies who somehow find their way to the top either through sheer determination to buck the system, raw talent, or good luck. These might be migrant nannies who understood their worth and developed a professional career on the nanny market while getting their papers or additional qualifications.

A second tier in child care's caste system is home to a key nanny demographic in New York City—the Caribbean nanny. She can come with or without papers. For some employers she represents a hardworking and reliable asset to a family. Other employers might view her as a commodity and someone to look down upon. Migrant women of color labor under the shadow of older yet persistent stereotypes in America, ones that can alienate her even from African Americans: the mammy and the help.

MAMMY: SLAVERY'S LEGACY

When I heard white women say that Afro-Caribbean nannies "were just more loving and more maternal" than other nannies, I would feel uncomfortable. *Were* women from the islands more magically endowed with such abilities to rock, soothe, and nurture a new baby? Or were these assumptions based on something deeper, something unconscious, on a darker mythology that pervades the collective consciousness in the Americas like a sinister echo? Was this the resurfacing of the "magical Negro," that endearing black character who endows the white protagonist with a magical transformation at the expense of his or her own progress? I didn't in truth know the answer, so I began to speak to women of color about it.

Nandi Keyi is my friend and a former nanny. She also penned the novel *The True Nanny Dairies* in 2009. In part as the title suggests, it tells the *other* story in American child care: the nonwhite nanny narrative. It's a book that both informed and initiated me into a fiercely protected sanctum of Afro-Caribbean child care. This passage from *The True Nanny Dairies* cuts to the heart of black child care:

But the boy's whiteness welded on my blackness was the sum total of what I had become in America: a stroller-pusher doing the daily drudge through Central Park on aging knees, stepping and stumbling under the bridges, through the valleys, up the hills, past the rills, shrubs, ponds, swans, frogs, grass, statues, tunnels, squirrels, joggers, cyclists, swings, slides, sand-boxes, monkey bars, children, lovers, moats, pastures, fountains, rocks, ducks, fish, algae, geese, hotdogs, ices, food carts, and trees. Just a stroller-pusher bent on preserving the image of the American Mammy, as little white dreams rooted and blossomed out of my black, f*****g nightmare.[7]

What was the nightmare? I wondered as I approached Nandi's apartment in Brooklyn one summer day. I had some idea, but it was not my idea to assume.

Nandi eloquently framed it as "the no legitimate path" to the American Dream experienced by many women from the islands. The woman of color who arrives in the United States without papers can quickly fall into a role within a system that already has her pegged as a second-class person. Alongside this stigma can come a deeper-rooted shame, beyond domestic work, that in and of itself can lower any worker's self-esteem. In Nandi's words:

I think the shame was also deeply self-inflicted, as it was steeped in my knowledge of the historical fact that I was doing work African American women fought and died to escape. In the core of my being I felt that the resentment of African American women was justified, and that created and deepened the shame. But there's quite a bit of collective shame to go about. I recall my first employer, a white woman from Britain, being absolutely scandalized and contrite that there was a black woman at home taking care of her little blond baby. She apologized to me frequently for the power she wielded over me, and I had to reassure her that I needed this work. That dance between white woman employer and black nanny can be diabolical.[8]

Nandi told me how she had often walked "head-down" through the streets of Manhattan and elsewhere, and not just to avoid the scrutinizing or patronizing nods of white people. The worst glances that Nandi hoped to escape would come from black Americans. They would pierce Nandi through her skin and fill her with a loathsome sense of *shame*—a word that arises again and again among Caribbean nannies.

In order to better understand how the legacy of human enslavement affects African Americans and all women of color to this day, we must first examine the myths and the facts that surround the stereotype of the plantation mammy or house servant—an enslaved woman held in bondage under a system that legitimized their inhumane treatment over generations.

Mammy

In American folklore, the enslaved house servant known colloquially as the mammy is portrayed as having loved her slave owner's children as her own flesh and blood. She was also viewed as being in a powerful role. The plantation mammy was attributed with exaggerated maternal instincts and—dare we say it—with primal instincts when it came to infant nurturance, thus freeing the white mistress for more genteel roles. Through this warped lens, the system that held her and her offspring to human bondage for hundreds of years was exonerated. After all, did it not appear that mammy enjoyed and even relished her role in the slaveholder's world?

In reality, the African American woman on a cotton plantation who was forced out of sheer survival to escape daily torture and rape in the fields and who chose to love and care for her captor's children was often a miserable, abused woman. African Americans understand this connection painfully, and so do the women of color who push Caucasian children today in glimmering strollers.

Many of today's foreign nannies experience a kind of bondage—not one of impending torture, of course, but one of ceaseless drudgery with no escape, of little to no respect, or of any legitimate pathway to a better life. This is not to say that these women are entirely powerless. Like all immigrants, they harbor the same ideals and dreams of progress as do all migrants. But unlike other demographics, immigrant nannies of color without papers often lack the proper entry and runway to personal success in America—and herein lies one of the greatest detriments to modern child care: our current immigration system.

If you believe this idea to be too radical, let's explore it further. How does the mammy myth affect perceptions of migrant women of color today? Simply this: that white assumptions about the plantation mammy are also routinely made about black migrant workers today.

In a review of Micki McElya's *Clinging to Mammy*, Susan L. Blake explores the extraordinary lengths that Caucasian Americans go to in order to collectively maintain the myth of the faithful black worker.

The mammy, McElya observes, is the most visible character in the general myth of *the faithful slave, that paternalistic narrative of slavery as reciprocal affection and loyalty rather than coerced and uncompensated labor* that has excused slavery and its legacy of racial discrimination and violence since at least the 1830s, and which, McElya argues, persists today.[9]

Is there a tangible connection in white assumptions about women of color in domestic work that runs from the plantation to modern domestic work? I believe so, and perhaps more than one.

In 1912 an unknown African American woman in domestic service shared her experiences. Her words have traversed 100 years into the present, and yet much of what she spoke of continues to exist today in terms of attitudes, duties, and pay for women of color. I have added in brackets aspects of domestic work that remain unchanged.

I am a negro woman, and I was born and reared in the South . . . I will say, also, that the condition of this vast host of poor colored people is just as bad as, if not worse than, it was during the days of slavery. Though today we are enjoying nominal freedom, we are literally slaves. And, not to generalize, I will give you a sketch of the work I have to do—and I'm only one of many. . . .

[Hours] I frequently work from fourteen to sixteen hours a day. I am compelled by my contract, which is oral only [no fixed contract], to sleep in the house . . . .

[Live In] I not only have to nurse a little white child, now eleven months old, but I have to act as playmate or "handy-andy," not to say governess, to three other children in the home, the oldest of whom is only nine years of age.

[Duties] I wash and dress the baby two or three times each day, I give it its meals, mainly from a bottle; I have to put it to bed each night; and, in addition, I have to get up and attend to its every call between midnight and morning. If the baby falls to sleep during the day, as it has been trained to do every day about eleven o'clock, I am not permitted to rest. . . .

[No downtime or breaks] And what do I get for this work—this lifetime bondage? The pitiful sum of ten dollars a month! [Wages] And what am I expected to do with these ten dollars? . . . Of course, nothing is being done to increase our wages, and the way things are going at present it would seem that nothing could be done to cause an increase of wages.

[No representation] We have no labor unions or organizations of any kind that could demand for us a uniform scale of wages for cooks, washerwomen, nurses, and the like; and, for another thing, if some negroes did here and there refuse to work for seven and eight and ten dollars a month, there would be hundreds of other negroes right on the spot ready to take their places and do the same work, or more, for the low wages that had been refused.

[Surrogacy] . . . If none others will help us, it would seem that the Southern white women themselves might do so in their own defense, because we are rearing their children—we feed them, we bathe them, we teach them to speak the English language, and in numberless instances we sleep with them.[10]

The experiences of an African American domestic worker in 1912, some might argue, are chronologically too close to actual institutional slavery to accurately represent a cultural departure of white assumptions about blacks. Remember that we are specifically looking at white opinions about black domestic workers first and African American judgments about black domestic work for whites second.

If we move forward to the 1950s to a book by a white author about black domestic service, one that spawned a movie and a storm of criticism, we can see that the mythology about black domestic workers is still very much alive.

Kathryn Stockett's book *The Help* is an astute snapshot of America's pre-civil rights history. In it we see the daily indignities that black servants experienced in white employers' homes. For this reason, from the

1950s on, African Americans pursued almost any other type of employment rather than continue to operate—albeit voluntarily for a wage—in service under an institution of white oppression.

Critics of *The Help* point out that the book primarily details the desires of the white protagonist. It exaggerates the bond between the central black nanny and her white charge. *The Help* perpetuates uncomfortable white beliefs about black nannies, bringing them forward to today. Namely, these are:

- The woman of color loves your children in a magical way;
- She is probably better suited to nurturing your children than to anything else, such as her own professional or economic advancement;
- The woman of color enjoys domestic servitude—it's her realm!
- A woman of color who advocates for herself within domestic servitude is seen as being uppity or an angry woman or a troublemaker.

More faithful narratives about black servitude from the 1950s do exist. Willie Mae Wright, a black domestic worker from the South, told a white woman, Elizabeth Kytle, her account. Remarkably, Alfred Knopf published it in 1958. In the book Willie Mae speaks about the dangers of sexual exploitation and of beatings and degrading talk by employers—common occurrences that strayed not too far from the plantation field. These negative conditions simply reinforced the pain and suffering that blacks had endured for centuries at the hands of whites. It is no wonder that from the 1950s African Americans in droves abandoned any work that left them feeling subservient.

Women such as Willie Mae Wright and the fictional Aibileen Clark formed the core of the African American female work force for almost a century. In 1940, 60 percent of all employed African American females were domestic workers. For them, the indignities were innumerable, but so were the efforts to establish agency over one's life, to survive those thousand small cuts with one's head held high. Most domestic workers moved to other employment at the first possible opportunity, even before passage of the Civil Rights Act of 1964. By 1980, only 7 percent of employed African American women were domestic workers. Oral history interviews reveal a world that is largely gone and which few African Americans mourn.[11]

As most African Americans today would rather do anything other than work as a nanny or housekeeper in a white home, non-American women of color fill that gap for domestic labor, and the judgments against them from African Americans can be harsh.

The sight of a woman of color pushing a white infant in a stroller is a powerful visual reminder of America's racist past. As feminist writer Roxane Gay, puts it:

I watch movies like *Rosewood* or *The Help* and realize that if I had been born to different parents, at a different time, I too could have been picking cotton or raising a white woman's babies for less than minimum wage or enduring any number of intolerable circumstances far beyond my control.[12]

Yet today for black Americans there *are* women of color "raising white babies for less than minimum wage" and often precisely because their immigration status creates "intolerable circumstances" beyond their control.

While the glares of disgust from African Americans can be visceral on the sidewalk, such work can also generate negative feelings from relatives back home in the Caribbean, where expectations for success in America run high.

The protagonist of *The True Nanny Diaries* experiences it firsthand via her father, who in speaking of the protagonist's sister says that "because she went to America and make sheself something. She doh fart around like you. *Yuh shame meh.*"[13]

For the author of *The True Nanny Diaries,* only significant changes in the U.S. immigration system will enable migrant women of color to get on track for advancement. The economic shackles of an undocumented status simply reinforce assumptions made by both white and black Americans.

Yet even in this racially charged environment, younger nannies of color are pushing the boundaries in child care. An American-born African called Amara,[14] the daughter of Ugandan parents, had these thoughts to offer:

Based on my experience in the child care industry, I can say that I've witnessed two types of privilege at work. The first, racial or "white" privilege, is one that I obviously [as an American-born African] do not hold. It seems, from my perspective, that young white nannies are typically held in the highest regard. They are *among* the rest of us but not *of* us. The common assumption is that they have chosen this career only as a temporary means of supporting themselves while they pursue a bigger and better career (unlike black or Hispanic foreign-born nannies, who can't do any better).

Then, there is class privilege, which I *do* hold. However, this privilege isn't quite as visible—I've always felt as though it was something that I had to prove before reaping its benefits. For example, it was not until I'd gotten to talking with some of the moms around school about my past, private education, multilingual upbringing, and world travels that they began to offer gems like:

"I like you because you aren't like other nannies, I know that sounds bad but, you know what I mean!" or "Wow! You're more educated than I am! Imagine that!" These shocked reactions (which I took as insults thinly veiled or perhaps even unconsciously veiled as compliments) caused me to think about my place within the nanny hierarchy.

I feel that I occupy a liminal space within this system. I don't quite fit in with the young white nannies all the way at top who can interact with mothers without any fear of being snubbed. However, on the other hand, I also don't fit with the minority or foreign-born nannies, who sometimes seem suspicious, distrusting, or even resentful of the white nannies and their bosses—and many of whom have advised me to "remember what color I am because THEY do. Even if they pretend they don't." . . .

While I feel lucky to work for a family that treats me just as they would treat anyone else, it's a difficult position to reconcile in the arena that seems to be the school grounds. I sometimes feel as though I should pick a side. Am I a privileged but confused young girl navigating postgrad life the best I can or am I simply 'the help'?[15]

Another young African American nanny whom I know feels that there has simply been "enough time" between the 1950s and today and that her choice of work while she puts herself through college is nobody's business: it's just a job. Class for sure goes some way toward removing women of color from assumptions that some whites and blacks hold—both of the younger nannies quoted are middle class and college educated. Yet as Amara puts it, there is always an imperative for these nannies to prove their class status before they can reap the rewards—that is, social inclusion. In doing so they also pay the price of alienating other women of color in communal spaces such as the schoolyard or the playground.

Race in the Home

For parents interviewing and employing women of color, there is the temptation not to discuss the issue of a nanny's race to children. We like to think that our children when exposed to diversity will grow up color-blind, but in a city such as New York that's next to impossible. Not only is racial diversity everywhere, but it can also raise awkward questions such as "Why are a lot of homeless people brown-skinned?" and "Why are nannies mostly brown-skinned?" These were two questions I actually heard children ask their parents or caregivers as they walked about the city.

In the book *NurtureShock,* authors Po Bronson and Ashley Merryman explore race in a chapter titled "Why White Parents Won't Talk about Race."[16] The crux of the chapter is that when white parents don't talk to their children about race, children construct their own assumptions, often negative. For example, children might believe that all house cleaners are brown-skinned or that all nannies are brown-skinned just because that's what they see in their own homes. Parents can look for ways to talk about the racial differences between people—perhaps with the same confidence that they discuss gender equality or gay relationships, with *different doesn't mean unequal* being the usual argument.

There are other ways children pick up clues about race. They might hear their parents groaning in hushed tones about "lazy nannies" while eyeing a group of black nannies. Caribbean women often get labeled as "bench-sitters" or as being "lazy" on parent forums because they cluster in groups in the playground and don't always helicopter their charges.

Caribbean nannies are well aware of this stereotype. They told me that in their cultures back home the adults would sit and talk to one another while keeping an eye out for the kids. They believe that American children are too mollycoddled and micromanaged and that children should be given a little space to "be." But when a child strays or begins to do something unsociable, you can be sure that one of the watchers will sound an alarm—and it's that action that rarely gets acknowledged.

There are other casually racist assumptions made about nannies from the Caribbean, the Philippines, and Latin America. In academic books and blogs and magazine articles about foreign-born nannies, these women might be routinely dismissed as being not very well-educated or as being Third World. In truth, many migrants held professional or academic positions back home, but due to their local economies those jobs didn't pay enough even to live on. It takes great tenacity and intelligence to migrate to a new country. Western observers tend to overlook these virtues. Negative stereotypes exist for a reason—because enough of us believe them to be true.

Black nannies are not self-sacrificing, magical, or overzealous caregivers, and neither are they lazy or uneducated or universally poor. They are individuals who have journeyed to America to create a better life for themselves and for their families. They come with their own narratives of triumph and challenge. With immigration reform and child care regulation, migrant women of color will be in a better position to demand higher wages, have protection under the law, and stay in or leave domestic service on their own terms.

Until that day, the industry of child care continues to operate much like a caste system, with a clear hierarchy of workers. It isn't always a strictly black and white delineation, however, for some of the most oppressed workers are lighter-skinned women.

PARALLEL LIVES: HIDDEN WORKERS

As we have already seen, unlicensed child care can have a more sinister side. It is not only an industry that pedophiles, dishonest, and mentally ill people can freely enter—it is also a system that enables a sometimes brutal exploitation of its workers.

In America today, some domestic workers—nannies, maids, and house-keepers—labor under the most appalling conditions, akin almost to slavery. When I first began to research narratives for this chapter, I had originally wanted to call these workers "invisible" in reference to their being hidden away from public scrutiny within their own ethnic communities, working for wealthier compatriots. That was a mistake.

When I spoke to advocates and organizers, they quickly corrected me: "These workers are not invisible—not to one another; they just lead parallel lives." The women I speak of are South Asian in origin. They can come from such countries as Tibet, Thailand, Sri Lanka, India, Pakistan, and Bangladesh.

As South Asians, a percentage understand how the experiences within India's caste system, as members of the Dalit or untouchables, can be socially transplanted into U.S. child care. The stigma of being from a lower caste in India and elsewhere infers with it an inherent spiritual inequality in a stratification based on religious ideology. When South Asian women arrive in the United States they enter into another hierarchical system governed by such diverse factors as race, nationality, an ability to speak English well, immigration status, and the strength of one's own ethnic group in the host country.

For migrants such as Caribbean and Filipina workers, being able to speak English has enabled their demographic to set up strong networks of support within the United States. To some extent the same can be said of Hispanics, although this has more to do with geographical proximity. Within these ethnic environs, new immigrants can quickly assimilate and begin their search for work through word of mouth.

Filipina, Thai, and Tibetan Nannies

When we discuss different types of child care workers, it is easy to fall into stereotypical thinking. Filipina nannies, for example, are regarded as industrious, educated workers. That reputation can quickly become one that is exploited with heavy workloads, including housecleaning or excessive academic tutoring without appropriate compensation. Similarly, Tibetan women who are culturally raised with enlightened spiritual practices can be seen, as a consequence, as useful gurus for unruly children or as trendy child care accessories. Thai nannies often convey a natural serenity that comes from being raised to be socially polite, but this can be seen as passivity and compliance and can lead to their exploitation.

For other South Asian migrants, being stereotyped as beasts of burden is an experience that they bring from home. Some have been trafficked by members of their own families or village leaders. Foreign diplomats might have brought them from local staffing agencies in the Middle East. Once in the United States, these workers can simply disappear into nightmarish worlds of harsh treatment. These migrants often fight tooth and nail to get to America just to escape appalling domestic conditions such as forced marriages, rape, torture, or imprisonment for their political beliefs. Many are women who arrive in the United States without any knowledge of English and with scant funds.

I wanted to find out what it felt like to come here out of total desperation. Where did South Asian women go first? What kind of work was initially open to them? Did some of them end up working for American families?

I spoke with Nahar Alam, a fellow at the Petra Foundation and the founder of Andolan (meaning "movement"), a nonprofit female domestic workers' group aimed primarily at Indian, Pakistani, Bangladeshi, Sri Lankan, and Nepalese women. Her own story is revelatory.

Nahar

When Nahar was just 13, she was forced into an arranged marriage with a police officer in Bangladesh. Upon entering her new home, Nahar learned that her husband already had a wife and four children—including a son a year younger than herself. The new arrangement did not go well for Nahar, and she suffered terrible physical and emotional abuse as a result. She tried to escape six times, but in Bangladesh women have very little power and are totally subject to their husbands. Despite this period of intense suffering, Nahar continued her education on her own. Previous to this she had only made it to the seventh grade in school before being pulled out by an early marriage. Like Afghan girls under the Taliban who continue to learn in secret, Nahar would borrow books from a friend's family and devour them in order to self-educate.

During this time, incredibly, Nahar not only adopted her younger brother's daughter but also started a women's organization. Nahar's focus was on learning and teaching skills such as writing and sewing as a way for women to empower themselves. Eventually Nahar was able to apply for a government program to raise poultry—another invaluable way for local women to earn independent money. But Nahar's husband and his family constantly interrupted her endeavors, forcing her to take more extreme measures to escape. She ultimately began to look for a way to leave Bangladesh.

Through family connections and a great deal of negotiating, finally in 1993 Nahar was granted a visa to come to the United States. Her daughter couldn't accompany her, because in Bangladesh there is no legal recognition for adoption. With a heavy heart, Nahar recalls of her arrival: "When I arrived in the United States, there was no one to greet me at the airport. I spoke no English and had almost no money." Typical of many new South Asian immigrants, she headed to Queens, New York City and shared her lodging with a family.

Her first job was in a garment factory, where she was paid 35 cents per finished piece. When by her 15th day she realized she had only earned $35, Nahar wisely concluded that she needed to find another kind of job.

The only work open to women such as Nahar in these situations is domestic work: cooking, cleaning, and child care. But these positions don't come cheap in terms of human cost.

For example in her first job as a live-in domestic worker for an Indian family, Nahar earned just $50 a week cooking, cleaning, and providing child care. Language was an issue with Nahar and her employer attempting to communicate in broken Hindi and English. As a young woman living in a stranger's home, Nahar became the unwanted focus of her employer's husband, who would call her during the day when she was alone. Feeling uncomfortable, Nahar told her boss.

In this twilight world of domestic work even substandard wages can make way for no wages. Soon after her revelation, Nahar was given just a day's notice that she had been fired and that her employers had found an Indian woman who would work for lodging. Suddenly Nahar was homeless, and her troubles almost overwhelmed her. Fortunately and at the last minute, she discovered that a friend's mother was visiting relatives in Queens. Nahar asked the woman if she could temporarily stay with her.

Nahar's second job in America was in Long Island providing elder care. This type of crossover caregiving—for the very young, then for the elderly—is a significant labor market for migrant workers. It was a full-time live-in position that paid $145 a week. Her employers were kind and encouraged Nahar to attend a course in English at Hunter College on weekends.

Nahar was clearly determined not to give up on her American Dream, and the few spare hours she had were spent at the public library learning English by reading books. She was also resourceful in getting part-time work as a Bengali tutor. This employer, Rana Qureshi, was a member of a nonprofit organization for South Asian women called Sakhi. Rana encouraged Nahar to apply for a position with Sakhi as a domestic worker coordinator. In Nahar's words, "She was very nice to me."

In her last domestic job for employer Razia Hashmi, Nahar cared for a newborn and a five-year-old boy. Her employers treated Nahar like a family member. They would eat together and provide Nahar with rides to her classes. They attended a demonstration that she had organized against a former bad employer. Later they even helped her write a résumé and apply for the Sakhi position. These gracious people exemplify how employers can individually contribute to the successes of women such as Nahar.

Eventually in 1996, Nahar was hired full-time by Sakhi to organize a group of South Asian immigrant women who were being exploited, underpaid, and abused in domestic work. A year later Nahar's group officially split from Sakhi and named itself Awaaz (meaning "worker's voice"). In 1998 Nahar founded her current organization, Andolan.[17]

From my conversations with Nahar, I discovered that the cloistered path of a South Asian migrant is fairly typical. Upon first arrival they tend to stay with a relative or someone they paid to receive them. They might sleep on floors and share meals with entire families. They will take jobs in sweat factories, sometimes working over 12 hours a day 7 days a week depending on contract demands. These jobs are illegal, and hence the pay is invariably low—often less than a dollar an hour.

Sweatshop conditions are generally so dreadful that migrants quickly seek other types of work within their own communities and often in live-in positions. This extreme form of economic codependency can easily lead to verbal and physical abuse, being overworked, and being denied appropriate payment. Generally—but not exclusively—the people who hire them first will be wealthier members of their own South Asian countries.

I asked Nahar how hard it was to obtain her U.S. visa:

I had help from my family and friends—they understood how much I was suffering but it wasn't easy. I had to prove I had a relative here in the U.S. and that I would not be a burden. I couldn't bring my daughter though as my husband prevented me. It was hard to leave her.

What problems do South Asian migrants, especially women from Bangladesh, experience?

Language is a huge barrier, because language is a gateway here. You need to understand what your papers say of where to go for jobs. We bring skills from our home countries, but we cannot express how we can do things to employers. This limits us in the beginning to work for people from our own ethnic and national regions.

How do new immigrants learn English?

The library was my sanctuary. I believe they save people's lives. I would take free classes and use the educational aids. I could sit and look at magazines. I don't think people appreciate how powerful the libraries are for immigrants.

How Important is Immigration Reform?

I think it has to be done properly. There are huge trust issues in our community: for example, after 9/11 back in 2001 when people from our religious community were urged to come forward and get registered for homeland security reasons. So many South Asian men got deported because of that. I don't know if immigration reform will work unless there is implicit trust and a guarantee of not being deported.

What About Diplomatic Immunity, Would you Like to see That Removed?

I think the problem begins before domestic workers reach the U.S. There are agencies in the Middle East who recruit and "sell" workers to diplomats, and they tell the workers all kinds of lies. Then the workers get two contracts, one in English and one in their own language, but they are not the same. The workers don't understand the English contract. Then when the workers arrive, they are told more lies to keep them afraid and to stop them going outside. That's when the abuse can really begin. It has to be a global effort.

Nahar continues to help South Asian women escape exploitative servitude in New York City and elsewhere. Her organization Andolan has even helped to bring lawsuits against abusive employers. She enables South Asian workers in other ways too, assisting them in locating resources to learn English and by mailing to prospective employers (via job ads in community newspapers) what is required of them under the law.[18]

Over time and with help from organizations such as Andolan, many South Asian domestic workers are able to advance their English skills and get better-paying jobs. That's when they can begin to blend with other Asian nannies on the child care scene. It's at that point that they encounter American employers. Perhaps someone like you?

Despite all of their personal struggles, I have found South Asian women to be fiercely strong. They see their lives as meaningful and their journeys as successful. Ultimately they regard their sacrifices as essential for their children and families.

Lucy

So many times I have wondered what it feels like to leave one's husband and children, one's parents and village, and risk all to care for American children. I understood the economic incentives, but I also wanted to find out how these nannies coped and sometimes even thrived thousands of miles from their loved ones. So, I contacted Lucy,[19] a village schoolteacher who had left her children behind in Sri Lanka.

It was a crisp June morning when I met up with Lucy for an interview.[20] We were in a Manhattan dog run where the strong aroma of canine urine and disinfectant clouded the sweet scent of the apple blossoms. Lucy was walking her employer's dog. Lucy had been employed as a housekeeper/babysitter for the previous two years, and her duties included, as is obvious, dog walking.

My name is Lucy, and I was a schoolteacher in Sri Lanka. In America I work for people, taking care of two girls. They are 3 and 6. I am good with the girls because I have three of my own back home. I know how they tick. Today is my [eldest] daughter's birthday. She is 10.

March 1, 2010. I'll never forget that date. I came on a visitor visa. Five weeks before I went to American embassy. It wasn't easy; I had to show them a bunch of stuff. That I was an educated person; teachers are good, no? Better than most back home, I had good job, a small house. But even so, life was hard. You can work hard in Sri Lanka, but you don't get nowhere because of corruption. You need powerful people, relatives, to get you into good positions, like a policeman or something. You get stopped in the street, you have to pay a fine—just for no reason because it is a cop. Same thing with local government; you don't get nowhere in business or building a house unless you pay, always paying. I wanted a different life for my children.

My tourist visa was good; then I overstayed. On TV they say all the time people like me are criminals. Let me try to explain, but maybe you won't understand. In my country, people go hungry; they have no power, and they live very badly, with no hope of ever getting better. They just see the same thing happening to their children, like cycle. Then there are some with all the power. They decide everything. If they get jealous, something bad happen to you. Even though my husband and I had good jobs, we knew it could be taken away from us.

Okay, let me explain it like this. The U.S. dollar is worth 130 rupees [2014], so when I send home $500 a month, my kids, they get 65,000 rupees! You know what that gets you in my country, a good school? No, the best school! Medications! Good food like meat, milk, and eggs! Good clothes! Good shoes! With that money, my parents can bribe people to help my brothers, my cousins, to get powerful jobs like be cops. My money saves my whole family! I cannot earn this money even as a judge or a lawyer back in my country. But I can earn that being a nanny or cleaner here.

I love the kids I work with. They fill the hole in my heart. My heart has this, how can I say it, empty space where my kids' memories should be. I get to put the memories of these kids here in my heart. I get to keep these memories because they are mine. I have the memory of teaching S [the child she cares for] how to wash herself or the memory of wrapping D [the child she cares for] up in a towel after bath, night after night. I got the memory of D asking me smarter and smarter questions about the world, like "Who makes the rain, Lucy?"

When these girls I look after smile or skip, I think "that's what my girls are doing now back home," and I just squeeze them, these girls, hard like this. I feel like God takes that love, and he send it to my girls.

Coming to America was my husband's idea. He said to me, "Go to America for a year just to make some money, then come back. We can make a business and live well in Sri Lanka." I didn't want to leave my kids. But my mom, she say, "Listen to your husband—you go and make a difference to our lives." He promised me I would stay in America for 12 months, but he lied. After 12 months, he told me he had spent all the money on our children's education, and I had to stay longer for us to build a house, so I thought "Oh well, I might as well stay another year and work."

But a year turned into two, and you know I just stayed longer. I felt very angry. But I was a good wife, so I stayed. Then stuff happened, like my grandmother died and I couldn't go to her funeral. My brothers got married. I couldn't go to weddings. Then one day, I got a letter from my mother—she told me my husband had left our children with her and he had spent all my money on alcohol and that he had taken another wife. Can you believe it? I just cried. I found a second job at weekends. I had to work-work-work because I didn't want to stop and think. My husband he suddenly doesn't have any money to give to my mother. He says, "I don't have job." It's a lie because he drinks and gambles his money away. So now my girls only have me. My family only has me.

The night before I left for America I put my three little girls to bed, and they didn't know I would be gone in the morning. I sang to them, I read to them, I held them in my arms until they fell asleep one by one, and I did not shed one tear. After they fell asleep I cry all night like someone had taken my heart out. I did that; I put them to bed knowing I would be gone in the morning, not knowing when I would be back. I was strong because I thought we would be better family because of it.

My kids don't even know we're not together, him and me. It would be too bad for them with me so far away. So we pretend we are together. They think Papa is away working somewhere. But I know he is with another woman. Sometimes my eldest daughter she tell me, "Mama, I stopped drinking milk, so you come home sooner." Kids, they don't understand. She tell my smaller kid, "Don't ask Mama for something new. You keep her in America." She doesn't understand I pay for everything. Every month, every dollar I send home is spent, it's gone. I'm in a trap like animal.

If I go home now, we will have nothing again. It will all be for nothing. My family back home needs money every month. But I have a plan. I want to bring my girls here so they can be free. I want them to go to American schools and work hard. Maybe the law will change, and I will be able to become an American.

I come here and work hard. People know when they hire illegal. I tell my boss when I took job. I said, "I don't have papers," and *they are lawyers*. They said, "Fine, we don't mind, so long as you are good at your job." They both work. They make lots of money, two houses, nice cars, private schools, but they never see their kids. The girls are beautiful. I call them my little angel hearts because they stop my heart from breaking. I do everything with them. I cook for them. I put them to bed. They love me. I know that. Sometime I worry that I love them too much. The parents don't notice things like I do. They just buy them lots of toys, but the kids, they just want you to be with them.

When you are illegal you live day to day. Like for example, I have no doctor. I haven't had any checks as a woman since I came here. The other day I get knocked off my bike by a cab, but I didn't go to hospital. I have cuts and bruises, but I can't go to hospital. My mother, she send me medication from home. If I get sick, I have to look it up and ask my mother for medicine. Also, if there are police, like in subway, checking backpacks, looking at driving license, I get nervous. I have to walk to another station but not make it obvious. I get scared just to look at a cop. If something happened to me, I couldn't go to police. Every day, you live like you don't exist. I'm here, but I am not here. Like I'm a ghost.

My husband said coming here would give us all a better life. In some way it has. It showed me what kind of person he really is. It showed me I could be strong. It showed me my kids could be strong. Maybe it will all be worth it. I think maybe I will have my kids with me again. People here so lucky; they forget what their own parents and grandparents did for them to be here. I have no regret. Freedom is more important than money. I want my girls to be whatever their heart tells them to be. This is a great country.

It was only after I had taken this interview that I became aware of my own privilege: health insurance, papers, and public safety. Lucy endured an enormous burden, but the value of her labor was immeasurable. She was the golden goose, her family's lifeline, but not theirs alone. There was also an uncomfortable suggestion of surrogacy, an alien transplant of love in the midst of so much personal heartache.

I had seen the burning in other nannies' eyes when I told them I had a green card. I immediately materialized into an undying object of hope, as if somehow my status could be conferred. Lucy and I are immigrants. Our path to America started out the same way, through tourist visas. Now we were poles apart. I wondered, despite the extraordinary care Lucy provided two American children, whether there was a penalty being paid. I put this question to Karen Kaufman, PhD, LCSW:

Lucy's predicament is sadly common for many foreign workers, undocumented and forced to live in the shadows. Having left her home, family, and support system, Lucy may be vulnerable to depression, hopelessness, and other mental health problems. When her service is no longer needed with the current family, future employers may prey upon her illegal status, thereby increasing her desperation with long work hours, few benefits, and fewer choices. The lack of access to health care and other benefits of legal residency will exacerbate her already desperate situation.[21]

In some respects Hispanic women, those who have migrated from Mexico and South America, share a status similar to that of South Asian workers in child care's hierarchy. They too can be cast into subservient roles that open them up to exploitation. Most of the Spanish immigrant women I spoke to said that the first job in America is always the worst. This is because certain employers know that new migrants will work for next to nothing for that first crucial American reference—of course, only if the employer is so inclined to provide one at the finale.

Teresa

Teresa is typical of this type of worker. She is a bright, joyful person who is eternally grateful to be living and working in the United States now for well over a decade. Her English is good, and with her stockpile of references she is able to look for child care work at local market rates. Still, she says, employers see her as a cleaner-cum-babysitter as opposed to what she feels she actually is, a nanny.

My name is Teresa. I am 33 years old, and I come to USA in June '99. I have 15 years living in the country, and I came from Mexico because the economic situation in my family deteriorated with the illness of my father, and the economic livelihood of my family and my four brothers who were still in school depended on me. Arriving here at 21 years of age I worked at first preparing salads and deli sandwiches, but because my English was limited, I was forced to work as a maid in Brooklyn sleeping in six days a week and working more than 12 hours a day. I had to do all cleaning, cooking, washing, ironing, and babysitting for a weekly salary of $180. Although there was no abuse from this family, I think I was abused having to work long hours and hard work for such low pay. My friends were not so fortunate; some were verbally abused and made to sleep in basements in low light, without air conditioning or heating, and to scrub the floors on their knees.

Crossing the border was one of my worst experiences. It took more than three months trying to cross into Tucson, Arizona, walking all night for three days; the first time we walked from 6 p.m. to 9 a.m. each night. We finally made it to a hotel in Tucson, where we went days without eating until we were picked up and taken to a safe house. We stayed there one month because it wasn't safe to fly into NYC at that time. We then traveled by ground to Nebraska and were stopped by a police patrol. They realized that we were undocumented and put us in jail for three days. Eventually we were released, and after spending $1,300, we were deported. I could not give up now because I could not afford to.

We went back to Agua Prieta, Sonora, in Mexico determined to cross again. So we crossed and were caught after we had walked half the night. We were detained a day and a night, then released. The third time we attempted to cross again and to get to Tucson, where we had arranged to meet a truck. The American police also stopped this truck, but this time they wished us good luck and let us pass.

From there we went to a safe house where we ate a meal, bought ourselves new clothes, and purchased three tickets for LGA airport in New York. The total cost of crossing was $4,300—a fortune for our family back in Mexico—so I had to work a long time to pay back all of the money that was loaned to my friends and I. This is often what happens to us when we come here to look for work.[22]

Nahar's, Teresa's, and Lucy's stories are the same as millions of others. Today women like them are attempting to enter America with the ambition of staying and working. Rightly or wrongly, they come in droves because there are jobs here waiting for them and employers willing to hire them. The debate continues as to whether comprehensive immigration reform will weaken or strengthen America's borders.

As Nahar pointed out previously, all reform in terms of human rights has to be a global initiative, because human rights are not a geographical lottery. We will not stop impoverished workers attempting time and again to come to America in search of a better life. Their communities are already here. Comprehensive immigration reform is a step toward integrating these communities into our economy and our society. For South Asian workers, this cannot come too soon.

Universal human rights includes a child's right to a safe and loving home environment. Across the world, millions of children live in abject fear on a daily basis. Some fear being trafficked into guerrilla armies; others fear being sold into prostitution or being sent to toil in factories. Yet others, small and vulnerable, feel afraid of the stranger who comes each day to tend to them. For some of these children, their fears will prove to be well founded.

Chapter 5

Hostage Takers: When the Time Bomb Goes Off

WHEN NANNIES BECOME KILLERS: SHOCK, COLLECTIVE DISASSOCIATION, AND AFTERMATH

Nanny time bomb: it reads like an oxymoron. How can a person paid to care for our children—a nanny—be linked with a terrible weapon of war, a time bomb? I originally coined the term back in 2004. It became the title of my blog in 2009 because of what I had begun to see in Manhattan.

A time bomb can silently tick away while all about it people move in normalcy, ignorant of its potential deadly blast. When a time bomb explodes, its devastation is immediately felt in terms of massive shock, injury, and death. As we have seen with school shootings or with suicide bombers, some people carry within them the seeds for destructive behavior. Although statistically small children are more likely to be killed by their parents, a relative, someone they know, or a stranger, a few criminal nannies also murder children. These people are ticking time bombs.

The idea of a child care provider fatally injuring a child is not new. The most high-profile crime in America that I can recall was the Louise Woodward case. It was all over the news in the United Kingdom mostly because Woodward was English. When I started to work as a nanny in America, I could see that certain conditions within the industry itself *could* lead to more fatalities, more injuries, and more personal heartache. The title of this book was therefore deliberate. Not all time bombs kill people outright; some maim or lightly wound bystanders. Other civilians are emotionally and mentally scarred by a time bomb because of what they saw or heard. Indeed for miles around a time bomb's detonation, entire communities can be deeply impacted by just one remote device. It's the same in child care.

New York City

The most recent case that gripped the nation's attention was the double homicide allegedly perpetrated by a former New York nanny named Yoselyn Ortega. It involved the murder of two small children left in her care. It is to date perhaps the most extreme and terrible abuse of trust between a family and a nanny.

On October 29, 2012, at 5 p.m. I posted this on my blog: "The skies of Manhattan are a brooding charcoal. Black clouds hang over the skyline like an apocalyptic doom. Hurricane Sandy is on her way but New Yorkers are already in the eye of a storm."[1]

Indeed, collectively our city was. In the months and years that have lapsed since then, threads of the accused nanny's life are coming together. The consensus is that Ortega suffered a psychotic breakdown after a long bout of depression and financial troubles. These critical facts about her were hidden from her employers.

Ortega's employer, Marina Krim, a pediatrician by training, was a stay-at-home mother. The family lived on the Upper West Side of Manhattan. Kevin Krim was a senior vice president at CNBC Digital. The Krims hired Ortega after the birth of their third child. Ortega, originally from the Dominican Republic, was a U.S. naturalized citizen. She was introduced to the Krims via a friend. The Krims even traveled to the Dominican Republic and met Ortega's relatives.

In cautionary tales, we instinctively search for things that can point to a tragedy. As humans, we like to solve problems; it's in our nature. In this instance and with this crime, we are left helpless and ruined by the knowledge that a trust was simply broken, the kind of trust that we all—as parents and as nannies—routinely enter into.

Unknown to her employers, Ortega's personal life had begun to seriously deteriorate. Although the Krims paid their nanny well, Ortega was complaining of being "broke" and "tired" to neighbors and friends. This eventually came to her employer's attention, and the Krims, concerned about Ortega's financial problems, had helped her look for a second babysitting job. Ortega had also recently paid a visit or visits to a psychologist. She had begun to lose weight, looked haggard, and was increasingly withdrawn and anxious.

From time to time we all go through periods of extreme stress. Our friends and family will rally to help us. Mentally healthy individuals eventually bounce back, but there will be times when we don't look or act our best. In those situations, our loved ones and employers don't expect us to suffer psychotic breakdowns. Sane people often choose to take time off work and get help if they feel they are on the verge of a breakdown.

Ortega was not a sane person, and yet she managed to work within child care. In other words, there could be *no writing on the wall* in Ortega's case.

Aftermath

When something this seismic occurs in child care, the clues in terms of public impact can be gleaned from general responses immediately after the event. A few hours and days later, the New York City moms I spoke to had expressed their shock in a number of ways: physical upsets such as vomiting and diarrhea and alternating between bouts of anxiety and tears and complete disbelief and shock. Other parents simply felt numb. They rationalized the event away as a tragic but random act and one that could not be anticipated or prevented. On the Internet, parent message boards and mommy blogs were awash with posts and articles, as working parents now attempted to second-guess the most intimate strangers in their homes: their nannies.

Curiously, the responses of nannies were a little different. While all nannies expressed horror and sympathy for the family involved, a tiny percentage suggested that there was more to the story than meets the eye. There have also been hushed remarks between caregivers, the gist of these comments being that only now do privileged people grasp the impact of low wages, immigrant work, and unfair demands routinely made upon nannies. A couple of nannies have also expressed concerns over a backlash against foreign workers. Conspiracies are where people go when they cannot fathom an event as it stands. *How could anyone hurt a child? What does that say about me?*

Ortega's crime put all nannies suddenly on public trial. For migrant workers, there was a keen feeling that a witch hunt would ensue. After all, hadn't Ortega—a foreign worker—presented herself as a good enough nanny? But behind the scenes, all was not well. We now know that Ortega had a long history of mental illness. Congress has not sufficiently addressed the potential of mental illness among child care workers. It remains a deadly and potent cause of concern for parents, however.

In the same year as the Ortega case, another crime highlighting mental illness in child care came to light. Elzbieta Plackowska was a suburban Chicago housewife, a mother, and a nanny. On October 30, 2012, she murdered her seven-year-old son and the five-year old girl she had been hired to care for. Plackowska claims at first that she had killed her own son because she was angry with his father, her husband, for frequently working away from home. Plackowska's excuse for murdering the child she cared for was that the girl had witnessed her killing her own son.

In time, however, Plackowska told the police that she had been plagued with thoughts about the Devil. She also complained that she had been working three jobs and getting very little sleep at night. Her father had recently died.[2]

Mental Illness

What the Ortega and Plackowska cases demonstrate is that someone who *already* has a disposition toward mental illness can be tipped into more deadly psychotic behavior when subject to a random cluster of arbitrary stresses: the death of a parent, a history of alcohol abuse, altercations with family members, financial stress, and marital problems.

Parents cannot know these facts if they are hidden from them. It is the unlicensed industry of child care, with its lack of universal regulation, that is flawed. Background checks as they exist today often do not or cannot uncover mental illness in candidates. In fact, routine background checks can even fail to catch troubling personality traits such as violence, addictions, public disorders, and a propensity toward pedophilia.

It is therefore the failure of successive governments to enact federal regulation that would protect families against mentally ill or otherwise potentially abusive caregivers.

One notable example of this is the case of Sarah Cullen, a woman who is now serving time for the death of a four-month-old baby boy named Cash Bell. Cullen's case raises a red flag over the industry of child care in much the same way as Ortega's crime does. It demonstrates that parents are often rendered helpless to the potential of abuse in a caregiver.

Allegedly Sarah Cullen had worked in various day care centers where there had been reports made against her for the rough handling of children, but none of these complaints made it to an investigation or to a public record.[3]

In so many of these cases, a baby is fatally injured in what was once termed shaken baby syndrome; it is now commonly referred to as abusive head trauma.

Abusive Head Trauma

"Abusive head trauma (AHT) and shaken baby syndrome usually refer to the same thing," according to Karen Miles, writing for Baby Center LLC.

"When a caregiver shakes and injures a child, it's sometimes called shaken baby syndrome. Shaking a baby is the most common form of AHT. It occurs most frequently in babies younger than one—typically when an adult is overwhelmed by a crying baby and tries to get him to stop. AHT is also the term doctors use to describe a serious brain injury that results from blunt force. Receiving a blow to the head and being thrown or dropped cause similar injuries to violently shaking a child, so doctors refer to all such injuries as AHT."[4]

AHT is caused in a momentary lapse of judgment (when a baby is dropped accidentally or knocked against something) or can occur in a moment of frustration and rage, as when a baby will not stop crying and a caregiver becomes overwhelmed. A baby might then be vigorously shaken, causing its head to move violently back and forth. In this action, an infant's brain literally knocks inside of its skull, causing massive internal bleeding. Similarly, an irate caregiver could slap or hit a crying baby or throw it roughly down into a crib or onto a diaper-changing mat.

The immediate impact of this action often causes bleeding within the developing retina, leading to blindness, impaired brain function, and sometimes death. The damage of this kind of action can also severely injure the infant's neck, spinal cord, and other bones.

In the case of individuals such as Cullen who have a history of incapability dealing with small children and Louise Woodward, a person who allegedly lacked the maturity in coping with the demands of a young baby, the merging of such a caregiver with a newborn is particularly dangerous. Indeed, in both cases it proved fatal.

Hidden Dangers

Sarah Cullen's employers found her via a reputable online nanny agency. She appeared educated and experienced and had CPR certification. She was also a mother. For Cash Bell's parents, Cullen ticked all of the right boxes. What they couldn't know was that Cullen already had a history of anger issues.

Shaken baby syndrome, or AHT, first hit the headlines in 1997, when a British au pair named Louise Woodward was arrested for the death of an eight-month-old baby named Mathew Eappen. Five days after being admitted to the hospital, Matthew died from injuries related to a fractured skull and a subdural hematoma, injuries that are indicative of AHT.

Woodward's original conviction for second-degree murder would later be reduced to involuntary manslaughter on appeal, because the presiding judge stated that "the circumstances in which the defendant acted were characterized by *confusion, inexperience, frustration, immaturity and some anger.*"[5] For Matthew Eappen's parents, these words would bring small comfort. Allegedly, the au pair agency involved in placing Woodward had given her just three days of actual training prior to engagement with her employers.

Both the Woodward case and the Cullen case demonstrate an astonishing breakdown in appropriate training for younger caregivers and the reporting of abusive behavior in day care to the authorities.

Routinely, online agencies will maintain a position of "we did the appropriate background checks" when faced with accusations of allowing abusive caregivers to slip through their net. While this is often true, it is not good enough. In lieu of comprehensive federal child care reform, day care facilities and nanny agencies must do more to follow through and flag prospective violators.

AHT Prevention

As we have seen, infants have intrinsic needs that are best taken care of in our absence by people who have the appropriate experience. In child care, this type of nanny is known as a newborn care specialist. These caregivers have significant expertise in handling the often unregulated demands of newborns. It might be a good idea for new parents to consider the services of a newborn care specialist until an infant has found its own schedule.

When your baby is ready for a long-term or full-time nanny, follow the tips in this book for hiring a good nanny. When sourcing a nanny via an online agency, do not rely on its standard background checks. Conduct your *own comprehensive background checks.* Always meet a prospective nanny's references and if possible meet her children. No matter how wonderful a candidate appears to be, purchase and fit a nanny cam and use it from Day 1.

I wish I could tell you that angels watch over our children in the world of child care and protect them from monsters, but they don't. We have been placed in their stead, and collectively *we* can work toward a time when no child dies at the hands of a bad nanny.

NANNY TRAPPED: GUILT, COERCION, AND PASSIVE-AGGRESSIVE BEHAVIOR

At once, a nanny may serve as a partner and a confidante while also walking a tightrope of serving as intended, *as hired child care help.* Moms often encourage nannies to love the children in their care as if they were their own—perhaps a simple concept at face value, but in essence a labyrinth of complexities emerges. I have seen mothers truly embrace the nurturing role of a nanny, only to be held hostage emotionally by her. New mothers are especially vulnerable to a domineering and patronizing nanny, someone who seeks to annihilate a mother's views on parenting. In these latter types of entanglements, the power balance is clearly off, sometimes leading mothers to lose their instinctive sense of boundaries and maternal confidence.

Amy

Amy[6] had become a first time-mom in the fall of 2012. Living in New York City she, like most other parents, had become engulfed in the storm of the Krim tragedy. In a highly vulnerable state, Amy hired her first nanny and went back to work full-time just five weeks after giving birth. Norma[7] was a pleasant woman who had come recommended from a friend in the neighborhood. An experienced nanny, Norma immediately assumed a position of superiority with her employers Amy and Jordan.

Going back to work so soon was tough. I had literally birthed another human being from my body, then, boom, back to work full-time I go. My hormones were raging. My body was both in recovery and in that bonding phase where you are literally in sync with your infant every second of the day. So, here we had this amazing, beautiful miracle, and I had to leave him with someone I had just met. On that score alone it was stressful. Add to that what had just happened to that family on the Upper West Side with the two murders by their nanny, and the ordeal of actually finding a nanny—it wasn't an easy transition.

We ended up finding a person through my friend, but we couldn't afford to hire her full-time to begin with, so my husband and I kind of patched a way through our jobs of making it like a 30-hour nanny job for her. She came and seemed committed. It was terrifying for me in the beginning. We lived on the West Side at the time, and it was right after, you know, so I would run home around 10 times a day to check on them (nanny and infant). I was a wreck, and I didn't get much work done. I was so scared.

So, one night, I guess three months later, she (the nanny) texted my husband and I and asked if we could be home early the following day, as she had something she wanted to tell us. Now, it had taken forever to find someone, and I was just getting comfortable with her. Plus, we were just finally getting back into the groove with our lives and work. So I thought "uh-oh, what's coming?" I was in a panic. I needed to know what was going on! I had meetings in the morning. I knew I wouldn't sleep that night. So I asked her what was going on. She replies [by text] "Don't worry, everything is fine" and that she would tell us tomorrow.

So, that night when we came home she's sitting there with another woman. She tells us, "I'm leaving. I found another family that can pay me more, but don't worry because my friend is going to take this job with you." I didn't know what to do. I couldn't quit my job. I was hysterical. I was very angry, and I felt ambushed, but by the same token I knew that there was nothing I could do. The following morning this other woman was going to come to my home and take over the care of my baby. I was completely handicapped. It's not like I could assert myself. I didn't know what my rights were.

I asked Amy if she felt as though she had been taken hostage.

Oh, totally. I knew there was absolutely nothing I could do. This woman would be in charge of my son all day—the next day and beyond. She was my nanny's friend. I couldn't yell or scream at her [my nanny]. I had to make these women feel that they were right. I had no choice. It was a set-up. I always expected that if she wanted to quit, she would give us two weeks notice. I mean, it's personal but it's also business. I expected her to be more professional. In the end I felt like it was nothing to her. Like my baby was so connected to her and she could just leave him. So it was horrible, and we ended up taking on the new person.

It was hard because the first nanny came highly recommended by a good friend. We checked her references. This new person we didn't know at all. Our previous nanny had pushed her on us. So that was really challenging. I'm ashamed to say at the time that we just went with it. I didn't do all the right things. We did no checks. I was just so overwhelmed at work. I couldn't afford to lose my job. I was also in a state of shock. So life went on.

There was no time-out to sort stuff out. We just kept moving. The new person seemed very, very kind, and she seemed to know a lot about what she was doing. She talked about all the things she wanted to do with our son, the groups she would take him to, and it all sounded perfect to be honest. She told us she had worked in a high-end day care. In the beginning she was amazing. She would do stuff with our child that the previous nanny hadn't done.

Slowly but surely, though, with time I just started to feel that things weren't right. I can't explain it other than it was a feeling that what she was saying wasn't what she was doing. Things like she insisted on absolutely no TV even though we had told her "Look, when our son is napping feel free to watch TV and relax." Then we would turn on our TV at night, and it would go to some daytime TV channel. Other things surfaced, like that she wouldn't take the subway and she would have her husband come in and take them in their car. We found that out through a neighbor, so obviously she held him on her lap without a car seat. She would tell us she was doing things with our son, then later she would switch the story—so she couldn't keep her story straight.

This went on for quite a while. We began to realize that probably she wasn't a good fit for us. Like another thing, she could never remember our son's age. At first it was too much to believe. Other stuff too, like she would tell us he was napping, then not napping. Her stories didn't add up. It began to affect my work. I was so distracted with calling her up and checking in on her that I began to let things slide at work.

And she was always totally passive-aggressive. She would completely undermine me. She would question or dismiss everything I asked her to do. It was as if I was stupid. She would look at me and have this fixed smile, and I knew I had absolutely no power. She played that "I'm older than you—I know what I am doing" card a lot.

It was horrible. So my husband and I decided that enough was enough, but we were in the middle of moving, and all the while we were interviewing people to be our nanny—you know, in the evenings, at weekends. So we really just stuck it out with her in the meantime with the hope that it would change. Looking back, it was kind of weird or bad luck that literally no one else worked out at the time. But that's pretty much what happened. Either people found another job, or they just never called back—but we tried. I mean, we really tried to find another nanny.

The other thing that was completely off was that our nanny was extremely religious, like a born-again Christian, and my husband and I are secular Jews. But she would always preach to us, then she began to extend that to our son. She would pray over his food with him. She would talk to him about Jesus, and he's 12 months, so he was beginning to listen to adults. During the day he was listening to church music, and she would host Bible readings in our home. She was so bold about it, she told us—she didn't even try to hide it! It was actually so crazy that I think we almost couldn't believe what we were hearing.

One day she blatantly told us that if we didn't go to church, we were all going to Hell. She asked me what did I think would happen to our child if my husband and I went to Hell? This was what I was having to say "goodbye" to in the morning.

Then it started that she began to get all of this personal drama. She told us she volunteered in a church and helped with marriage counseling cases on the weekend. She felt like my husband and I didn't have a healthy marriage, and she wanted to offer us couple advice. So every morning, she would grill me on what I was doing for my husband. I would get it—reason being because my husband left for work before me and I would do the handover with our nanny. It was getting to the stage that I was constantly late for work.

Then there was a lot of just not showing up where she would cancel at the last second, and we would have to scramble to find alternative care. And we began to just get this sense that she was completely taking over our home, like charging her phone, leaving Christian literature everywhere, watching daytime TV. My mother-in-law would pop in unannounced and find our nanny watching TV or having people over we didn't know. It was crazy. My husband couldn't deal with her. He would leave early and come home late, so essentially I was the one "dealing" with her.

People might judge me for not standing up more, but you've got to understand that I had to go to my office every day and leave my son with this woman. Was I going to make her angry? Was I going to leave after an argument? I felt like she was in charge, that she had all the power. I didn't want to upset her or make her angry. My child's life was in her hands—even when I knew she was wrong. It could be about developmental stuff like napping, for example.

She started to tell me that our son who was 14 months old didn't need to nap anymore. I told her that I thought that he did. And she would just stand there with her arms folded and smile at me. So we would come home to our baby totally strung out, exhausted, in the evening. That little time I thought I had with him at night evaporated. It was horrible.

So it was getting progressively worse with her calling me up at 8:30 in the morning to cancel as I sat waiting for her, dressed for work. I couldn't go into work. I'd have to work from home or use my sick days. I was getting so stressed out that it began to affect my work—canceling meetings with clients or bringing my baby in and asking the receptionist to watch him while I met with people. Remember, too, that at that exact same time we had newly moved. It was so stressful.

Then one day we finally managed to find another nanny. She was everything our nanny was not. We checked out all of her references, and again she came highly recommended. Plus, we really liked her. Trouble was, I was now terrified to end it with our current nanny. I had this feeling that it would get really ugly. But we had no choice. I wanted her to leave. I wanted our home back. The other problem was that the new nanny couldn't start until January, and this was, I think, November. She had to give her other family notice, and with the holidays it just wasn't feasible for our new nanny to start until the New Year.

So those four weeks where we had to wait it out were like pure torture. I admit that I should have told our current nanny that we had found another nanny, but I was terrified that she would do something bad to our child. Luckily, my mother-in-law and a friend's daughter in the neighborhood agreed to take on a few hours here and there, and I asked my boss if I could work from home one day a week. Long story short, we told our then-nanny that we were reducing her hours due to budget issues from five days a week to two days a week in the hope that she would quit and find another job. I know—it's not my shining moment.

So, our nanny went down to two days a week, and the brunt of interacting with her was experienced by my mother-in-law, who decided she would just pop in multiple times a day. But by this time our nanny had just completely given up any semblance of working at all. For instance, she would not get up and turn the TV off when my mother-in-law popped in. There were no more tales about library visits, or playdates, or playground trips, none of that feedback. And I couldn't be transparent at all. So, I avoided her as much as I could. It was an extra burden on me, the guilt the second-guessing "does she know?" kind of thing.

Needless to say January came, and the new nanny texted my husband and I at the last second and told us that she couldn't start on the date she had agreed on. I got to tell you I was almost hysterical at that point. I mean, come on. *Really?* And she didn't have a clear start date for us—she told us she was dealing with a family crisis. We wanted to give her the benefit of the doubt. I mean, it happens. We were completely desperate.

But just knowing that it wasn't over was awful. I just felt trapped and hopeless and desperate. It was horrible.

Two things happened. One, our nanny told us she had to be gone for two weeks just out of the blue. We had discussed paid vacation. So, if we were away she would get paid—all the holidays. Then she could take one week off paid. So she had already used over a week on all the time she took off, like a day here, two days there. And this time she wanted to be gone for two whole weeks with no prior warning. I think she texted me at like 11 o'clock at night the day before. But this was what she normally did, so my husband would move his hours and stay home. I would do the same. Friends and relatives stepped up, and I realized we just jumped and moved to accommodate her whims. It had gotten that bad. My girlfriends thought I was nuts.

Looking back, it is almost like being in an abusive relationship. At the beginning it was amazing, and then slowly things began to change. And when you're already stressed out and in the middle of it, you kind of just let things slide. Everyone I spoke to just said "you've got to fire her immediately." And I would go home and think that I would do it, but then I just couldn't because we didn't have a plan in place. In my mind I couldn't afford to be so impulsive about it. I couldn't afford to get fired.

I asked Amy why it was so incredibly difficult for her to find another nanny. The entire child care ordeal had lasted over a year.

We signed up on a lot of websites, but I wanted to find someone peer-recommended. I was so afraid of everything with him [my baby]. I was a first-time mom, and you got to remember this was a few months after that terrible, terrible crime on the Upper West Side with the two children. I was one of those people who went up there to the apartment building the night it happened and laid flowers. I was a mess after that. I was obsessed with the case. It was beyond belief. It haunted me— it still does, to be honest. I was already nervous, but then after that awful crime—I think all parents had like post-traumatic stress, you know? I mean, that could have been me coming home and opening the door slowly, waiting to hear some noise— of your child, your kids. I read everything about the case, and I was just terrified, terrified of angering my nanny. I think it kind of just froze me, which made it hard to effectively look for someone else.

And not that, honestly, my nanny would have done anything that horrible, but you never know. It was a very scary scenario—I think for everyone. When I went to work the next day after the . . . the double homicide I was absolutely sobbing, and my coworkers who weren't moms told me not to think about it. And it's interesting that I didn't talk to any other moms about it. I mean, aside from the initial shock. I think we all maybe withdrew.

Anyway, so we still hadn't found a replacement, and we were still looking when one day our cleaner reached out to report what she had witnessed that day. She said that my son kept trying to get his nanny's attention, and she was ignoring him, watching TV, and was on the phone the entire time. Our cleaner felt distressed, as she thought my son was distressed.

That was it for me. That night I let her go. I didn't tell her why. I just said that my work situation had changed and that we didn't need her. I think it was over a weekend. I didn't want her coming back. At first she sent me a very nice message saying to tell our child that she loved him, etc. The next day she sent me a message saying I would have to pay her for two weeks and her vacation time—not sure what that last part even meant. She then sent a message saying if she didn't get her money she would take legal action. I never responded to her. We changed our locks, and that was it. For a time afterwards I kept leaving work to check on my son. I was fearful she would show up at the door or in the neighborhood and do something rash, but we never heard from her. My mother-in-law stepped in, thank goodness, for emergency care, and then very soon after that we found someone that we love and is still with us—yeah—we finally caught a break, and our new nanny is amazing. Incidentally, last year our former nanny she sent my husband (funny how it wasn't me) a text telling him to wish me a happy mother's day for her. It was strange, but—.[8]

What can we learn from this account? I think it contains some powerful insights. The industry of child care is riddled with ideas or myths about the parent-nanny relationship.

Myth #1: This is a voluntary engagement between two equals. You and your nanny are not equal. Parents have the power to hire and fire. They are also quite rightly the CEOs of the household. Nannies are at best supportive junior partners in the "Smith" home corporation.

Myth #2: My nanny is my best friend. Friends are generally not hired at an hourly rate. A genuine friendship may develop once a nanny is no longer employed, but it truly cannot begin until then. Good friends speak their minds, especially if they think we are wrong. A nanny will rarely do that. She will almost *always* tell you what you want to hear. On the other hand, she *is* a working partner. You will need to have a healthy working relationship with your nanny that includes her ability to discuss subjects, even some that might be difficult for you to hear.

Myth #3: My nanny is a part of our family. While a nanny may temporarily feel like a member of the family, in the long run she isn't. Nannies have families and children of their own to love and dote on. Yes, nannies will grow extremely fond of your children, and that is a unique relationship. So, cherish the bond between your nanny and your children, but don't try to codify or own it. Nannies view the professional caring of children as a career.

Myth #4: My nanny would never talk about me behind my back. Most nannies do talk about their employers, just as most parents talk about their nannies. So, if you as an employer want to confide in someone, it's better to talk to your friends.

Until the industry of child care is regulated and reformed, the parent-nanny relationship will continue to resemble a mishmash of tangled emotions, resentments, miscommunications, and expectations. Many nannies complain about their working conditions, yet they fail to advocate for themselves. This doesn't help anyone. If you are looking to hire a nanny, do lead with a working agreement. A good agreement or contract will help to eliminate any misunderstands up front. Treat a nanny like a working partner, not as some invisible subordinate. Also, avoid the temptation to project onto her your own child care fantasies or fears. She is not a best friend, a coparent, or a servant.

A good nanny has been described as being a wife to the wife or a surrogate sister. I'm not sure that's apt. While a good nanny often acts like a family's diplomat—a person who balances the needs of every member— she is primarily your child's ambassador, always seeking her charge's best interests in his or her world.

In the long term and in the wider world, a nanny is a child care professional, governed by a desire to advance, to be treated fairly, and to be properly compensated. It can be that simple.

THE 1 PERCENT: PRIVILEGE, POWER, PAY

"She (Mrs. X) looks down at the paper for a few moments while I shift my weight from foot to foot."
"This is a little higher than we originally discussed."
"Well, the original list I gave you was two weeks ago and I've accrued over sixty hours since then."
She sighs and starts counting out twenties and fifties, slowly sliding them back and forth between her fingers to ensure that none of the bills are stuck together. She hands them over, her Hermes limoge bangles clanking together.
"It sure is a lot of money."[9]

No other novel to date explores working for the 1 percent as a nanny better than *The Nanny Diaries*. The book's excellent satire has done much to highlight how some members of the superrich relate to their employees.

Annie Braddock is an archetype we see often in child care: the educated nanny, the college babysitter, or the graduate babysitter. These nannies are the canaries of modern child care. Economically caged, they temporarily plunge deeply into the child care industry with a keen sense of social awareness. They didn't come into child care from another country, leaving their kids behind to give them a better life. They were born here, and they believe that a better life is their birthright. Hence, what they experience as caregivers is vital to understanding the systemic descent of the child care industry. Most important, their experiences working for members of the 1 percent can be some of the most insightful.

Jennifer's Story

I found my very own Annie Braddock via my nanny friends. She was characteristically young, smart, and well-meaning. A few times during our interview, we had to stop as she broke down in tears. She had taken a break from college before going on to earn a master's degree to earn some extra cash as a nanny. And like Annie Braddock, she worked for an extremely affluent older stay-at-home mom. The father was largely absent, being a successful hedge fund manager. The household employed an entourage of staff, including a housekeeper, a personal trainer, a chef, and a personal assistant. Jennifer[10] was a live-in nanny.

The first thing that happened was, I think I didn't sit down for a straight 12 hours a day consistently for 6 days a week for like 12 months. My boss was always home or around but not present—if you know what I mean. It was obvious to me that she wasn't the least bit maternal. They had a nanny from the day the child was born, and by the time I arrived they had gone through a couple dozen nannies—which I thought was odd. I was micromanaged the entire time. She would flag with post-it notes the meals the chef would make every night. She left me a daily itinerary. I also had to provide her with detailed reports on our day's activities. The kid was a little monster. He just really needed someone. I feel like no one was really listening to him. It took me a few months to calm him down and get him to listen to me.

I got up at 6 a.m. prepping breakfast. Even if he was in preschool in the mornings, I was always given chores to do: sort clothes, clean specific toys, research craft projects, look for books she chose. She always made sure there was always something for me to do. I had zero downtime. It made me extremely nervous.

The child was used to his mom not being around at age four. That made me sad. I was always being judged, like she would question every single thing I did. Like nitpicking. One day we created a very intricate project, and the mom came upon us and freaked out. I had strayed from her list of activities, and we were making a mess (which I would have cleaned up). The child was happy and enjoying himself, but as soon as his mom came into the room he got upset.

Every week we had to collect 12 books from the local library, read 3 a day, and then return them. He could not choose his own books. He could not keep his favorite books. Our books were prechosen online and reserved. I would always just agree with the mom. It was easier. Meal times were stressful. I was required to prepare all the breakfasts and lunches a week in advance. I had to list everything and give it to a personal shopper. Everything was allergy-free, organic, and honestly a bit bland. There was little room for spontaneity. It closed me down. I'm a very creative person, but in this job I just became a robot.

Every time she was around, the child wouldn't talk, and she got it into her head that I was being mean to him. It was just that he didn't want to be interrogated by her. It was odd. My bond with the child was so intense because I was with him every day for six days a week for what was to be a fourth of his little life. We did everything together. On my day off they hired another nanny, so he was never with his parents alone—ever. I think that's what made it so heartbreaking. That he needed me so much.

At this point Jennifer paused to cry. It was difficult asking her to continue, given how traumatized she clearly still was over this connection to the little boy. But we needed to get to the finale—what went wrong and why she left.

Okay, so fast-forward to 8 months, and I was contracted to stay for 12 months. That's what we had agreed on, and I kind of figured, you know, that after that time when I went back to college that I would be allowed to stay working with him maybe on the weekend or in the evenings. The weekend nanny had indicated to me that she wanted to move on. So, anyway, I just saw this continuum of taking care of him. I guess I'm just naive.

So, everything to do with this child was on a strict schedule. I think I said that—right? The mom had fixed times for when he ate, she scheduled like a g-zillion classes and activities for him, and he's like four, you know? There were times he was so exhausted he would beg me just to hold him and let him nap. But I knew that was not allowed. It was hard trying to keep a tired child awake, especially if he hadn't been well.

Oh, right, regarding sickness. So, he got really sick once, like sneezing, and he had a runny nose, and she would wear latex gloves, and when he was crying she would hold him at arm's length. Like she was horrified if any of his germs landed on her. But she absolutely would not allow me to comfort him—even though he reached out to me. I thought that was so mean.

So, one day he [the child] woke up 20 minutes early. He had fallen asleep earlier the day before because he had done a class and had literally fallen asleep in my arms at bedtime 20 minutes early. The following evening the mother kind of hissed at me. She said "I'm putting him to bed today, as he woke up too early today, and you are not keeping him on his schedule. This is unacceptable." I was like "okay," so she put him to bed, and guess what? He fell asleep on her too—20 minutes earlier than scheduled.

Look, it's not that I was happy, like I had proved her wrong. I just figured okay, now she understands you can't help it when a kid falls asleep. Then she told me that I was right in a backwards way. I said, "Yea, when kids are tired, you kind of have to let them sleep." She took that as a personal affront, and she snapped at me. I said, "I agree with you on a lot of things, but on this I just think kids should be allowed to sleep."

The next morning she asked me to take him to school. I thought that was odd. I never took him. That was what she did. On the walk to school he and I talked about all the things we would do that evening—our little plans—and I hugged him and told him I loved him. When I came home the movers were packing up my room. I was fired. She told me I had to leave immediately. I never saw him again.

I bumped into the housekeeper recently, and she told me that since me they have employed three other nannies. They all came and went, and that the little boy was now out of control. She said when she gets her coat on he clings to her and begs her not to leave. He tells her "you won't come back like Jennifer didn't come back." She thought it would make me happy to know that, but it just broke my heart.

I don't understand why his mom had him. She clearly did not want to spend any time with him, which is awful, and then to fire anyone who would actually love him is cruel. She never allowed me to say goodbye in a way that would make sense to him. Like, he's four, you know? What do you think he felt when he came home and I was gone? It was so bizarre, because everyone knew how much I loved him and how good I was with him. I watched *The Nanny Diaries*. I thought it was similar except I didn't have any downtime at all.

I asked Jennifer if this experience had changed the level or depth of care that she now offers to children.

Yes—because of that awful experience I now put some distance between me and the children I care for. Because I think it's kinder to the children in some way. I was so invested before; now I think I'm more actively disassociated. You wouldn't know it on the outside. I do everything right, of course, but in my soul and in my heart I keep something back. And that's the conflict. Because I'm a naturally nurturing person, and I hate walking on eggshells. I want to fall in love completely with a child so they know even if they are not my own child that I value and adore them. Everyone deserves to be loved. I do feel like there should be some regulation in the way human beings treat one another. These people should not be allowed to be so cruel to little children no matter if they are the parents or if they are rich.

I wondered if Jennifer thought that there might be wider long-term implications for the 1 percent and for society as a whole, given the way some of them treat their own children and the people who are there to help care for them and given how much influence the 1 percent wield in our lives.

I feel like the children learn this behavior and that they become the same cold-hearted disassociated people unconnected to other people. They grow up believing that other people are not equal. There's no hope for them being kind. They end up being screwed up, and they become powerful people in our society, so our society gets more mean.[11]

This was a compelling idea, and I wanted to take the subject further.

Eve

I talked to Eve, one of the caregivers I had interviewed in the "Surrogates" section. I was looking to make a definitive link between the emotional disconnection the very wealthy have with their children and the emotional disconnection that some members of the 1 percent have in society in general.

I lived in for four years with the family, and I guess it took six months for the reality to set in. What I mean by that is, that even though I lived in a huge penthouse in a very expensive part of Manhattan, I was in a cage of sorts. I had a room so small, it made dorm rooms look luxurious. I didn't have my own bathroom, and the bed was a kid's bed, something you would find acceptable for a child, not an adult, certainly not for long-term accommodations. I never ever felt comfortable in the house. Everything cost thousands and thousands of dollars. For example, the personal assistant told me that they (parents) just paid $60k for a painting—an ugly painting if you ask me. It was at that point that I asked for a raise. I was earning $50k a year. That's 24 hours a day 5 days a week. The child's baby monitor was in my room, so I was on call. The parents never had a monitor in their room. She was my absolute responsibility. Yet somehow the care of their child was worth less than a painting in the hallway.

I shared the space with another live-in staff member, a divorced woman who was the housekeeper, and her daughter, the cook. On the weekends the parents would go to their country house and take a weekend nanny with them. On the weekends I was alone in the apartment with this other family. We shared a kitchen, so I never ever felt like I had any real space of my own. I couldn't host friends or family, for example, because the communal areas were so loaded with expensive pieces of art and furniture that I was nervous about spilling a drink or breaking something. The housekeeper also took it upon herself to police the rooms when the parents were not home, ready to tell on me if I had a guest over. It quickly became uncomfortable, as it became clear my room, although rent free in an expensive city, was my own little jail cell.

There came a point when the housekeeper became abusive. I feel like she was threatened by my role in the family. She had been working in the family for nine years when I was hired, and suddenly she had to serve me, simply because my bosses insisted I sit and eat with them. The housekeeper attempted to blackmail me one evening after I made an innocent mistake. being new to this house. She saw my error and said, "I won't tell Mr. and Mrs this time so long as you do what I say." When I told her I wasn't going to be blackmailed, the housekeeper became a nightmare. When we would pass each other in the house, she would stare right through me or she would yell at me, curse at me, get in my face. She also felt a distorted sense of power, given her seniority within the family. Had I been undocumented or a younger nanny, I think she would have been in a better position to abuse me, because I would have been more vulnerable and less confident about standing up to her.

After several other verbally abusive incidents, I finally decided to tell my employers about the verbal abuse. Despite the seriousness of her behavior toward me, they maintained her position in the family another three years, until they recently moved on, of their own accord.

Interestingly and sadly, the housekeeper and her daughter were undocumented in America, and my employers knew that. The housekeeper was not my favorite person, but her daughter was lovely, and people in that position, who work so hard for so little, have no real choices. My employers are fabulously wealthy and could have easily sponsored this family, but they chose not to. That is such codependency.

So I came to the family when the child was two years old. She (the child I care for) had a baby nurse from birth to two years of age. Then I kind of took over, and when I say took over I mean I took over. I became the most important person in her life.

The circumstances were such that I was actively encouraged to plug in 24–7 and be the full-charge nanny. I became the attachment person. I was given that role. I was paid to provide that service, which is a weird way to put it. I was the alpha person. They [the parents] made it plain that I was to be that person in the child's life. There was a point about a year ago that I thought about leaving because I was worried about her getting too attached to me, but then I realized that all they would do would be to hire another nanny. So I didn't want that to happen— because she's little and she needs someone now. She needs to feel safe as a small child. She needs to know someone is there for her. That's what I do for her. It's my gift in a way that will never ever be acknowledged perhaps even by her. And that breaks my heart.

I asked Eve why she thought this child's parents had decided to have a child if they were both so clearly disconnected to her in her early childhood. Her response was astounding.

It's a competition. They [the parents] are competing for their father's attention [the senior member of the family is an extremely wealthy individual] because one of the parents has a sibling who had already started a family. On a professional level they were both on equal footing, very successful in their respective fields. But the fact is, daddy has all the money. They are tap-dancing for daddy basically. They're saying to daddy, "leave me all your money." It's a class thing— a dynasty thing. If you want to understand how psychopathic the ruling people are, just look at how they raise or don't raise their children. It's all about the money. For wealthy people to inherit family wealth, they have to produce heirs. These people produce heirs to keep the money and power within their families.

They are not raised to have empathy or attachment. If anything, they are raised by the people who have no power. But at some point the kids realize that in order to inherit the power and the money, they have to become the same disconnected people that their parents are.

Eve has a two-year plan to stay with the child she cares for because she wants to see her through some definitive developmental stages. And after Eve leaves, she intends to stay an integral part of the child's life—for the sake of the child's emotional health. But I pointed out that I'm not convinced that the parents concerned have the emotional integrity to respect her unique bond with their child, especially if they are threatened by the connection between nanny and child. The idea came as a shock to her.

I said, "I need you to listen to me. I understand that you need to have a plan for your life, an exit strategy, and that when you leave this child it's never going to be easy—the emotional fallout, etc. But you have been such a beautiful presence in this child's life. I mean, in years to come, she is going to be doing things with her own children that you did with her. That's your gift—that's a nanny's gift to the children we care for."

"Yeah, right," Eve responded, "it never occurred to me that when I leave they wouldn't let me see her."

I wondered about the broader implications of attachment disorders among some members of the 1 percent and whether that could affect our society. The most powerful family dynasties actively engineer our society—they run the top 500 Fortune companies, they occupy supreme political positions. Are we becoming less compassionate because of the choices made by a few damaged individuals? I looked at Eve and posed this question. She paused for a moment before responding:

I had a date recently—incidentally with a very wealthy guy—and he asked me what I did for a living. So I told him "I'm a nanny," and he grew very quiet. Then he said, "you know I'm successful, right? But I'm still in therapy. You want to know why? My nanny was around from when I was a baby until I was 10, and then one day she was gone. My parents never told me why. I guess now she was just fired. Until this day I cannot properly attach to women because someone I loved very deeply just disappeared from my life." That's when I realized the power that nannies have in these families.[12]

The Value of Attachment

Edward John Mostyn Bowlby, a British psychologist, psychiatrist, and psychoanalyst known for his pioneering work in attachment theory, was driven to the subject in adulthood in part by his own childhood suffering. Raised in a typical upper-class manner, Bowlby rarely saw his mother except for a few hours a day. He was left primarily in the care of a nanny. When Bowlby was nearly four years old, his nanny, whom he deeply loved, abruptly left the family. For the small boy, as Bowlby later related, this was the equivalent of losing a mother. This early loss subsequently drove Bowlby's interest in early childhood attachment as a profession. Indeed, he developed most of the fundamental ideas behind attachment theory.[13]

Therapists believe that factors that contribute to impaired attachment include multiple caretakers—a regular turnover of nannies or the abrupt dismissal of a nanny who has been the primary caretaker since a child's infancy. Clearly, the emotional legacy that nannies leave behind runs deeply in the families who employ them—all families, affluent or otherwise. More important, nannies can profoundly affect the children they are hired to care for. Without recognition of the impact that nannies have in children's lives, we will continue to see trends of nonattachment in child care. Unresolved attachment can also span many generations.

Attachment problems are often handed down transgenerationally unless someone breaks the chain. As a parent, an insecurely attached adult may lack the ability to form a strong attachment to their child and provide the necessary attachment cues required for the healthy emotional development of the child, thereby predisposing their child to a lifetime of relationship difficulties.[14]

If you were raised by emotionally distant parents, it could be a real challenge to be present in your own children's lives. Take courage in the knowledge that you can break the chain of detachment. There are therapies available that have been proven to improve attachment between parents and their children. It's never too late to start or learn. While it might feel easier to hire an emotionally solvent nanny and to outsource that kind of care to her, ultimately our children enter this world yearning for a parent's attention. A nanny is a supplement to a child's emotional life. His primal attachment must be with his parents.

In your absence, when you are at work, you will want to be replaced by an extraordinary person. Only an emotionally solvent caregiver can help to fill the void left by parents. It is not her role to replace you as the central attachment figure. It is her job to nurture and comfort your child when you are gone.

Chapter 6

Avoid a Time Bomb Now: Preventing the Unthinkable

PREVENTION: PROFILING GOOD NANNIES, DETERRING BAD NANNIES

The search for a *good nanny* can resemble a quest for the Holy Grail. False starts, trails that lead nowhere, and convincing fakes litter the path to an accomplished caregiver. But it *is* entirely possible to successfully navigate the labyrinth. I have walked this path from the other side, and I understand the pitfalls. I've also partnered with child care experts, agency owners, and parents who have found Ms. Right. By now you will have acquired a basic understanding of the different types of caregiver available. Here's a refresher:

Newborn care specialist. A caregiver who specializes in the needs of newborn babies, including but not exclusively establishing sleep and nap schedules, breast-feeding or formula feeding routines, umbilical cord health, colic, constipation, etc.

Infant/toddler nanny, manny, babysitter. A caregiver who provides full-time or part-time full-spectrum child care generally in the home. A nanny is a female caregiver; a manny is a male caregiver. A babysitter is often a part-time caregiver who works to a more flexible schedule, such as evenings and book-end child care, such as taking kids to school and picking them up after school and working on weekends.

Child nanny, manny, babysitter, tutor caregiver. A caregiver who provides full-time or part-time full-spectrum child care generally in the home. A tutor caregiver is a person with academic experience in education who specializes in intellectual enrichment.

Older children nanny, manny, babysitter, tutor caregiver, housekeeper caregiver. A caregiver who provides full-time or part-time child care generally in the home. A housekeeper caregiver is a person who acts as an adult supervisor in the home but does not directly manage older children and is more of a house cleaner and manager.

All children nanny, manny, babysitter, tutor caregiver, mother's helper, au pair. A caregiver who provides full-time or part-time full-spectrum child care generally in the home. A mother's helper is person who assists a parent in the home. Duties can include running errands, grocery shopping, personal assistant, and cleaning as well as some child care. An au pair is a younger generally foreign-born person who lives in with a host family and offers part-time child care in exchange for cultural enrichment.

Stage #1: Where to Start?

Where does one begin the journey for a good nanny? There are various choices open to parents:

1. A nanny agency
2. Professional online child care list site
3. An open source general listings site
4. Word of mouth, peer recommended (mom to mom)
5. Notice boards in common spaces such as a pediatric office, a store, or a community board (generally a self-posted ad by a nanny)
6. Social media sites
7. Apps
8. On-the-spot solicitation (you observe a nanny in action and offer her an interview)

Realistically, parents can utilize all eight avenues of engagement. Whichever resource you finally choose, the golden rule should always be this: a prospective nanny must come with multiple *credible* references.

Stage #2: Arrange to Meet the Candidate and Request References

Most employers will reach out to candidates via e-mail or phone depending on what form of contact an agency or an individual nanny has offered. Tip: try to get a phone number so you can speak to a prospect.

Hearing a person's voice and her choice of words can be a powerful first marker of suitability. Therefore, if possible, before you arrange to meet with a nanny, try to talk to her *first* over the phone. After an initial conversation, ask the nanny to prep references, then arrange to meet her in a *public space*. After all, this is an initial meet and greet.

First impressions count. When you meet a prospect, observe her personal demeanor closely. How does she appear when she first arrives? Is she on time or even a few minutes early? Is she late? Does she seem harried? Does she provide a valid excuse for being late? How is she dressed? Is she smartly attired, or is she overly casual? Does she seem relaxed and confident? Does she pick up on your mood or tone? Does she maintain eye contact when answering challenging questions? Does she listen attentively, or does her attention tend to wander? Does she seem arrogant? Is she alert, or does she look tired?

While CPR training, early childhood-themed education, and caregiving experience are vital, so is a prospective nanny's ability to express a full spectrum of care. Equally important are a nanny's nonverbal and verbal skills. Even newborns need to be spoken to, played with, and given regular eye contact. In light of this, when you first meet a potential hire, it's essential that you listen for the subtext. Here are some points to observe during the meeting.

What is the quality of interaction between a prospective nanny and your child? Does the tone of her voice, her facial expressions, or her physical handling convey an inherent tenderness and ease? Your child deserves a nanny who is emotionally robust enough not to take the child's behavior personally. How does your prospective nanny deal with your toddler's childish antics, for example?

Your nanny should appear to be fulfilled in her private life. Does she look happy? Is she a single parent or a sole breadwinner? Is her extended family in the United States? Does she like where she lives?

A good nanny views her position as an opportunity to make a definitive contribution to another human being. Why is she working in child care in the first place? Is it primarily because she thinks she's good at it and that it feels relatively easy for her to undertake? Or does it come from a deeper yearning to enrich a child's life? If she is a transient child care worker, someone headed to another vocation or pursuing higher education, why did she choose to work in child care and not in some other sector?

Is the candidate still in touch with any of her previous charges? If not, then do ask why. These are all good topics to bring up in that initial encounter. Does the prospect squirm or seem irritated by your questions? Did she bring along the references you asked her to? These are indications of how motivated she is in working for you.

Check, Check, Check

If you just click with your nanny and your children adore her on sight, then the temptation could be to forego background checks. That would be a grave mistake. Some employers feel uncomfortable asking discerning or personal questions. If you are such a person, you can outsource that side of the process to an accredited nanny agency or a security company. You will not want to verbally offer a job to a candidate until you have had all of her checks completed.

References: What to Ask For

It is an unfortunate fact that some nannies have their friends provide job references. I've had two nannies tell me this. I've been asked to pose as a mom and provide a reference. So it goes on. When a prospective client calls to get a reference, the nanny's friends are primed to *recommend* her in glowing terms. In light of this, you should definitely request a landline number and a face-to-face meeting with a nanny's previous employers, preferably in their homes. An insistence upon a face-to-face meeting with former employers will deter a prospective nanny from forwarding bogus references.

Here are some references to ask for:

Personal references. A new nanny should be able to provide at least two personal references. They should be professional people in good standing and not relatives. Find out from the nanny her relationship to each individual. You should ask for landline numbers only (if possible), not cell phone numbers. This will weed out potential fakes. Business numbers are good because they can be easily verified. When you speak to the references, listen carefully to how they respond to these questions:

What is your relationship to X?
How long have you known X?
Why do you think X would make a good nanny?
Have you observed X with children? What stood out for you?
Is X a responsible person? In what ways is she?
Do you consider X to be trustworthy? How and why?
What do you consider X's strengths to be?

Employer references. You may not be able to talk to the nanny's current employer, but you should talk to at *least two recent employers in your locale.* You must insist upon only talking to a previous employer for whom the candidate provided *child care,* not other services such as housekeeping, cooking, or cleaning, as these are not automatically transferable skills.

How long did X work for you?

What was her job description?

Did her duties change over time? Why?

Why would you recommend X for being a nanny for a newborn, multiples, toddler, etc.? Do you consider X to be a responsible person?

Can you give some examples?

Was X on time and reliable? How so?

Do you consider X to be a loyal person? What does that mean to you? Can you give some examples?

What do you consider X's strengths to be?

Why did X leave your employment?

Would you hire X again? Why or why not?

What did you personally like about X?

Is there anything you feel she could work on?

Was X responsible in your home?

Did she ever have to respond to an emergency? What happened?

Is X generally a healthy person?

Is X punctual?

While speaking to and meeting adult references is mandatory, if possible you could also try to talk to the reference's children. If the reference feels it is appropriate you could arrange to informally meet, say in a playground, to see how the children behave. You might want to bring your own children along. You could casually ask the reference's children if they miss their former nanny. Are they still able to see her? Do the reference's children appear well adjusted? Are they spirited, happy, and confident? A nanny's former charges can often tell you as much as anything written down on paper.

It's good to remember too that perfectly behaved children are not always the mark of success. As parents, you already know that small children can be difficult. They are bundles of demanding energy that turn apartments upside down. Babies, toddlers, and children need constant attention, affirmation, and touch. When they cry, they need to be picked up and fed and changed. They wet beds, they tip things over, they fight, they struggle, and they don't always listen. Do the reference's children seem normal, or do they seem to be putting on a show for the adults? This could indicate that their former nanny was too strict or authoritarian.

Criminal history, motor vehicle, and medical references. If a potential nanny's personal and employer references are positive, parents should then check for criminal behavior and for her motor vehicle history. If you feel that it is appropriate, you could ask to contact your prospective nanny's medical practitioner. The latter might indicate whether a nanny has been prescribed antidepressants or sleeping pills recently, medications that might impair her ability to perform or suggest an underlying mental health issue.

Identification. You will need to ask the candidate to produce personal information that legally identifies her, including:

- A social security number/card or a valid work permit
- A thumbprint (optional if she has little in the way of documentation)
- A valid passport and a driver's license number (be sure to see the actual license)
- Proof of date of birth
- A current utility bill in her name proving residence

A passport and a driver's license should be photocopied and retained somewhere safe. If the references and background checks are satisfactory and if the referee's children appear happy and well adjusted and genuinely seem to miss their former nanny, the chances are that you have found a potential hire. However, the next stage is the most crucial: the interview.

Stage #3: The Interview

At this point you are ready to bring the prospect into your home. It's important for both partners to be present during a formal interview, because it's a joint decision. If it is not too disruptive, it is also good to introduce a potential nanny to your children in their own environment.

If you have a newborn, you might want to see how the nanny reacts to a fragile, helpless infant. Does she ignore your baby while holding her? Does she seem confident as she interacts with your child? Is she overly functional with the baby, or does she demonstrate respect for a newborn's body and needs? Your baby can be a good guide on the energy emanating from a nanny. Infants need to feel safe and connected. They can sense if someone is hostile or insecure.

Your baby will need to fall in love with her new nanny. She will need to learn from her how to become an engaged, complex, and responsive person. In order for that to happen, a nanny must first possess those attributes and in abundance. How does one measure qualities such as empathy, pleasure, joy, and social confidence in a prospective nanny? It can only come through posed questions and an intense observation of her responses and her behavior.

Questions to Ask during an Interview

There will come a time during the interview when you will want some undisturbed (kid-free) time to drill down on some important questions.

One of you (parents) could take the children outside or put them to bed, or you could have a relative help out. In fairness to nannies, it can be challenging concentrating on important questions if there is a crying baby or if boisterous children are in the room. So, set aside some adult time just to talk. Lead with the structure of the job: a proposed salary, hours, duties, benefits, job commitment, and the length of paid vacation. Then drill down with these types of questions, and be sure to take notes:

When can you start working?

Will you ever be available to work evenings or weekends?

Will you be available to travel with our family for weekends/vacations?

How much direct experience do you have with my child's age group?

Why are you a nanny?

Why are you looking for a new job?

What different age groups have you cared for?

What's your favorite age range? Why?

Do you have any formal higher education?

Did you complete high school?

Do you have any formal early childhood development education or training?

Do you have any first aid or CPR training?

Do you like to drive?

Can you swim? How well?

What common early childhood ailments are you aware of?

Have you ever had to deal with an emergency?

How many ways can you take a child's temperature?

What about your life has led you to this type of work?

Aside from child care, what have you accomplished or achieved in life that you are really proud of?

What are some of the challenges of working in child care?

What are your beliefs around discipline and boundaries?

What kinds of activities would you organize on a rainy day?

What are your opinions on napping, bedtime routines, nutrition and feeding, diaper changing, potty training, enrichment, downtime, and media?

How would you comfort my child in my absence?

At what level of anxiety or distress would you call me/inform me?

What are some of the rules you've followed in other households that you think work well?

Which rules don't work for you?

What is your preferred salary range?

Are you willing to do any light chores while our baby is sleeping or our children are at school? Which ones?

Would you perform the Ferber method (allowing babies to cry themselves to sleep) if asked? Why or why not?

Have you ever had to deal with a life-threatening emergency? What happened?

How do you feel about in-home camera surveillance (nanny cams)?

Are you a religious person? If yes, what religion are you? What religious traditions do you observe?

Do you intend to share your religious beliefs with our child?

What are your views on child nutrition?

Our children are special. What makes you special?

What do you know about emotional intelligence (EQ)?

How do you feel about children making a mess?

What (different) career would you do/have if circumstances permitted?

Trial Runs

If you feel that the interview went well, you can arrange a supervised session where you observe a prospective nanny interacting with your children for an extended period of time. This is a paid session. Trial runs can also help you in making a final selection if you have more than one candidate you like.

During a trial, you will want to gradually pull back and observe things. It's important to provide clear instruction, of course, particularly if you have a young baby, but avoid the temptation to micromanage. You will want to see how a nanny deals with prolonged interactions, such as long dialogues and problem solving with your children. Can she occupy your baby without overstimulating him? Does she simply follow your children's demands, or does she take the lead where necessary?

Is a nanny creative without being domineering during playtime? Can she play scary dragons as easily as she can play with dolls? (This will help if you have boys and girls.) Is the nanny comfortable with allowing imaginative play to unfold? Is she able to debate logically when asked difficult questions? Arrange for multiple trial sessions and in different locations so that you can see how a nanny supervises your children in a playground or on the sidewalk. With each session, move further and further into the background. At one point you might even want to leave the room or an area for an extended period of time to see how a nanny manages a child's anxiety.

In addition to asking searching questions and observing a nanny through trial sessions, you also have two tools at your disposal when screening a prospective nanny: body language and personal intuition.

Body language rarely lies. You can tell a great deal about a person by how she reacts when your carefully primed children enter the room, tip over her coffee, and jump all over her. If she smiles through grinding teeth, she's probably not at ease with children who fully express themselves.

Parental intuition. Evolution has equipped parents with a powerful instinct that has worked brilliantly for millennia. *How do you feel about this nanny?* Sometimes you have no rational explanation for it—something about her just doesn't feel right. It's okay to move on to the next person. Trust your intuition.

So, you're at the stage where all of the candidate's references are returned with glowing recommendations. The interview and trial sessions all went swimmingly. Your children already love her, and you feel in your gut that she has all of the right credentials for the role of a nanny. Are you ready to make her an offer and give her a start date? Not quite. As with all financial relationships, documenting a verbal agreement in the form of a contract helps to avoid confusion later on. What should a good contract contain?

Creating Your Contract

A contract ensures that all parties are aware from the get-go what is expected from them. It is a legal document that can be held up in a court of law. It should include awareness of and compliance with state laws. Contracts create job security and employee longevity. Contracts are the Magna Carta of the child care industry in that they outline services, rights, and compensations awarded. They cut down on miscommunication, resentments, and misconduct later on. Below is a sample of what a work contract should contain.

Section A

Personal Information
Nanny's full legal name:
Nanny's social security number:
Nanny's passport number:
Nanny's work visa number/expiration date:
Nanny's driver's license number:

Probation Period
2 weeks: Dates _____
1 month: Dates _____
3 months: Dates _____

Starting Date
Weekly hours:
Weekly salary or hourly pay (first year):

Overtime policy:
Rate of increase annually:
Rate of increase per new child:
Any benefits provided such as sick leave, holidays, etc.
Payment of social security, income tax, etc.
A fixed payday (nominate a day of the week):

Section B

Agreed upon Responsibilities
With children:
In the home:
Outside duties:
Extra Duties:

Section C

Household Rules and Personal Standards (Parents' Outline)
Rules to be followed regarding television, diet, transportation, etc.
Media allowance/content/gadgets permitted:
Diet:
Allergies:
Transportation (radius of permitted travel, modes of transport):
Other household rules:

Confidentiality Clause
Do you agree to maintain our family's confidentiality outside of our home?
Circle yes or no.
Yes
No
Add comments:

Section D

Termination of Employment
Period of termination notice mutually required (circle period).

1 week
2 weeks
3 weeks
4 weeks

Section E

Dismissal and Resignation

Should either party act contrary to the terms of this contract, termination of employment and contract will occur immediately. Add additional terms/clause here.

Section F

Agreement

On (Date)_____ this contract of employment was made between
Employer (print full legal name)
Employee (print full legal name)

The signing of both parties in agreement to all terms was witnessed by _____ as witness under the laws of governance in the state of _____.

Signature of all parties:

Employer: _____ Date:_____

Employee: _____ Date:_____

Witness:_____ Date:_____

Employer

Congratulations. You have created a job, and you are now an employer! With employment comes a responsibility to observe state laws governing domestic labor. In Chapter 7, I go into depth about the nanny tax because it is such an important subject. Here are other considerations for new employers.

Insurance and Health Care

You will need to speak to your *insurance* provider about adding a disability policy to your home insurance, because should your employee have an accident in the workplace she will be entitled to compensation to cover a loss of earnings and medical bills. You will also need to speak to your *accountant* regarding declaring and filing your nanny's taxes. Nanny agencies in your state are excellent resources for calculating employee benefits such as vacation, overtime, and sick pay. What about health insurance? While some employers don't see this as their concern, it actually makes sense if your new baby's caregiver remains healthy. Health insurance isn't just there for when we get sick. It provides otherwise healthy people with prescreenings, routine blood tests, and access to generic medications at low cost. Can you add her to your plan?

Unfortunately not. "Because she's not a family member, your nanny can't be covered on your plan," according to Julia Quinn-Szcesuil. "And even if you own a business, she can't be covered as an employee of your business because she's technically a household employee. The difference may seem minor, but can cost you thousands if she is injured or gets sick and your insurance company refuses to pay because she's not really a business employee, but a household employee."[1]

The good news is that under ObamaCare she can now shop around for an affordable plan. Unfortunately, as an employer you cannot fill out a form on her behalf. And if she has an accident or gets sick in your home, your insurance likely won't cover her.

You can look up your state's insurance guidelines at http://www.naic.org/state_web_map.htm. Once you have indicated your state, you will be taken to a site that offers a wide range of information on laws and regulations. It's important that you choose "Health" under the main menu, as that will lead you to the requirements you are subject to as an employer in your state.

If you want to avoid a lot of bureaucratic red tape, simply head to http://www.naifa.org/practice-resources/client-management/160 and select health plans. The website will help you search in your local area for a broker who is an association member. You can make a call on behalf of your nanny, request the most affordable plan, and request the paperwork.

Transition

Once you have hired a good nanny, there are steps you can take to ensure a seamless transition. Talk to your children about the change that will shortly be taking place. It will help the new arrangement run more smoothly if you can take time from work and oversee your nanny's placement within your family.

If you are replacing a nanny, your children may express conflicted feelings regarding their previous nanny and the new one. They may need time to grieve as well as to adjust to their new caregiver. If you cannot take time off work, it's good to make yourself available via the telephone for your nanny. Equally important, you can take calls from your children to check in with them.

In the beginning, you will want to set up definitive ground rules for everyone so that the kids understand that you and their new nanny are on the same page. Have clear guidelines on issues such as the following:

- Diet (allergies, gluten, sugar, fast food, etc.)
- Media time (how much per day, what type of media)
- Homework (when does it get done, assisted or unassisted)
- Household chores (who does what, when)
- Compliance to a nanny's authority (no backtalk, questioning, or rudeness)
- Bedtime (absolute deadline for lights off)
- Playdates (activities and location)
- Separation anxiety (what to do when the kids get really anxious)

In those early weeks and months, you will want to be closely aligned with your children and your nanny. Staying alert to your children's behavior will indicate how good your nanny is for them.

You might want to create an information pack for your nanny in case of emergencies. For example, your nanny will require the contact number/address of your local family physician or clinic. She will also need the number and location of the closest hospital. Another invaluable document to have is a letter giving your nanny power of attorney if you are unable to be at the scene of an accident. Prior to handing her this information, it is essential to tell her what medications your child is allowed to take and if your child has allergies. Insist that your nanny program all of the emergency numbers into her cell phone. Update the information when necessary.

Ordering In, Snacking Outside

Another area that often requires repetition is nutrition. If you do not want your child eating fast food on a weekly basis, let your new nanny know beforehand. Keeping a food diary and stocking up with whole foods will lower a nanny's temptation to purchase fast food. Also inform your nanny at the outset what treats your child is allowed to have.

Developmental Milestones

Nutrition, nap times, and potty training should be procedures that you have full control over. If you don't want your nanny napping your child for hours on end during the day, say so. Potty training and weaning (off formula) can be very stressful for an infant. Some nannies have very definite ideas about when a child should pass through a developmental stage. Early communication on the subject will ensure that your wishes will be upheld. As always, being on the same page when it comes to a child's development will enable that child to progress without anxiety or confusion.

In those early days, it is particularly important that you look out for signs that your child is not happy with the new arrangement. Separation anxiety is of course normal, especially if you are transitioning back to full-time work. But if your infant or toddler becomes extra fussy or clingy as soon as your nanny arrives, you might want to seriously consider why.

The greatest tool in your armor for monitoring the behavior of a new nanny remains the nanny cam. Your in-home surveillance should begin immediately. I would advise parents not to inform a nanny where a camera is located. Your nanny must be observed as she goes about her normal daily business. That's the point of surveillance.

SURVEILLANCE: NANNY CAMS, DISCOVERY, ACTION

Lisa Belkin's 2007 article "Knowing Noreen," which appeared in the *New York Times Magazine,* opened with this paragraph:

When the author learned that her children's former babysitter had been arrested for assaulting two elderly men in her care, she needed some answers. For starters, what is trust? We trust strangers not to poison our food in their restaurants, not to drive drunk when we board their buses. We trust loved ones . . . we hire office workers after a few hours of interviews . . . we go to a doctor based only on the fact that our neighbor seems to like him. We hand employers our Social Security numbers, and valets our car keys, and bank tellers our balances, and nannies our children.[2]

Although the above-mentioned nanny never physically harmed Belkin's children, she had caused one of them to say that "Noreen scares me." Belkin had checked out the nanny's references. There had been certain signs toward the end of her employment but nothing to suggest that her nanny could be capable of serious assault. Then one day Noreen let slip that she had in effect fooled Belkin in some way:

She [Noreen] turned to me [Belkin] and said, "One Christmas you wrote me a note saying that I must have come from a loving family to show such love." She took a deep breath and looked me straight in the eye. "Wow, did I put one over on you." Her voice was steel. Icy. Scary. She seemed pleased with the pain her words had caused.[3]

As it turned out, Noreen had endured a traumatic childhood with a violent father who was eventually sent to prison. My point in using this example is to demonstrate that emotionally damaged people can end up working with the vulnerable: children, the elderly. They seem to easily get past first base.

If a bad nanny has managed to breeze her way through multiple reference checkpoints and an interview and secured herself a job with your family, how can you protect your children from her? There is only one foolproof way. You need to observe her with your kids when you are not home. In other words, monitor her with a nanny cam. This might seem an extreme measure, but it's really just common sense. It's not invasive. It's your right as parents to protect your children in their home. Many parents use this method to observe the care that their children are getting or *not* getting. The many recent cases of nanny abuse caught on camera serve as a reminder that abuse by nannies goes on.

"I just felt like something was . . . off," said a parent quoted by Jennifer Johnston in a story for the *Daniel Island News*. The young mother installed a web cam, hoping to find a simple explanation for her veteran nanny's seemingly sudden change in behavior. But when she first logged in to the web cam live feed, she was irked to find that her four-month-old son had not been moved from the spot she'd left him in hours before. When the nanny finally picked the baby up and he spit up on her, his mother was horrified to witness her nanny yell and then forcefully place him in the baby swing. She went straight home and fired her nanny.[4]

Thankfully, the most extreme forms of abuse—shaking, slapping—are quickly caught by nanny cams, and in-home surveillance remains the most effective parental safeguard. But a nanny cam shouldn't be an impulse purchase. There are five things parents should think about first before buying one.

1. Do we tell our nanny we installed one?
2. Which nanny cam is best?
3. Where do we put it?
4. Is it legal?
5. Troubleshooting.

Disclose or Not?

There are two schools of thought on the subject of disclosure. It goes something like this:

- *The Yes Camp.* Telling a nanny that she will be monitored during the course of a working day creates a working environment of mutual trust. It also raises her game. On-the-job performance scrutiny is routine in most other sectors, so parents should explain it as such and need not feel weird about revealing it.

- *The No Camp.* Notifying a nanny will simply nullify a nanny cam's most effective features: measuring the quality of care offered and catching potentially dysfunctional actions early on.

Comments made by nannies online who had discovered a hidden nanny cam runs roughly 50/50. Half reported feeling startled, betrayed, and violated, and equally as many nannies, while surprised to find a nanny cam, were not overly perturbed. Collectively this group felt that they were doing their job and had nothing to be anxious about. Clearly, then, the choice to disclose a nanny cam or not is a personal one.

Which Nanny Cam Is Best?

Nanny cams are hidden in everyday objects such as teddy bears, clock radios, wall hooks, and other commonplace objects. They use two basic technological forms when recording, and your lifestyle will dictate which one is best.

1. A stationary camera (recorded data) connected to a VCR or DVR that records video internally *that parents view at a later date.* Pros: affordable, easy to set up and use. Cons: makes for time-consuming and often monotonous viewing, which can lead to complacency.
2. A web cam (live streaming data) using a wireless transmitter that allows real-time remote viewing by a working parent. Pros: connects parents to their children 24–7, thus acting as more of a live surveillance tool. Cons: more expensive, can generate obsessive snooping and a distraction from the day job.[5]

Reviews are a great resource. Websites such as http://spytechinc.com/nanny-cam-guide and nanny-cam-review-toptenreviews.com offer technological advice. For more hands-on peer reviews, parents can turn to Amazon.com, Care.com, Thehonestreviews.com, Nannyreviews.com, and Babycenter.com.[6]

Where to Put a Nanny Cam?

The purpose of a nanny cam is to monitor the actions of a caregiver in her daily routine, so it needs to be placed where a nanny spends *the majority* of her caregiving time. A nanny cam cannot be placed where a nanny's personal privacy would be violated, such as a bathroom or her bedroom.

Is It Legal?

Nanny cams are legal in all 50 states. However, in 15 states (California, Connecticut, Delaware, Florida, Hawaii, Illinois, Louisiana, Maryland, Massachusetts, Montana, Nevada, New Hampshire, Oregon, Pennsylvania, and Washington) *it is illegal to record audio without express or written consent of the nanny being filmed.*[7]

Troubleshooting

When purchasing your nanny cam, ask the following questions:

1. Is the nanny cam a good visual fit for our home? (Teddy or I-Pod?)
2. Which brand is best? (Price is a good indicator.)
3. What is this nanny cam's range of vision? (Spyhole or panoramic?)
4. What is its storage space?
5. What is its battery life?
6. Which recording mode does it use?
7. What are the resolution and video quality?
8. How easy is this nanny cam to set up?[8]

Nanny Abuse Outside the Home

If you suspect your nanny of maltreating your children outside of your home, you still have viable options. You might want to take a morning off work and shadow your nanny. You could enlist the help of a trusted neighbor, friend, or relative. A third-party individual who is not recognized by your nanny could follow her sporadically as she goes about her daily routine. Bad nannies are not that discreet—they'll mistreat your child in a crowded park or shopping mall or on a sidewalk. If possible, you or associates should attempt to capture your nanny's mistreatment on camera. A third course of action would be to hire a private detective.

A Spike in Nanny Cam Horror Stories

Predictably, the rise in nanny cam deployment has seen a rise in footage on national and local networks. ABC's *20/20* recently ran a segment featuring a mother named Whitney Matney from Arkansas. The segment followed a familiar theme. A young professional mom, Matney had hired a high school acquaintance named Melissa Medema (after a thorough background check and positive recommendations) to look after her one-year-old daughter Raylee. From the get-go Matney began to notice changes in her child's behavior. Raylee became extra clingy and, most telling of all, appeared frightened *just as she was about to be left alone* with her nanny.[9]

Matney decided to install a hidden camera: the Mini Alarm Clock Hidden Cam. The footage soon revealed nanny Melissa shaking and smacking a clearly distressed Raylee. What happened next?

After reviewing the footage, Matney immediately called the police. She showed them the evidence and pressed charges. The nanny was arrested and charged with "endangering the welfare of a minor," the lowest-level felony charge. This lesser charge was applied because Medema had not left any marks on the child's body or caused extensive damage. This is a major loophole in child care. In as little as three years Medema could have her record cleared, leaving her free to pursue other nanny jobs.

Matney decided to pursue the cause of child protection. She began to actively advocate for the establishment of a child abuse registry. Her campaign has culminated in a bill that could be presented as early as 2016 in Arkansas.

Therefore, Arkansas would be the first state to have such a bill if it passes. Anyone who had been criminally *convicted* of child abuse in Arkansas would be listed on the public registry for anyone to see. What the bill and Matney's abuse case demonstrate is the importance of protecting all children, not just children in Arkansas, from serial abusers. What we need is a national registry of child abusers.

One of the more telling aspects of the Matney case is that the nanny seemed at some point to be aware of the possibility of a nanny cam. Toward the end of the nanny cam's footage Medema approaches and looks directly into the camera. Then calmly she turns it around to face the wall.

Another high-profile crime of nanny violence to date is the so-called Ugandan nanny cam case. The video has gone viral, with an estimated 20 million hits worldwide. This case, too, follows a familiar theme. A nanny is attempting to perform a routine function: to feed or put a child to sleep. The child does not cooperate to the nanny's satisfaction, and this provokes a sudden, violent reaction from her. The nanny continues to attack the child until her anger subsides. How can parents preempt this type of offender?

A *criminal nanny* can be a manipulative, cold-hearted creature whose antennae are sharpened against detection. But she can offer some telltale signs:

- She often looks sullen.
- She can be very controlling and unwilling to follow your instructions.
- She is critical of you as a parent and/or your children.

- She is passive-aggressive, turning up to work late, "accidentally" burning things, not answering the phone, or calling in sick at the last moment.
- She is not demonstrative with your children but is short-tempered and overly strict.
- She does the bare minimum of what is expected of her.

Remember also that your children will provide the most powerful hints if a nanny is behaving badly.

- Your child isn't happy to see the nanny and has become anxious and withdrawn. (Your nanny may be speaking harshly to your child and relying on punishment, verbal or physical, to make sure he or she follows her rules.)
- Your child sports bruises or cuts. Are they really caused by accidents? If they are, were those accidents preventable or caused by a nanny's neglect?
- Your child often looks unkempt and dirty (odors, runny nose, dirty hands and feet). A nanny can do everything else right, but if she doesn't keep your child clean, she's endangering your child's health. Failure to keep a child clean can also point to a general lack of interest from a nanny.
- Your child has started cursing or acting mean. If your child is using words you'd never say or behaving inappropriately, chances are these bad habits are being picked up from your nanny. If he is being aggressive toward other children, his toys, or the family pet, he might be mimicking his nanny's own aggressive behavior.
- Your nanny's stories don't add up. Never tolerate someone who steals, lies, or deceives you in *any way*. You have to be able to trust your nanny for the relationship to work.
- Your child suddenly becomes withdrawn or sad or wets the bed or acts out. While this could be due to a move, a new school, or some other such event, it is worth checking that it isn't because of your nanny.

If you are about to become a parent for the first time and need to employ a nanny, buy a nanny cam and use it from Day 1. If you're concerned about a current nanny and suspect her of mistreating your children, buy a nanny cam now.

Action

If you have clear evidence—material that can be upheld in a court of law—that your nanny has abused your child, you must immediately remove your child from her care. Your instinct might be to raise hell and confront her with the proof. If you do that, she may simply walk out and disappear without ever facing charges. If you are unable to deal with her in person, have a friend or a family member call her. Remember, your objective is to *buy time and keep her within reach of the law.* Your friend could say something like "Fran and Mike have to take little Danny out of town for a few hours to a last-minute family function [funeral, wedding, birthday], but Fran needs you here in case it gets too much for Danny and they have to come home."

Report

If you have a partner, both of you will need to take time from work to deal with the crisis. If you are a single parent, reach out and accept help from your family or friends. One of you must immediately go to the police and present the evidence. If you have identity information such as a copy of your nanny's passport or driver's license, current address, or social security number, give that information to the police. Inform your lawyer if you have one, or hire one. Press charges.

Help

Your child is now in urgent need of specialized help, both physical and psychological. A full medical examination will rule out the potential risk of concussion, fractures, and internal injuries and bleeding.

Psychological Damage

There are professionals on hand who can help with this specific type of trauma. For example, though you might tell your child over and over again that the abuse was not her fault, she may feel as though she is in big trouble for not telling you. Your nanny may have told your child vicious lies or threatened to kill him if he spoke up. Your child may have formed a deep attachment to *a criminal nanny* and despite the abuse does not want her dismissed. An older child might blame you for working full-time or may go into denial completely and say that the abuse did not even happen.

Therapy

You will need help. Your family will need to heal collectively. Nobody but a criminal nanny is to blame. You may hear and see painful evidence in court. A criminal nanny might seek to capitalize on misplaced feelings of guilt. You and your partner cannot be divided on any issue. Your child will need to feel completely defended by a united front. If you are divorced, bury any differences with your child's other parent and work together. Your child becomes top priority over work, your ex, ego, and guilt.

Revenge

A criminal nanny's actions might be so distressing that you are tempted to take matters into your own hands. You may feel like exacting a form of rough vengeance. Ultimately this instant revenge does little to ensure that a criminal nanny is kept from damaging other children. If you do not report a criminal nanny to the police and press charges, you are allowing a perpetrator to remain at large. Trust that justice will be done in the court system and that a criminal nanny will face consequences.

A convicted nanny will experience the humiliation of an arrest. She will feel disempowered when taken into custody, just as she made your child feel disempowered. She will have no rights and will be subject to the scorn of fellow prisoners. If she is undocumented, she could be barred from the United States with a permanent record. If she is a U.S. citizen, she will receive public punishment and will be placed on an offender's database. Justice will be done. Parents like to think that they can protect their children from every terror this world has to offer. The truth is, sometimes a monster slips through the net. It does not mean that the parents failed their children but that a mistreated child was failed by the nanny.

Some child care books argue against hidden cameras. Some advocate popping home unannounced. If you have any doubts about hidden cameras, here are some things to think about.

Videotape or a feed stream with clear visual and audio showing a nanny mistreating a child is the best evidence. One person's discovery of mistreatment of a minor by another and that person's testimony is subjective; it can be contested in a court of law. Criminal nannies who are informed about hidden cameras during a job interview are more inclined to go elsewhere.

That's the beauty of nanny cameras.

MANAGEMENT: TRANSFORMING PERFORMANCE, TRAINING, AND REVISITING DAY CARE

Parents, particularly mothers, ultimately want a nanny who is proactive and competent. Some nannies just miss the mark but are otherwise good-enough caregivers. Sourcing a new nanny can be both exhaustive and expensive. So, the idea of transforming an existing nanny through direct management can be an appealing one.

Apathy in the workplace is a particular problem for employers—any employer. In the home, however, it does not affect profitability; it directly impacts our children. How can you determine whether your nanny is apathetic?

- Pop in from time to time *unannounced* and see what your children are doing.
- Ask your children to talk about what their nanny has fed them that day.
- Follow your nanny periodically (or have someone follow your nanny) to the park and observe how she monitors your children—whether she plays with your children and/or allows your children to play. If she doesn't do any of the aforementioned, what is she actually doing?
- Talk to your children about what their nanny has done with them that day. Was there any reading or projects? Was there any playtime that involved their nanny? Were they able to play with their friends and make a mess in their own home?
- If your child is preverbal, you can ask your nanny for a detailed account of your baby's day. Offering her a journal is one easy way to track their activities.

If you have discovered that your nanny does the bare minimum of what is required, you will want to sit down and discuss what it is you *do* require from her. Using a simple checklist for daily requirements such as the one below will make it obvious that you are watching her behavior. Subsequently, she will either buckle down or move on.

- Give your nanny a journal and have her log her hourly activities.
- Nanny to read between two and three books a day with children.
- Insist that she play at least one game with children per day.
- Organize playdates with children in your child's class or neighborhood, and limit playdates with your nanny's sphere of friends.
- For children under two years of age, restrict all media including a nanny's iPad and smartphone. For older children, limit TV and all media to one to two hours per day. Offer for use only selected DVDs, Tivo, or preselected parental programming filters.
- Insist that your children play outside every day (in fair weather) and that they frequent different parks and playgrounds.
- Collectively schedule library visits, museum trips, classes, and other local activities so that your nanny cannot exclusively coordinate excursions with her friends in the neighborhood. Ask your nanny to make suggestions. Your aim is to motivate her so that the end result is not you micromanaging *but her taking the initiative.*
- Mention to your nanny that you will be requiring feedback from your children on a daily basis.

Another area that needs scrutiny is the food a nanny provides for children in her care. As previously stated, one of the most common sights I've encountered is nannies feeding their charges cheap convenience foods. The eating habits of even the wealthiest children, those I observed at least, were sometimes substandard and tailored purely to suit a nanny's needs. How can you prevent a nanny from feeding your child junk?

It's simple. Stock up on organic and whole food produce, and forbid your nanny from feeding your child anything but the food that you provide. While occasionally a snack-on-the-go might fall outside of your control, most treats and snacks can be wholesome *and* convenient.

It's easy to want to clamp down on an apathetic nanny through micro-managing, but that only creates more work for you as a parent. Plus, it could be counterproductive, making a nanny resentful or even more apathetic. If you are frank with your nanny about what you are looking for and if you take the lead in directing your child's day for a period of time—while offering your nanny a space to step up with ideas and activities—you will soon discern if your nanny is capable of performance enhancement.

Staying in touch and reviewing what your child does on a daily basis, even if that means you tacking on an extra paid hour or two per week for your nanny to check in with her, is a large part of managing employees. As with all aspects of the job. using a good nanny cam during this time will demonstrate if your nanny is on the same page.

Did You Hire a Cleaner or a Nanny?

It can be a difficult task on the surface to see the difference between a cleaner and a nanny. It feels nice to come home to a spotless home, folded laundry, and scrubbed children in clean pajamas. Busy moms might appreciate that extra domestic touch, but what about the kids? Ask yourself whether the following description for what I term the *perfunctory nanny* sounds like your nanny:

- Your home is constantly spotless.
- Your nanny talks about what she did to your home, not what she did with your children.
- Your children seem able to amuse themselves when nanny is around but are needy and demanding on weekends.
- Your children wince when they accidentally make a mess.

The perfunctory nanny is just that: perfunctory. She will ensure that the kids don't electrocute themselves or dangle out of the window, but she might not do much else for them. If your perfunctory nanny has endeared herself to you and your family and is not a tyrant with a mop, you might want to gently insist that she leave certain chores around the house undone. Gradually speak to her about the importance of play and activities. Simply take the daily checklist provided for an apathetic nanny and ask your perfunctory nanny to follow the same daily activities. Check in with your children to see whether their nanny has become more absorbed in their world.

In the event that your perfunctory nanny cannot adjust and if you can afford it, you might want to hire someone else for a few hours a day to play exclusively with your children. In time you can adjust schedules so that a strictly perfunctory nanny becomes the primary cleaner and an occasional babysitter.

Remember that although this type of nanny may appear conscientious and house-proud, she is actually a person who is unwittingly placing more value on a home than on your children. She may also lack key skills required for the good quality care of children. Over time, such negligence can damage your children emotionally. Parents instinctively know how to juggle domestic chores with their children's needs—perfunctory nannies may not.

Another type of caregiver who can be enhanced with great success is the youthful babysitter, whether an au pair or a college babysitter.

Getting the Best from a College Babysitter/Au Pair

It is essential to establish clear house rules from the beginning regarding Internet access, cell phone usage while on duty, and whether or not boyfriends are allowed to drop in on nights she is babysitting. Ensuring that your college babysitter understands and follows your household rules will prevent the scenario of them against you.

What a college babysitter has in energy she may be lacking in experience. Newborns and small children are especially vulnerable, particularly when they are ill or undergoing a developmental change. Providing a college babysitter with up-to-date child care information, basic CPR training, and continuous on-the-job coaching will protect your most precious members from a college babysitter's mistakes.

Semester breaks also free up your college babysitter's availability for extra hours, but be wary of creating resentment by suddenly demanding a full-time schedule. Semester breaks might mean your college babysitter has a thesis or family commitments to attend to, and it would be unfair to encroach upon her time without prior notice.

It has been my experience that most college babysitters make good short-term babysitters. They are smart, bouncing around with their charges like puppy dogs. They can also have great imaginations. A few, however, have been glued to their gadgets, chatting and texting friends while junior heads off out of the playground. Some have been short-tempered because they lack experience or because they have hangovers.

College babysitters often do not lack ideas for creative projects, nor are they famous for their housekeeping abilities. They also know some of the best cultural institutions to take our children to. College babysitters can make ideal supplementary tutors. They are eager to learn and have the energy to match our children's. In short, college babysitters are wonderful human resources. Engaging them on that level and as a team, with you firmly atop as the head, will help to provide them with the leadership they need.

Performance Enhancement

The decision to employ a nanny, with all of the effort it entails, is as essential a component to a happy childhood as a nutritious diet, the right schools, and a stable, loving home life. But what if you find a wonderful nanny who has not heard of EQ and doesn't know how to apply it, yet clearly embodies it?

Orientating your nanny from the get-go in the *practical* basics of emotional health will greatly increase your child's access to what he or she needs throughout infancy. It also provides a nanny with structure. I have prepared a free printable guide, "A Nanny's Practical Guide to Emotional Intelligence," that will be made available via my website (http://thenannytimebomb .blogspot.com) within six months of this book being published for you to give to your nanny.

This handy guide will introduce your nanny to the rudiments of EQ. For your convenience, I have reproduced some of the guide here. This section is created and aimed at nannies, so the language used will reflect this. The pronoun "your" in relation to a child or baby indicates a nanny's charge, not her own biological child.

What is EQ?

EQ is "A form of social intelligence that involves the ability to monitor one's own and others' feelings and emotions, to discriminate among them, and to use this information to guide one's thinking and action."[10]

EQ helps us to understand people in our everyday life. It's the ability to respond and interact socially. If we look back to our own childhoods, wasn't there someone who seemed to be everyone's friend? How did that person act? Were they kind and slow to anger? Did they listen well? Most important, did it make you feel good just being around them? If so, chances are that person had EQ.

How do we learn EQ? Years ago, acquiring EQ was much easier. Most of us lived in communities where an extended family tree of grandparents, siblings, cousins, and friends mapped out a vast emotional landscape. In this template, children learned the rules. Everybody took a turn in this. Most important, in this environment children experienced love expressed through touch, social skills developed through child's play, boundaries created by adult example, and a sense of worth by feeling a part of a group or clan.

This wasn't a perfect system, of course, but it did provide a foundation for community living and civic responsibility. Today, modern families often consist of mom, dad, and the children. Often, parents are working full-time. How can infants, toddlers, and children learn EQ when parents are absent? Simple: they can learn it *from you* (their nanny).

It is likely that you—as a working nanny—already know most of what is written below. Consider this as a handy guide to implementing the various stages and the tools required for teaching EQ. Here are some developmental stages:

Three Months Old: What's going on?

Emotions

Opening up. Infants develop deliberate responses and a calm interest in people, smiling at those around them.

Social Skills

Attention and regulation. Does your baby turn to look at you when you make sounds or facial expressions?

Practical applications

Eye to eye contact is crucial. When you pick up your infant, look straight into the baby's face. Let the baby's eyes meet yours. Talk to the baby as you maintain eye contact; otherwise, it could feel a little intimidating for the infant. Once you have consistently captured your baby's attention, make expressions (happy ones), coo, and make ga-ga noises but also talk normally. Turn your face so that the baby has to move to follow your eyes. Talk, sing, even read to your newborn.

Physical touch is crucial. If you can, carry your baby about in a sling so that she or he can feel your body. Cuddle and hold your baby as often as you can. Despite what some people might caution, you can never spoil a baby! Gently massage a baby after a bath, and periodically allow a baby to stretch naked in a warm room.

Learn the distinctive sounds your baby makes. The way in which your baby cries or murmurs will also communicate how the baby is feeling. Is she hungry? Is he tired? Does the baby simply need a hug? Is baby bored? Regular tuning-in will make your baby feel seen and will embolden the baby to try new sounds.

Even in those early days a baby can become bored, so try new thing/toys and engage your infant. Play music (classical or light pop) and let your baby feel sensations such as warm water on his or her feet and hands. Move a favorite toy from side to side so that baby's head must turn to locate it. Play with your baby!

Take baby out in good weather so that your infant feels the warm air, a breeze, and the sun (although never direct sunlight without protection). Let the baby see new objects and hear the exotic sounds of the outdoors.

Having floor time with the baby 30 minutes to 2 hours per day.

Warning signs. If baby does not demonstrate any interest in you or to any external stimulation, inform the child's parents immediately.

Additional Milestones

There are other important stages of development that a child will navigate from 5 to 30 months of age. These will involve the development of fine motor skills such as the act of a child feeding him or herself establishing bipedal balance and walking, and gaining control over bodily functions. It is vital that a caregiver is informed about the best practices for assisting small children through these stages.

5–9 months old
10–17 months old
18–30 months old

Potty Training and other Milestones

We have added potty training here as a milestone worthy of specific consideration because we believe it is a fundamental stage that can be commonly mishandled by even well-intentioned caregivers. If performed wrongly, this stage can set a child up for guilt for the rest of his or her life. We have witnessed nannies calling normal childish habits such as touching private parts, picking their noses, wetting underwear, and missing the potty "filthy," "dirty," "disgusting," and "nasty."

The consequence of this is that a child begins to look upon its body with a sense of self-loathing. Minor events such as spilling milk or getting muddy suddenly become intolerable to a child who has been told that clean equals good and dirty equals bad. Such reasoning can establish a basis for later neurotic behavior.

Potty training should not be a forced event. Enforced potty training with no compassion is very distressing to a toddler. Today pull-up pads and rubber sheets are available so that accidents need not entail mammoth laundry bills. When a potty is seen as a game with no great emotional attachment, toddlers are naturally drawn to them. I was fortunate to closely observe a mother who was very relaxed about potty training, pacifiers, and infant feeding bottles.

The result? The child in question pretty much potty-trained herself at an earlier age than her peers. She also phased out pacifiers and bottles with relative ease. Society's insistence upon rigid schedules and developmental timetables do not allow for a child's individual needs.

A good nanny neither enforces nor denies her charge's progression in terms of potty training. If handled properly, potty training is a rite of passage that gives an infant a real sense of achievement. If mishandled, potty training can lead to lifelong feelings of shame. If you are a nanny who was raised by a strict mother, you must make the effort not to impose your own rigid rules on your charge. This is a once in a lifetime stage in a child's life, and it can never be undone. So, go with your child's flow and make this important development a time of joy and personal triumph, for that is your gift to your children.

Clean-up themed games—in and out. Challenge and reward your toddler for helping you tidy up after a mess. There's nothing toddlers like more than to feel as though they've contributed. At this stage they also like to put things in boxes (and take them out again), so perhaps create boxes with multiple objects inside for the infant to play with.

Meaningful play—acting it out. As caregivers, we can encourage role-playing games with our toddler. Such games prepare our charge for the real world. Games with themes such as

- Mommy, daddy, and baby
- Going to the store (pizza, café, grocery store)
- Going to school (teaching toys)
- Having a picnic
- Building a castle, a home, or an obstacle course
- Fantasy games (kings, queens, dragons)

What Is Floor Time Again?

Dr. Stanley I Greenspan defines "floor time" as "face-to-face interactive play."[11] As it suggests, floor time means literally getting down to a child's level by playing on the floor for at least 30 minutes a day. It also requires taking ourselves to a child's level in terms of imagination. But what good does floor time do? Greenspan defines floor time further:

It's one of the best ways to help babies exercise their growing nervous systems and to master their most important new mental abilities. In floor-time play, babies learn to coordinate their senses—sights, sounds, smells—with their movements, all guided and orchestrated by their emotional interests, such as smiling back at you, reaching for something you're holding, and making funny sounds back when you make sounds at them.[12]

Floor time with children involves giving one-on-one quality attention. It could take the form of playing a game or talking to the baby about her or his day. It demonstrates to the child that you are actively tuning in to the child's frequency. If you have more than one child to take care of, try to find time to connect one-on-one with the older child as well as the younger one.

Collecting a child from school or putting a child to bed also allows for one-on-one floor time. Having that special time alone can take place when a younger sibling naps. Remember, during this time you should be warm, empathetic, and nonjudgmental. Take the opportunity to find out what an older child feels about household rules, school, or some of his peers. When this type of interaction occurs regularly and is intentioned, it communicates to the child that he is seen and loved.

Ultimately, floor time requires that you care. Children can detect a phony but will forgive a genuine, if clumsy, attempt to connect. Unless you are really dedicated in your motives, do not push floor time. Some nannies don't get modern youth. They treat preteens and teens as though they were toddlers. This causes resentment. In fact, if you are not good with older children, look for another position and work exclusively with infants. Maybe that's where your gifts in child care naturally lie.

Today, many children are scheduled with enrichment or activities to the point that they have very little downtime or available floor time with a parent or a nanny. Learn about floor time and be prepared to adapt as your charges grow older. Excellent reference sources are *The Challenging Child* and *The Four-Thirds Solution* by Dr. Stanley I. Greenspan. As caregivers our education never stops, and that is the beauty of working in the child care industry.

Revisiting Day Care

Plato and Socrates spoke about the crèche, or collective nursery, where children of a republic could be raised away from parents by professional nurses. Crèches have existed on grand scales in Europe, Russia, and China under the socialist banner, both left and right.[13]

Today, many working mothers resume employment in as little as two weeks after giving birth. They simply cannot afford to stay home. In such situations, it would be optimal to have a nanny give one-on-one care to the child at home. Sustained one-on-one care is highly beneficial as long as one's child care professional is a committed, qualified person.

Child care reform will lead to an increase in the annual income for nannies. As a result many, low-income or single-parent families could find themselves outpriced. What do such families do then? Choose day care? Some day care facilities simply do not have enough staff or a progressive approach toward child care. Some are merely run for profit, and the majority can be hampered by excessive regulations. Such day care centers often depend on unskilled workers employed on low wages.

A study conducted by the National Institute of Child Health and Development found that only one-third of infant child care providers have received any specialized training in child development, and only 18 percent have received a bachelor's degree or higher in this area.[14]

Another worrying factor in day care centers is the amount of disease spread among large groups of children.

Children in day care still are at nearly 100 percent greater risk for contracting life-threatening diseases such as hemophilus influenza and meningitis. They are four and a half times more likely than home-cared children to contract infections and nearly three times as likely to need hospitalization. Day care children are significantly more at risk of contracting upper respiratory tract infections, gastrointestinal disorders, ear infections, salmonella, herpes simplex, rubella, hepatitis A & B, scabies, dwarf tapeworm, pinworms and diarrhea.[15]

Higher standards of hygiene and smaller groupings of children must be a key component of modern-day care centers. Good day care centers provide children with nurturing personal care from professionals on a consistent basis. I believe that the best care would be provided if the same caregiver(s) could tend to the same children throughout their formative years. This type of consistent care enables a child to develop attachments. Day care environments should also mirror a child's own home as opposed to a kindergarten. This could include a private area where a child could retreat to lie down on a bed or a sofa *at will,* allowing that child to follow his own rhythm.

A private place where the child can store a personal toy and books would counter the constant need to habitually share, often with older, bigger children. Infants and children need one-to-one care and interaction. Children require floor time or attunement, and they also need downtime. These conditions are a natural part of the cycle of home life. A similar environment could be created in day care centers. For example, day care centers could provide:

- Modern, professional child care with a government subsidized sliding-scale fee so that even very low-income families could meet payments.
- Day care centers would recruit professionals at a minimum entry-level requirement even if that meant including voluntary nonaccredited courses.
- Child care professionals working in these facilities would be able to continue their training vocationally, attaining work credits that would contribute toward their education/courses while on the job.
- Each child care professional would only be responsible for a minimum of three children under the age of two or three children aged two to five.
- Classes in EQ held for child care professionals and parents could be offered in the evenings or on weekends to day care workers.
- A daily schedule implemented in day care centers would equally balance supervised play among the children, with one-on-one nurturing (floor time), stimulating small group activities, and quiet time in a calm environment.
- Day care centers would offer developmentally appropriate toys that are not exclusively plastic or based on TV shows.
- A salary linked to some type of collective benefit such as health care for child care professionals in day care could ensure job loyalty.
- A national policy of pairing the same children annually with the same child care professional should be encouraged for bonding.

For those parents who are considering using a day care center for child care, how can you get the best from day care? Here are some key points to look for when visiting a prospective day care center:

- Is the day care facility close to your job/home? This will give you ample opportunity to drop in unannounced to see how your child is being cared for.
- Is the facility overcrowded? How much square footage of space is allotted each child? Can a child walk freely about a main area, or does the child have to push through an assault course of strewn toys, staff members, and children?
- Is security tight, or can just about anyone walk in? Are there security codes/pads and multiple doors guarded by security staff before one reaches the children's area? How are adults checked in and checked out?

- What security and background checks are conducted on *all staff* related to the day care center? Janitors, cleaners, administrators, and security staff should undergo the same police screenings and background checks as the children's minders. Does your day care screen for potential pedophiles?
- What sign-in requirements are in place? Can a UPS guy get past first, second, and third checkpoints simply by waving a parcel? You will want your toddler ensconced in an inner sanctum.
- Will your infant be passed from pillar to post, or will the day care, to the best of their ability, guarantee a primary person to care for your child for a number of years? Consistency of care ensures normal emotional development as well as development of verbal and motor skills.
- Are staff trained in how to lay a baby to sleep safely? Should a baby be allowed to cry itself to sleep (Ferber method), or should it be picked up and cuddled? Does the staff check on sleeping infants every 15 minutes? Are there enough clean cribs available for a baby's individual nap routine? Do the sheets and bed linens look clean?
- Are the floors, walls, kitchen/dining area, play areas, and toilets clean? Who is responsible for the industrial cleaning of the day care center? What chemicals do they use to clean floors and walls? (Some industrial chemicals are toxic and particularly harmful to small children.)
- Does the day care center allow for lunchtime breast-feeding visits and periodic breast-feeding visits?
- Are the floors, rooms, and corridors cluttered? Are personal items, electrical equipment, and tools ever left lying around?
- Is the facility well lit and well ventilated, or is it dingy and dark? Children require plenty of fresh air and light in order to grow and feel happy. Is there access to nature in the form of a rooftop garden, a local park, or an exterior garden?
- What minimum qualifications do the day care staff have? Are the child care providers fluent in CPR?
- Are toys, play structures, and play areas disinfected or cleaned on a daily basis? Are the toys new? Are toys and games changed periodically? What kinds of toys are procured? How do they relate to childhood development?
- How often are infants' diapers changed? What age is potty training conducted? How is potty training conducted? Do staff wear plastic gloves when handling diapers and vomit? Is the staff required to wash hands periodically?
- What is the day care center's policy on admitting sick children? You will not want your three-month-old infant in the same room as a toddler with a fever.

- Does the outdoor play area meet industry standards? Is the play area fenced in? Does it border an alley, wasteland, or woodland?
- How long has your child's prospective caregiver been working with this particular age group?
- What food is served at lunchtime and for snacks? Can you provide your own food for your child?
- What is the child-to-adult ratio? This has to be the single most important question any parent considering day care will ask. If you infant is below 12 months, the child-to-adult ratio should not exceed three infants to one caregiver.
- If your baby is a newborn and used to attachment caregiving, will the staff periodically wear a carrier for the baby?

Once you have considered the preliminaries of a particular day care center, you will want to be sure that staff involved in working with small children are be trained in the following areas:

- Child development
- Surveillance (what does the day care offer in terms of direct video monitoring?)
- Behavior management strategies
- Common childhood illnesses
- Procedures for preventing contagious disease
- Immunization standards
- Injury prevention
- CPR and general first aid
- Nutrition and health
- Exercise
- Medication administration
- Children with special needs[16]

You will also want to know what the staff turnover ratio is. This will enable you to gauge how long a primary caregiver is available for your child. Longevity is an essential component of an infant's development from birth to three years of age. You will want to ensure that your infant/toddler isn't going to lose his or her primary caregiver on an annual basis. Here are some good tips:

- Observe how a primary caregiver interacts with the infants in her care. Does she simply sit back and make sure they do not hurt themselves? Or does she periodically single out an infant for one-on-one play, cuddles, and stimulation? You will want the latter attitude in a caregiver.

- Does the day care center routinely tolerate unruly or violent behavior? Such behavior can cause distress in small infants if left unchecked. It can also be intimidating for toddlers to be around a bigger child who bullies and screams.
- What discipline methods does the day care employ? Physical abuse such as smacking, shoving, shaking, grabbing, and dragging are strictly prohibited by law. Verbal abuse such as name-calling is deeply humiliating to a child and must be a prohibited form of conduct. Isolating and putting a child in a time-out too often is a highly counterproductive form of discipline. Withdrawing food and snacks to counter poor behavior is a cruel practice. Emotional abuse such as withdrawing affection and attention in response to poor behavior is an inappropriate form of discipline. Find out *exactly* how the day care's staff provides loving guidance to correct antisocial behavior.
- Will you have to pay extra for collecting your child late?
- Will you have to pay for days when your child is not present in day care?
- Finally, ask other parents what their experience of the day care center has been.

Ultimately, you will want to ensure as much one-on-one care as possible for a child under three years old. Consistent, stimulating, and nurturing care for infants is vital to their development. If the staff of a particular day care appears stressed, if the atmosphere is rowdy and out of control, and if the place feels and looks grubby, go elsewhere. If the day care costs per week are on the same level as a local nanny, then you might want to consider hiring in-home one-on-one care for your infant.

Is there a day care model that exemplifies a high quality of care? I've long believed that day care could be a safe and affordable option for working parents as opposed to hiring a nanny, an option that may become cost-prohibitive with regulation. Good day care facilities can be hard to come by, however. In New York City, day care can run the gamut from crowded, noisy rooms in private homes to high-end centers that push the envelope in terms of early childhood development.

While I was reviewing good examples of day care, I came across Explore + Discover, an early childhood development facility in New York City. I visited the center and immediately came to believe that its model could be a template for all day care centers. I asked Explore + Discover cofounder Daniel Koffler the following questions.

What is an average room size? How many adults to infants? "For infants and toddlers 3 months to 9 months old, we have 8 babies to three teachers. For the 10- to 17-month room, we have 10 babies to three teachers. For the

18-month to 23-month room, we have two teachers to 12 children. The toddlers also have a bigger physical space in terms of classroom size."

How are infants grouped? "We group our children according to motor capabilities. Our 3–9-month classroom is for babies who are still moving primarily on their backs and tummies. The 10- to 17-month-old children are newly mobile, crawling, striving to be upright, taking first steps. The 18- to 24-month old toddlers are more secure in mobility, walking, and running and climbing."

Are you more Montessori based in your ethos? "We are a best-practices school that is influenced by the Reggio Emilia approach. We share the belief that children are born learners, competent, curious, and creative. We co-construct the curriculum with the children by noticing and capitalizing on their interests. We also honor the children's work through our documentation efforts, sharing the learning with parents on a regular basis."

Are infants allowed to follow their own rhythm/schedule (napping, snacking, feeding)? "We see care (in the form of feeding, sleeping, and diapering) as part of our curriculum, an opportunity for bonding and for learning. Our teachers work in partnership with parents to create a seamless transition between home and school. In terms of napping, we follow the lead of the youngest children while also respecting the schedule set out at home. As children get older, their nap schedules change and so does the approach of the classroom, with children more and more naturally moving into a shared sleep schedule. In terms of feeding, parents provide meals and milk for the child at our center, and we provide snack. Youngest children determine when they will eat, and as children get older, a more routine schedule is put into place gradually."

Can mothers breast-feed and stay with fussy infants? What's your policy on nannies? "Mothers are welcome to breast-feed at our center. In fact, we have a nursing room just for them. We also offer a transition schedule when a child starts at the center, and this includes a home visit from a teacher to make parent and child more comfortable as they begin. Additionally, parents are asked to remain at the center until children have adapted to the new people and place. The center remains in close contact with parents as children become comfortable. All family and caretakers are welcome at the center."

What is your policy on sickness? "We do our very best to make Explore + Discover a healthy environment for our children. At the start of each day we do a quick health check. Children with fever, vomiting, or diarrhea cannot attend school until they are healthy for 24 hours. We monitor children closely to determine when they are under the weather and will call caregivers when something isn't quite right. We send children home to be checked by the doctor if we suspect pink eye or other contagious diseases."

How long is a baby's day? "A full-time day for children is 8:00 to 6:00, but we also have part-time morning and afternoon schedules available. Children attend five, three, or two days a week."

What nutritional support do you offer? "Parents provide food for children at our center. However, we do provide healthy snacks with fresh fruits and vegetables as well as a protein."

Can you break down a typical day for me? "The daily schedule is flexible in response to children's interests and needs. Each day includes periods of exploration both indoors (paint, clay, water, etc.) and outdoors (we have our own private play area with age-appropriate materials), sleeping, and feeding. Each classroom has an art studio and library as well as a collection of musical instruments. Teachers are trained to play the guitar and sing with the children every day. A music specialist and art specialist both work with the teachers and students twice a week."

What input for your facility has come from child care experts? "We are proud of the high level of professionalism and expertise in our school. Our educational director and director at the 26th Street site were both trained in early childhood education at Bank Street College of Education and are steeped in the literature and practice of excellent child care and education. Both have taught for over 10 years in the classroom and administered programs. Additionally, the associate director at 26th Street has a master's in early childhood education from Teachers' College, and she is currently enrolled in the EdD program there. Of our 13 teachers, 9 currently hold a master's in early childhood education. Our work has been influenced by many child care experts such as John Bowlby and Mary Ainsworth on attachment theory and a host of progressive educational thinkers from John Dewey to Howard Gardner, Loris Malaguzzi and Maxine Greene. We have been moved and inspired by the RIE approach [Resources in Infant Educare, see http://www.rie.org/] developed by pediatrician Emmi Pikler in terms of its respect for babies and the connections between care and curriculum."[17]

Sadly, most day care is not run like Explore + Discover, and most workers cannot afford to study for a master's in early childhood education, nor are they able to earn a living wage. Until child care in all of its forms is a federally subsidized industry, nannies and day care owners will be forced to stay affordable. But being cheap has its costs, and as we have already seen, our children can often pay the price.

Chapter 7

Child Care Reform: The Three Keys

WAGES AND TAXES

Back when I worked as a nanny in Tribeca, New York City. *Forbes* ranked the Tribeca zip code as the 12th most expensive zip code in the United States. The average salary among nannies in the neighborhood was $10–12 per hour. For live-in domestic workers and undocumented nannies, of course, it could be much lower. Rates haven't risen that much, if at all, ever since. But the cost of living in New York City has.

In a neighborhood such as Tribeca, paying $12 an hour for child care isn't typically underpinned by economics. It is governed by a market rate. Affluent parents choose child care at certain prices because most workers offer themselves for $12 per hour or less. Parents might also consider the day-to-day functionality of child care not to be a highly skilled profession and one usually occupied by transient workers, such as college students looking to pay their rent, or migrant workers, some of whom are undocumented. Hence, a certain wage is appropriated for the service in their minds and in those of their peers. For other parents, it is merely a case of detachment. Many wealthy people were themselves raised by low-paid child care workers and believe that such an arrangement is suitable to pass on. In all cases, they are wrong.

Nannies universally feel the pinch of a low hourly rate, especially if paid out by an affluent employer. As a result, some of the nannies I associated with spoke openly of sitting their kids in front of the TV to avoid work. Others might let the baby cry a bit longer before they got up out of a chair.

The fundamental reason given by these nannies as to why they avoided work was their *low hourly pay rate*.

These nannies felt morally justified in doing the bare minimum of child care because they felt economically exploited. Therefore, I offer that there is a direct correlation between low-grade child care and a low hourly rate. The vast majority of the avoid-work nannies encountered were employed by extremely wealthy people. The nannies' attitude was one of "you're rich but you pay me a low wage to take care of your kids, so I'll do the very least expected of me."

Until wages are increased for child care workers, this type of on-the-job apathy and behavior will continue to underscore the child care crisis. According to a 2012 study by the National Domestic Workers Alliance (NDWA):

Low pay is a systemic problem in the domestic work industry.

- 23 percent of workers surveyed are paid below the state minimum wage.
- 70 percent are paid less than $13 an hour.
- 67 percent of live-in workers are paid below the state minimum wage, and the median hourly wage of these workers is $6.15.
- Using a conservative measure of income adequacy, 48 percent of workers are paid an hourly wage in their primary job that is below the level needed to adequately support a family.[1]

In a city such as New York, personal service providers are plentiful. I wanted to examine the hourly rates of a dog walker, a freelance cleaner, and a nanny and what they did for that sum. Their detailed diaries can be found on my website www.thenannytimebomb.blogspot.com. Below I have reproduced a day in the life of a typical nanny who earns $12 per hour and takes care of two children.

7:00 a.m.: Arrive at work, clear up children's bedrooms, make beds, get toddler up and change diaper. Load some laundry, get pajamas out for that evening, and hang them in the bathroom. Make breakfast for older child and toddler and for mom and myself: scrambled eggs, bacon, and beans. Clear up dishes and load dishwasher, pack snack and drink for toddler. Get both children dressed for the day.

8:00 a.m.: Go to store to do the family shopping with toddler. Drop older child to school en route at 8:45. Walk down to an arranged playdate.

9:00 a.m.: While on a playdate, I help the other babysitter to prepare lunch for her kids.

10:00 a.m.: Playdate. We both decide as it's nice to take a stroll in the park. Play with the kids in the sandpit and on climbing frames.

11:00 a.m.: Leave playdate to pick up older child from school. Take children home and prepare lunch for kids, myself, and mom. Unload dishwasher, put washed clothes in dryer before toddler's nap.

12 noon: Clean up lunch dishes and reload dishwasher. Tidy dining room and kitchen. Change toddler's diaper.

I put toddler down for nap. Play with older child until 1:30 p.m., when mom relieves me for my half an hour lunch break; before I go the grocery order is delivered, and I must put that all away before I leave. (Note: Most nannies do not get a one-hour lunch break.)

2:00 p.m.: Get toddler up from nap and give him a bottle. Get both children ready for older child's judo lesson at 3:30 to 4:00 p.m.

3:00 p.m.: Leave apartment with two children and walk up Broadway. While older child is in judo class, I occupy toddler in lobby.

4:00 p.m.: Walk both children back to their friend's apartment for a one-hour playdate.

5:00 p.m.: Prepare children's dinner and feed them. Unload dishwasher and put dishes away; reload dishwasher with dinner dishes. Quickly mop dining room floor and wipe all table surfaces.

6:00 p.m.: Run bath for children and fold dried clothes and put away. After bath I get both children dressed for bed. Mom comes home with new clothes; I remove tags and plastic and put new clothes away in closets.

6:45 p.m.: Give toddler his bottle, read three picture books, and he falls asleep by 7:05 p.m.

7:00 p.m.: I then go and read the older child three stories and settle him for sleep by 7:30 p.m.

8:00 p.m.: Tidy playroom, unload dishwasher, and have a general tidying up. I am finished by 8:45 p.m. Sit down and watch TV.

9:00 p.m.: Tonight I am babysitting until 10:00 p.m. My regular hours are from 7:00 a.m. to 7:00 p.m.

The nanny's diary demonstrates her almost *continuous labor* throughout a working day. Her work is more emotionally demanding and multifaceted than that of a cleaner or a dog walker. A nanny is in perpetual demand by the children in her care, as an absence of her attention could prove detrimental, so why are nannies paid less per hour than other service providers? In fact, why are nannies paid on average less than any other person who comes into professional (nonrelative) contact with a child?

Take supplementary classes, for example. New York City classes for infants, toddlers, and school-age children are a normal feature of weekly life in the metropolis. A 45-minute art class can cost as much as $600 per semester. The majority of children I encountered were enrolled two to three times a week in art/music and gym programs. Exposure to art/music, exercise, and social interaction adds dimension to a child's life. Some extremely wealthy parents think nothing of the cost of such activities. Why, then, do parents often skimp when it comes to their child's daily care?

Some might counter that their child care budget has to incorporate all of their child's needs and that a nanny's wages have to be factored in against preschool costs. The alternative to providing a living wage for a nanny will undoubtedly save money for other expenses. Yet contained in that fact is the knowledge that low wages can produce a slow and prolonged misery for the recipient. There is drudgery in living from paycheck to paycheck without hope of saving for a rainy day. Such a person can be rendered incapable of loving or providing positive nurturing. Poorly paid nannies don't appreciate terms such as "competitive market based-salary." Nannies living on a competitive market-based salary will leave in a flash and often without warning. As Stanley I. Greenspan asserts:

Some may see these improvements (higher wages) as onerous and costly—*but remember, they are for our children.* Private college now can easily cost $30,000.00-plus a year, and parents plan for decades to be able to pay their children's tuition. *Yet the early years are even more important than the college ones. We mustn't continue to neglect or undervalue this most important time in our own and our children's lives.*[2]

If your nanny has not complained about her wages to you, I can assure you that she has complained to me and probably to every other nanny she's encountered. If your nanny seems reluctant to discuss money with you, it may be because she comes from a culture where it is deemed inappropriate to query wage issues. She may also be undocumented, in which case she doesn't want to rock the boat. Perhaps her wages are her only income and she is terrified of losing her job. Whatever the reasons are, the responsibility for providing a living wage lies with her employers.

What is the price of employee loyalty? Stanley I. Greenspan's excellent book *The Four-Thirds Solution* expands on the problem of the low-wage, no-benefits, no-future mentality and how it affects the quality of care provided by day care staff (and, by extension, nannies):

To create incentives for caregivers to provide intimate care and stay with their jobs for longer periods of time, we need to find ways to improve the wages of day-care providers. We can't give people the most important responsibility on earth—nurturing a baby—and pay them the most minimal wage possible. *If we do, we can expect competent individuals will look for better jobs paying higher wages—which is exactly what has been happening for the last several years as the American economy boomed.*[3]

If you wish to reevaluate your nanny's salary or if you are considering employing a nanny, how can you calculate what to pay her? How much a nanny earns pretty much depends on where an employer lives and what a nanny actually does. Here are some factors to consider when calculating wages.

Qualifications. Are you hiring a nanny with minimal babysitting experience who requires training, or are you hiring an experienced nanny who has over three years of experience and additional skills such as CPR training and child care education credentials?

Live in or Live Out? Will you be covering all of her food and utility costs and car insurance? Will she travel with you on vacations as part of your family, with paid downtime? These are important factors to consider, since the cost of housing in cities such as New York ranges from $12,000 to $24,000 or more per year (2015).

If your nanny is living in and you are covering all of the normal expenses that independent lodging incurs, you should factor in those costs against her actual wages. Then you should total that sum and compare it against the local salaries of nannies and day care workers in your area.

Supply and demand. Do you live in a rural area or a major urban hub? How many suitable candidates operate in your area? Do you live in a relatively affluent area? If so, the costs of living and transportation will be weighed against how much child care providers charge.

Hours. Do you need a nanny for part-time or full-time work? Do you require more than 50 hours per week? (Fifty hours per week is considered full-time for nannies.) If so, a nanny's weekly salary will need to be adjusted to include an overtime rate.

Duties. How many children will the nanny care for? If the nanny has to care for more than one child, the weekly rate should be increased by 10 percent per child and so on. For some, this percentage increase might seem unreasonable; however, I have witnessed far too many overburdened and underpaid nannies caring for upwards of four children at a time not to recommend such compensation. While basic services such as shopping and cooking meals for children and tidying up after them are all associated with child care, these duties should be discussed prior to employment.

Extra services. Some nannies may also provide additional household management services, acting as a housekeeper, a house manager, or a teacher. Such services usually demand greater responsibility and specialized experience for which a higher salary is desired and deserved. Professionally trained nannies with over five years of experience with a bachelor's degree or a master's in child care who also act as house managers can command wages exceeding $1,200 per week.

The U.S. State Department offers guidelines on what to pay child care workers. Nanny agencies should be able to provide local rates of pay for nannies.

Taxes. According to the Internal Revenue Service (IRS), a nanny is considered an employee, not a freelance worker.[4]

The above suggestions are guides only, but ultimately working parents must juggle household finances with their child care costs and determine what they can afford. In the event that you are simply unable to pay your nanny a better wage, there are other ways you can show that you value her work and time.

- Sit down with your nanny from time to time and tell her just how much you value what she does for you. Occasionally let her go home early or bring her in some flowers. Everyone thrives on appreciation, plus gratitude is free.
- Offer your nanny the provision of eating on the job so that she does not have to pay for her own meals.
- On birthdays or over the holidays, give your nanny cash, not presents that she may not necessarily need. Cash is king in child care.
- Do give her an end-of-year bonus, generally one to two weeks' salary. If you cannot afford that, $100 is better than nothing at all or an unwanted gift.
- Once a year, consider offering your nanny a small sum toward health care costs or prescriptions. If you cannot afford that, offer your nanny access to your medicine cabinet. Research facilities that provide free or low-cost health care screenings or services, and arrange for your nanny to take a health day.
- If you live in a city such as New York, consider offering to pay your nanny's weekly travel card. If you live in the suburbs, consider how much gas money or bus money your nanny spends to get to work.
- If you have in-house laundry facilities, you might want to extend their use to your nanny.
- If your nanny has a child or children of her own, consider allowing her to bring them to the job during public school holidays so that she does not have to pay for child care.
- Always try to pay your nanny during your own vacation or at the very least help her to find extra work while you are away.

If you treat your nanny well, you and your children will experience her loyalty and dedication in multiple ways. Nannies especially understand that money can sometimes be tight, and they appreciate it if you are honest and thankful for what they do on a modest salary.

Perhaps you've just hired a good nanny, and she declines your offer to pay her taxes. Alternatively, will hiring a nanny affect your tax bracket? Is our current taxation system antiquated and out of touch with modern family life?

On January 31, 2007, John C. Goodman, PhD, president of the National Center for Policy Analysis, made the following statement before the U.S. House Committee on Ways and Means:

The most important problems faced by middle-income working families today are not problems that arise from the nature of our economic system. Instead they are problems caused by outdated public policies. The basic structure of tax law, labor law, employee benefits law and a host of other institutions was formulated 50 or 60 years ago by policymakers who made assumptions about how life would be lived. From top to bottom, key public policies were based on the assumption that:

- Workers would work for the same employer throughout their work lives.
- Men and women would marry and stay married; and throughout their working years the husband would be a full-time worker (40 hours+ per week) and the wife would be a full-time homemaker.
- Workable social insurance (e.g., for unemployment, disability, illness etc.) could be managed by bureaucratic agencies because the consequences of individual choices are largely irrelevant, regardless of how perverse the incentives are.

Clearly, these assumptions no longer describe the world in which we live. Accordingly, institutions designed for the 20th century are unworkable and inadequate for the 21st century.[5]

Fair Labor Standards Act

Other elements continue to squeeze working parents in the workplace. Our modern labor laws in fact harken back to the Great Depression. In the 1930s the federal government enacted laws aimed at protecting laborers from unscrupulous employers. The result was the 40-hour workweek, a template designed for mostly blue-collar men—husbands and providers of a family. Over time, other rules were added that allowed employers to pass on the cost burden of benefits such as sick pay, collective health insurance, and pensions onto workers by deducting a percentage on pretaxed income. Unfortunately, the tax system just hasn't caught up with the times since then.

The fundamental change to the labor model has been the introduction of women—mothers. Since the 1950s, the number of women aged 25–55 entering the workforce jumped 75 percent. In 2012, roughly two-thirds (65 percent) of women with children under the age of 6 were either employed or looking for work. This percentage was up dramatically from 39 percent in 1975. Two-worker families now total 75 percent of all married couples. However, laws regarding taxes, pensions, social insurance policies, and employee benefit schemes continue to treat mothers as though they are still at home. How does this affect child care options open to working mothers?[6]

A record 40% of all households with children under the age of 18 include mothers who are either the sole or primary source of income for the family, according to a new Pew Research Center analysis of data from the U.S. Census Bureau. The share was just 11% in 1960.[7]

Mothers in the workplace face federal policies that have resulted in a labyrinth system of child care credits and exemptions that are arbitrary and also unjust to persons working for smaller companies:

- While the tax law has a credit for child care expenses, the maximum credit for 2006 was only $1,050 for one child and $2,100 for two or more children, an amount well below most families' actual expenses. Further, there is no tax relief for uncompensated care provided by a relative, friend, or family member.
- Parents lucky enough to work for an employer who provides a flexible spending account may set aside up to $5,000 of annual pretax wages to purchase child care services.
- Employers can provide an unlimited amount of day care on-site, all tax-free; however, if the employer provides additional compensation to the employee to purchase day care services, the benefit is taxable.[8]

If the domestic labor market was truly free, the modern needs of working parents, particularly mothers, would be accurately factored in. For example, two wage-earning parents might not necessarily wish to work the same exact hours outside of the home, so an arrangement of flextime would be beneficial to them and the corporations they work for. It would also dramatically reduce child care costs and provide children with more consistent care. Rigid tax and employee benefits laws make such arrangements generally impossible for people who need health insurance, pensions, and other benefits.

When hiring a nanny, parents are confronted with the task of filing a nanny's taxes. This can feel onerous at the best of times, especially if a nanny is reluctant to take a deduction out of her hourly rate for Uncle Sam. For nannies in particular, the cut taken by the IRS can feel peculiarly unfair. Unlike most other sectors, domestic workers are generally paid out of an employer's already taxed income, resulting in a double tax penalty on their wages. Add to this an already low hourly rate, and you get the picture.

Nevertheless, until tax reform occurs, if you're an employer of a nanny, you are required to report her income and pay employment taxes.

Nanny Tax

I contacted Kathleen Webb, founder of HomeWork Solutions, to get a better understanding of what is involved in declaring and filing a nanny's taxes. HomeWork Solutions is an excellent company that helps new employers navigate the rules set down by the IRS. We will explore three case studies to demonstrate the penalties of not filing a nanny's taxes at all or of filing them incorrectly.

W-2 or 1099?

Linda had hired her nanny in the fall and was paying her in cash every week. Linda had an accountant to handle her own income taxes, and when she hired the nanny her accountant told her that everyone treats their nanny as an independent contractor.

Linda was the first to admit that she didn't understand taxes and preferred not to deal with them. In her circle of friends, all the families paid their nannies in cash. After checking with her accountant, she felt very comfortable with this arrangement. Linda and her husband, however, were enrolled in a dependent care account and had contributed $5,000 of pretax money to help with their child care expenses. In order to get reimbursement for their nanny's pay, *they needed to provide the nanny's social security number* to the plan administrator.

In January, Linda's accountant helped her prepare a 1099 form to give the nanny, and that is where the trouble began. The nanny went to a free tax clinic run by the IRS's Volunteer Income Tax Assistance Program. After chatting with the volunteer about her job, the tax preparer advised the nanny that her employer *had likely misclassified her as an independent contractor* and that IRS guidelines state *that nannies are employees and should receive a W-2 form.* Moreover, the volunteer preparer showed the nanny that the misclassification would cause her to owe an additional $2,300 on her income tax return.

The volunteer tax preparer was correct. Nannies *are employees* and *should receive a W-2 form at the end of the year.* Linda was confused about the distinction between an employee and an independent contractor. She did some research and then contacted her accountant. Her accountant explained again that everyone calls their nannies independent contractors even though they really are employees. "No one wants to deal with the nanny taxes," he explained.

It's important that employers of nannies *understand the distinction between employees and contractors.* This is important, because employers of household employees such as nannies *file and pay employment taxes.* Contractors handle their own tax filings. Linda's accountant had steered her wrong, and there was some catch-up Linda needed to do to straighten things out. It was fortunate that Linda's nanny had only worked for her for a short time.

Online household employer payroll service providers can help employers understand what taxes they are required to pay. They can also facilitate payroll services so that paying employees is seamless. A good accountant can also help employers process an employee's wages and employment taxes. Employers can pay an employee's portion of social security and Medicare taxes—an option available to all household employers. *This can help employers convince their nannies to permit deductions from their wages.*

Gross versus Net Pay?

Susan was a licensed social worker and a new mom who had hired a nanny so she could go back to work. Susan and her husband had agreed to the nanny's request for a weekly wage of $600 take-home pay *after* taxes. Susan found that getting all of the reporting and tax calculations right—particularly when working from a *net take-home pay*—proved to be a headache. Why?

Susan and her nanny had agreed to *a weekly net pay without ever doing the calculations to find out what the actual gross wage was.* Susan did not know, in essence, *how much* she had *agreed to pay her nanny.* She was aghast to learn that she had actually agreed to pay her nanny *$800 gross per week,* or $41,600 per year, and that when her employer taxes were added to the mix her total cost was over $45,000 annually. Susan burst into tears when the enormity of her financial commitment became clear to her.

After running the numbers for a couple of different situations with an adviser, Susan decided that *she needed to renegotiate the contract with her employee.* Her tax expert created a chart of options that included the gross to net wage information for several different scenarios, including having Susan simply gross up for the social security and Medicare taxes and transferring the income tax responsibility to the nanny. Susan was now armed with the information she needed to have a difficult conversation with her nanny. Together they explored the different scenarios so they could work out a solution that they could all live with.

The nanny, of course, didn't realize how much the taxes added to her pay. But she was agreeable to a middle-ground resolution, with her employer still paying her $600 a week but *only net of the required social security and Medicare taxes.* The nanny understood that *she was on her own for her income taxes.* At her employer's urging, the nanny reached out to a payroll tax expert too and was educated on what her approximate income tax obligations would be so she could plan her finances.

Off the Books?

Mike and Joyce hired a nanny when their twins were infants. They agreed with the nanny at the time that they were going to pay her $500 a week *off the books*. The nanny worked out wonderfully and stayed with Mike and Joyce for almost three years but was let go when the twins started a full-time preschool/day care situation.

The family's needs had changed, and they found another part-time nanny to cover the after-school hours. Their former nanny, sadly, could not find another position right away, and out of desperation she filed for unemployment benefits to tide her over. Mike and Joyce received a letter from their state's Department of Labor indicating that the former nanny had filed for unemployment benefits, naming Mike and Joyce as her former employers. They had suddenly found themselves in a very sticky situation.

Mike and Joyce, like so many nanny employers, had heard that the nanny taxes were very confusing. As busy young parents, they very much wanted to keep things simple. Their nanny was agreeable to being paid off the books, as she too benefited (in her own mind) by taking home a bigger paycheck every week. No one likes paying taxes, and so long as everyone was agreeable it seemed like the simple solution. Right?

Unfortunately, their former nanny *was the family's employee under the law,* and Mike and Joyce were therefore legally responsible for employment taxes. A payroll tax expert explained that these employment taxes totaled about 18 percent of the employee's payroll—or $12,000 over the two and a half years their nanny had worked for them. She further explained that if they had treated the nanny's payroll legally from the very beginning, they would have collected $5,000 of this from the nanny via paycheck deductions.

However, at this late date the obligation to pay the entire amount was now completely on the family—*the employers.* Because the family's nanny taxes are collected as part of their personal income taxes, they realized that *they were going to have to amend three years of tax filings.* Additionally, their former nanny would be receiving W-2 forms for the years in question, and *she was going to have to file and pay her federal and state income taxes.*

Mike hired a household payroll and tax preparation service and was quickly registered with the IRS and the state and obtained tax identification numbers. Mike worked with a specialist to review his former nanny's pay history, and together they prepared *back-tax returns.* Mike began to realize that their new part-time nanny *also* had to be *paid on the books.* Mike paid the overdue state unemployment taxes. Together with his tax expert, he responded to the state's original query and put this part of an unpleasant employer chapter of his life to an end.

Mike learned about what to expect going forward—including how the state would communicate penalties and interest. He understood that he now needed to contact his personal accountant with the federal forms that he had prepared and *to file amended income tax returns, pay the tax, and expect penalties on those too.* Several weeks later, Mike's accountant had been able to quickly amend his federal tax returns and help Mike and Joyce get on a payment plan with the IRS. Mike and Joyce—as hapless new employers—had learned a painful and expensive lesson.[9]

What lessons can prospective employers of a nanny learn from these case studies?

- Nannies are not independent contractors who take care of their own taxes. They should not be sent a 1099.
- Nannies are the employees of those who hire them. They should be issued a W-2.
- When negotiating a salary with a new nanny, employers must indicate the difference between the net and gross of a nanny's salary.
- There are different options available under the law whereby both an employer and an employee can contribute toward income taxes and benefits such as social security and Medicare.
- Families who pay their nannies on the books enjoy tax credits that they can use against their child care costs.
- Household payroll experts such as HomeWork Solutions are there to facilitate employing a nanny lawfully and seamlessly.

If you are in a position to hire a nanny, whether a U.S. citizen, a green card holder, or an undocumented immigrant, you should lead with a primary discussion on what it means to be paid *on the books.* It should be clear to a candidate what you intend to declare and deduct from her wages. It is optimal to have this in writing.

A good percentage of child care workers do not have papers and therefore have no desire to be included in a tax return. This hampers the lawful choices of working parents. In the next section we will explore how immigration reform is a much-needed prerequisite in our quest for affordable and legal child care.

IMMIGRATION REFORM

Throughout the writing of this book, there have been several notable coincidences. On November 20, 2014, for instance, as I began to edit my final notes around immigration reform, the president had just announced his new measures aimed at an estimated 5 million undocumented workers living in the United States along with their children—U.S. citizens. Today Barbara Young, National organizer at the NDWA, invited me to attend a celebration rally in Washington Square Park, New York City. On this day too I had the privilege of speaking with Nahar Alam, head of Andolan, an organization that advocates for South Asian workers, and a fellow at the Petra Foundation about the subject of immigration reform. Something was in the air.

In his public address to the nation, President Barack Obama stated that millions of unauthorized workers could now "come out of the shadows." I'd heard that phrase numerous times from the mouths of undocumented workers. Being *illegal* for them was like living beneath an omnipresent dark cloud that penetrated every aspect of their American lives, separating them from their children, denying them health care choices, and exempting them from employment protection under the law. There was also the daily terror of being routinely stopped by a police checkpoint in New York City and possibly deported for not having the correct papers.

A significant part of the president's proposed reform was the ending of a program euphemistically called Secure Communities whereby local police can detain undocumented immigrants over minor offenses such as traffic violations or for simply not having papers. The president made bolder moves too toward creating a political culture of inclusion, acknowledging that

1. The United States has historically benefited from immigration. This had kept the country demographically youthful and dynamic through the merging of ideas and cultures.
2. Our current immigration system is broken. Some employers flout the law and hire undocumented workers so they can pay them less. This gives them an unfair advantage over their law-abiding competitors. Undocumented workers are already living and working in the United States. Something needs to be done to address this.
3. Immigration reform must include increased security at the borders.
4. The Republican Party has blocked previously proposed reforms. The president would now use his executive powers to push immigration reform forward.
5. Highly skilled undocumented workers and entrepreneurs would be allowed to stay.
6. Enforcement resources would now be focused on criminals, in a new "felons not families" approach.
7. Undocumented workers now living in the United States would be offered more protection from deportation. Requirements are that undocumented workers must have been living in the United States for at

least five years and have children who are U.S. citizens. In order to qualify, participants must come forward for processing. Once processed, immigrants will be required to pass a criminal background check. In return, they will receive a temporary stay against deportation. They will receive a social security card and a work permit and will be required to pay taxes.

What does immigration reform mean for undocumented domestic workers? What does it mean for Americans? I approached Ai-jen Poo, director of the NDWA:

I think, to bring recognition and respect to domestic work. I think removing diplomatic immunity should be an obvious step—no one should exist outside the law, and the pattern of abuse is too egregious to ignore; there's no excuse. Immigration relief/reform is an important first step, because an undocumented status has created a shadow workforce in our sector so that even when you raise wages, it's difficult to enforce because there's so much fear out there.

Living wages, tax reform, and good enforcement strategies are all core ingredients to secure the most basic of rights and standards. They are some basic building blocks for turning the industry [of domestic service] from the "Wild West," where everything is at the whim of employers' individual decisions, into a more stable workforce who can care for their own families and deliver quality services.

Why could immigration reform be good for America?

As time goes on, more and more families will need elder care. People are living longer, the baby boom generation is aging, and more people want to stay in their homes as opposed to go to a nursing home as they age. Workers will be needed to support the elders and people with chronic illnesses and disabilities in the home. We hope to provide both training and help in finding employment in elder care in the future [among domestic workers].

Would a bill that gave undocumented workers amnesty if they reported employer abuse help to stop the widespread abuse of domestic workers?

Yes, I believe so. That is why we've been involved in a campaign to win the POWER Act, which is essentially immigration relief for people who expose labor violations. We think this could really help address the root issues of fear and vulnerability.

In your opinion, should the federal government do more to support the costs and burden of sourcing good child care?

I do believe that child care should be supported much more comprehensively. Our families and work lives have changed quite a bit. And the need for child care and elder care has increased dramatically. Fewer households than ever before have a parent who can stay home with children or aging loved ones. And many families do not earn enough to pay for the high cost of care.

We need paid caregivers to fill that care gap, and we need more options in general for families. It's simply not sustainable for families to manage on their own in this economy, when so many people cannot find work, or if they do, often it's poverty wage work or piecing together work with unpredictable hours.

Ultimately, Congress needs to put more comprehensive child care supports in place—including subsidies for families, training, and good wages for the child care workforce. In the meantime, the president should do what he can. I'm not sure exactly what that is; perhaps it's to support states that are taking a lead in putting strong programs in place.

Do you believe that there is a child care crisis in the United States?

The U.S. has one of the worst records on maternity leave and prenatal care. We have a draconian tax system [and] a failing immigration system, and as a result, working families often have no other option than to spend 25 percent of their joint income on often substandard child care.

Yes, I do believe we are headed toward crisis and that we need to invest in our systems and infrastructure to meet our growing care needs. What exists is out-dated and insufficient. It's an opportunity to shape the future of care, learning from the perspectives of workers who are often left out. That's what the Caring across Generations effort is all about—shaping the future of care in a way that meets the needs of families and workers alike.[10]

I wanted to explore other measures that the current president or a future president could take that would help undocumented domestic workers who currently endure exploitation. So, I asked two immigration lawyers—Dan Berger of Curran & Berger LLP and Alena Shautsova of Alena Shautsova Law Office. Dan Berger offered this:

For domestic workers, I would create a toll free number that is given to domestic workers when they have their visa interview at the U.S. consulate. If the employer is not treating them well, according to the contract and the visa terms, the worker can call that number. The biggest problem is that they get into bad situations but are afraid of speaking out because they might lose their visas.

For domestic workers, there is a J-1 option for some nannies and B-1 for domestic workers. The employers don't always follow the B-1 rules. See http://manila .usembassy.gov/domestic-employees.html for details. It is tough to try to help nannies now—the best option is to do a full consultation with an immigration lawyer to brainstorm all possible options out of the many visa categories.[11]

Alena Shautsova made these suggestions:

I do not think that removing diplomatic immunity is realistic, because we would need to rewrite the whole body of international law. But, placing a law/executive order saying that diplomats cannot hire help other than through an authorized agencies can help. . . . An undocumented nanny has rights *now* in New York, and she is covered by antidiscrimination laws. There are laws that regulate minimum wage and hours a nanny can work. It is a matter of enforcement.

Adding a new category for the domestic workers is an excellent idea. Currently, it is difficult to start successful employment-based immigration for a domestic worker or nanny because the government regards each specific task a worker performs as a separate occupation. Let's say a nanny would also cook meals for a baby or wash a baby's clothes or clean a room. All three of those tasks are technically *separate occupations,* and the government would say that an employer has to hire *three different people! A visa that would encompass a combination of these jobs* and would simplify the immigration process for nannies and domestic workers is an invaluable solution. Maybe we could call it an H1D?[12]

Fast-Track Green Cards?

Currently, people have to wait three to five years to apply for U.S. citizenship from the moment they receive their green card. This is three years for those who received a green card based on marriage to a U.S. citizen. There is only one green card track that is fast, and it is for those who are in the *military and on active duty.* This is obviously a good idea given the invaluable service our military provides for our country. But we should ask ourselves: Do not domestic workers provide an equally vital role in our society? Alena Shautsova proposes that domestic workers who would qualify for a newly created H1D visa status could adjust—or apply to get green cards—much more quickly. This would allow nannies and domestic workers to live and work permanently in the United States almost immediately.[13]

If you employ an undocumented nanny and want to help her, it can feel like a helpless situation. Alena Shautsova makes these suggestions:

The only way would be [for an employer] to file for an employment-based visa, which takes too long to get, and if the person is already out of status, it will be impossible to utilize it. There are very narrow exceptions to it, and most workers would not qualify. Employers can help by providing education compensation and treating their employees with respect. However, in terms of immigration, unless it is a worker for somebody who is coming from overseas to stay in the U.S. and go back (in other words, a foreign diplomat or a foreign visitor), there is only one way of sponsorship: PERM application for a worker, likely to be regarded as an unskilled worker. But there are many great organizations that have a working knowledge of immigration law as it stands now. If you feel it is an appropriate conversation to have, perhaps you should try. Most undocumented workers are afraid of being deported despite their excellent caregiving skills and length of stay in the U.S. So, approaching the topic could prove challenging.[14]

If we recall the example of Nahar Alam, it is possible that a caring employer can do much to help an undocumented worker seek out her or his own long-term solutions. Hope springs eternal in the human heart, and having a support system of a sympathetic community and considerate employers can go a long way toward enabling an undocumented worker to find a path to citizenship. It's my hope that future U.S. governments will continue to make humane progress in this regard.

A continuation of immigration reform, beyond the current measures by President Obama and amnesty for all undocumented domestic workers as an end goal, are ultimately good ideas for our society. The reason for this is that undocumented workers are already here and perform a critical function in our society, allowing many of us to go to work and improve the lives of our own children. They already pay state taxes on the purchases they make and hence are contributing, albeit remotely, to our tax system; by working and living and buying among us, they are adding revenue to our local economies.

New immigrants are also the lifeblood of a thriving economy, providing a younger workforce who will one day be supporting our own social security payments. Tax collected from newly naturalized migrants also generates income for our local infrastructure, and in the long-term, as our society ages, we will need registered domestic workers to enable us to continue living in our own homes longer. Finally, bringing undocumented domestic workers in *out of the shadows* will make America a safer country. As Dan Berger puts it:

I think the best argument for allowing more immigrants is that people who are here legally are documented and go through security checks. For follow-up measures, they have to go through a security check every time a visa is extended or changed.[15]

Immigration reform is a win-win for everyone but is especially so for child care. As things stand now, as a prospective employer you can harvest the best care for your children when you source a good, loving nanny, whether she is documented or not. But you will not be able to run a police background check on her without flagging suspicion or arousing her fears. Ultimately the choice to hire an undocumented worker remains yours, but there are other ways you can comprehensively vet her:

- Documented or not, a nanny should be able to show some form of ID such as a foreign passport and proof of where she currently lives (a utility bill in her name, for example).

- Run your own background check. How long has your nanny been in the country? Are you able to see her entry stamp?
- Arrange to meet her past employers face to face. Ask them discerning questions (see my previous reference and interview checklists).
- Your nanny should have at least three references in your locality for you to check.
- Once you hire a nanny, be sure to closely monitor how your children react and interact with her.

These, of course, are not foolproof, hence the need for comprehensive immigration reform. This book is not advocating that you break the law as it exists today. Hiring a child care provider without documentation remains your personal decision.

FEDERAL REFORM

Thanksgiving was fast approaching as I wrote this chapter, and I was reminded how much America exists under a shadow of its Pilgrim past. The austere beliefs of those early colonists remain embedded in our culture like soil nutrients, invisible yet powerful seeds of unconscious thought systems. According to Puritan ideology, the family is God's minikingdom on Earth: sovereign, holy, and self-sufficient. Americans continue to struggle with the role that government should play in our private lives. Strict Libertarians argue that it has no place interfering with decisions made by parents—especially in matters such as child care.

Despite the influence of religion in America, the country operates under a secular system of governance, not a theocracy. The people and the government coexist under what is termed a social contract. This is a voluntary agreement between the individual citizen and the state. Our body politic is obligated to represent and protect the rights of every citizen from birth. In turn, each of us has a civic duty toward one another and to abide peacefully by the laws set by our government.

Within this system of governance, the family is not a sovereign state. For example, husbands can no longer rape their wives simply because of alleged conjugal rights codified in the institution of marriage. Mothers cannot beat their children to injury just because a religious book declares "spare the rod and spoil the child." Parents cannot send their children to work as opposed to school because they need the extra income. In all of the above instances, the government has wielded its legitimate authority to protect the individual rights of its citizens within the family unit.

In contrast, public opinion continues to struggle with the role of mothers within the family. If there is any further evidence of the role of religion on women's daily reproductive lives, one only need to look at current state laws regarding contraceptive devices and access to family planning services. Women are still ultimately defined as mothers, with society split as to whether mothers should or should not work during their children's infancy.

These are two powerful reasons why there is endemic ambivalence toward the subject of child care reform: either government has a definitive role or no role to play in the private child care decisions made by parents, and mothers either should or should not stay at home as caregivers.

A third reason for stasis on the subject of child care is capitalism. The free market is traditionally the place where families go to solve their needs: employment, housing, health care, and child care. But the free market has failed families. How?

The basic premise of a free market is that one purchases a commodity or service as low as one can and then increases the value of that commodity through application, use, or resale.

Does this work for child care? Paying a nanny or a day care worker or facility the lowest possible wage or fee and extracting the maximum amount of energy from that worker or facility to fulfill day in and day out the emotional care of children while replacing a parent, nominally a labor unit of higher intrinsic value, and thereby freeing that parent to go to work to earn a greater yield of income *is a capitalist success story*. In theory it should work, but in practice it often doesn't.

What the market cannot take into account is that nannies and day care workers are human beings, not commodities. They can react unpredictably under certain forces and pressures. Children are not goods to be handled by a service sector. They too can react dramatically to the stress of low-quality care. The free market alone therefore cannot solve the issue of child care, nor should it rationally be expected to.

Is it time to turn to the federal government for universal child care? This is not a revolutionary thought. In fact, it's happened before.

In colonial times, working families frequently worked on farms, in urban cottage industries, or along coastlines. The kids were kept close to home, and supervision was largely the occupation of both parents and extended family members. As larger towns emerged and commerce became more complex, dame schools—a relic from Europe—were used to temporarily educate and supervise small children in their parents' absence. Older boys were apprenticed into guilds or into their father's trade. Girls were sometimes sent into domestic service to wealthier homes or used as caregivers for younger siblings at home. After 1776 and well into the 19th century, various charities and churches instituted nurseries and primitive day care centers to absorb the working poor's children as their parents migrated from agricultural labor to city factories.

In the 19th century nurseries became fashionable among the elite for educating small children, whereas day care with an emphasis on hygiene became the mainstay for working families. German immigrants brought with them the concept of the kindergarten, a place where toys and books were used to educate young children. During the American Civil War, women were able to join the war effort on both sides as nurses through makeshift day care centers.

During the Gilded Age, upper-class families employed European nannies and au pairs dressed in starched uniforms. Expensive boarding schools for boys and finishing schools for girls were the next step after a short in-home stint with a governess. In cities such as New York, the working poor—swelled by massive immigration—continued to labor in crowded tenements making clothes or small artifacts. As such, they had little choice but to rely on local ethnic fraternities and neighbors for child care help. In the worst cases, older children as young as six years of age were left all day in sole charge of infants.

It was the rise of a powerful middle class, however, that saw the notion of the stay-at-home mother presiding over a few servants (the help, generally consisting of immigrant Europeans and migrating African Americans from the South) becoming the cultural ideal. Yet outside of this social demographic it was not the national norm.

In the Great Depression when temporary employment programs were instituted, working, widowed, and single mothers were given access to government-approved child care facilities so they could earn a wage. In the 1930s and 1940s, these Works Progress Administration centers served as many as 40,000 impoverished preschoolers in some 1,500 centers across the United States.

The single most important act taken by the federal government occurred just eight months after the attack on Pearl Harbor in December 1941. As it became apparent that America had dramatically joined World War II, federal funds were immediately marshaled so that mothers could join the war effort. This was known as the Lanham Act. Child care became readily available for children as young as two years of age. The Lanham Centers, as they became known, received a whopping 50 percent in funding directly from the federal government. During the next two and half years $2 million dollars was provided to help run some 3,102 centers nationally. In other words, when a crisis hit the country, the government rapidly responded to child care needs.

During this extraordinary cooperation between the government and the states, children would spend 12 hours a day, six days a week, in child care centers. The better centers employed all of the features that mark modern-day care and kindergartens: outdoor and indoor play, the use of toys for educational advancement, scheduled naps, and creative expression in the form of painting, playing with clay, and exposure to musical instruments. Some of the centers provided nourishing meals and supplements such as cod liver oil and orange juice. Parents paid a small fee toward these costs.

After the war ended and as soldiers returned home, the government switched its focus toward providing affordable housing for families and jobs for men. Funding dried up for the day care centers, and by 1946 most of the centers had closed. The government and the media encouraged mothers to simply go back the home to raise children. Once again public opinion swung strictly to the conservative right, setting the scene for the women's civil rights struggles of the 1960s. Rosie the Riveter did not want to go quietly back to homemaking.

What can we learn from America's historic association with nonparental child care? It is this: the idea that mothers were traditionally homemakers is flawed. The majority of American women since our country's founding have worked and helped to support their families through their labor—alongside men. The ideal of the angel in the house is a limited and somewhat privileged middle-class concept originating as late as the mid-19th century. Child care has always been a requirement for working women, and they have sourced it via their communities, churches, or other charitable institutions. The affluent have consistently used child care in the form of nannies, nurses, governesses, and boarding schools. The federal government has a long history of supporting child care centers, especially during a crisis such as the Civil War, the Great Depression, and World War II.[16]

The above abbreviated history of child care owes much to Geraldine Youcha's incredible book *Minding the Children: Child Care in America from Colonial Times to the Present*. In the book Youcha exposes our society's traditional reluctance to push for comprehensive child care by quoting a Californian nursery school administrator, Hanne Sonquist:

We've done it and don't choose to look at it. How quickly we repressed that movement after the war. The standard line is "Mothers should be home with their kids"—the guilt quotient is enormous. The choices in our society to date have never been in support of children, families, and women. I personally am unwilling to say society is not able—we are not willing.[17]

With all of this in mind, what could child care reform look like?

A PROPOSAL

This book has made the case that the institution of child care is in crisis and needs to be regulated—now. It has also demonstrated that our tax and immigration systems urgently require an overhaul. We have explored how today, hardworking parents struggle to find good enough yet affordable child care with little substantive support from the federal government. We have seen how in times past the federal government has had both the will and the funds to secure affordable child care for working mothers— generally in times of national crisis. With all of these factors in mind, we can collectively urge that the federal government do the following:

1. *Provide universal paid maternity and paternity leave.* This should be available after the birth of a new child or after an adoption.
2. *Allow flexible work schedules.* Grant businesses (large and small) the freedom to offer progressive workplace practices and career options, including flexible work hours, remote work, and a temporary opt-out (one to three years) of a career path to raise small children, with no position penalty upon return (same salary and title).
3. *Provide benefits for all workers, full-time and part-time.* This includes access to collective health care, tax credits against child care costs, pension schemes, and unemployment.
4. *Provide affordable and registered day care.* This should be available to all parents who need it *as a basic citizenship right* (based on a family's combined annual salary).
5. *Create a national nanny registry.* Such a registry would register all child care workers in a government database, one that requires all child care workers to have an identity card. This database would offer new parents documented registered nannies in their area. Registered nannies would be paid a living minimum wage and would be protected from exploitative employers. Perhaps more important, a register would effectively identify mentally ill, pedophilic, dishonest, and abusive nannies. Such nannies would be blacklisted with full exposure, including a valid photographic ID, all legal names and known alias names, and a social security number.
6. *Introduce a low flat nanny tax code.* This code would allow nannies to access health care benefits and social security easily without overly burdening their employers.
7. *Ensure fair wages for all women.* Working women, mothers, and domestic workers must receive equal pay for equal work.
8. *Allow for sick days.* All workers (fathers and mothers) should be permitted to earn and accrue paid sick days to cover absences due to caring for their children.

9. *Enact immigration reform.* All undocumented domestic workers and nannies who are currently employed and providing a function should be granted immediate amnesty and *some type of pathway* to citizenship.[18]

Would child care reform change options for new parents?

Yes, and profoundly in the positive. Imagine a government database available to all parents that showed registered and vetted child care workers in your neighborhood. This would be a free open-source website with no hidden fees. Nannies registered in this system would have provided detailed information including biometrics such as a photograph, a fingerprint, and a tax ID for security clearance. As part of their selection for inclusion, these nannies would have undergone comprehensive background checks: medical, credit, and criminal. In addition, they would have undergone a *mandatory* psychological evaluation.

All of the registered nannies could be issued a work permit, a national card that identifies them as an approved workers for children. In return for voluntarily complying with registration, these nannies could qualify for free or low-fee weekend or evening certified training classes in early childhood development, infant and toddler nutrition, and first aid, such as CPR training.

Nannies could opt to specialize in certain areas such as caring for multiples, newborns, toddlers, older children, children with special needs, etc. By attending classes, individual nannies would be able to enhance their profiles, making them more attractive to prospective employers. This practice would encourage nannies to take control of their own professional advancement within the industry. In turn, both the industry and families would benefit from motivated, educated workers.

In terms of hours, nannies could opt to work part-time or full-time, even dividing their work hours between more than one family. Registered nannies could receive subsidized health care and access to social security through a new tax code. As part of their membership, nannies could be eligible for new employment placements—that is, automatic access to open positions within their community—once a previous job had ended. This could effectively end a nanny's constant need to hustle.

In response to our current immigration crisis involving potentially millions of undocumented workers, the new registration scheme would offer all working undocumented nannies amnesty from deportation, immediate entrance to a temporary visa program, and eventually full assimilation. In other words, child care reform would open up a pathway to citizenship for its workers. In turn, this would generate tax revenue and universal accountability within the child care industry.

Employers of registered nannies who qualify (based on their annual combined income) could be recipients of direct government subsidies to offset a raised minimum wage for child care workers through bigger tax credits. The government could also begin to implement new measures for parents in the corporate workplace. This would include a revision of the standard workweek, allowing for more flextime opportunities and more remote work from home.

Corporations that are evaluated as being eligible (the larger international corporations) could be compelled to provide *even more* services for on-site child care for their workers. Parents would need less child care if they were able to work flexible hours, alternating shifts with their partners so that one of them was at home at least a third of the time.

Finally, all new immigrants who wished to enter the child care workforce in America would have to first apply for a nanny visa or some type of provisional worker program scheme. They would need to prove that *there was a need for their labor*, such as a family willing to hire them. Those who required basic skills such as learning English would be helped to gain those skills. This practice could help eradicate the impetus for migrants to flout immigration laws and unfairly compete against other child care workers. We must protect the existing child care workforce, so specific quotas would need to be established.

As part of comprehensive child care reform, every day care center would be evaluated to determine whether it meets a federally approved standard of care in terms of its workers, its environment, the toys and books used, and its adult-to-child ratio. Draconian rules that have only benefited elite day care centers could simultaneously be reviewed. Highly restrictive coding and zoning laws have made being a day care provider both expensive and onerous. This has not served the interests of ordinary parents.

Day care centers specializing in education aimed at underserved communities in the poorest areas of the country could be subsidized by both the government and local corporations. This approach to public education through corporate sponsorship schemes relieves both the taxpayer and individual parents, and it directly benefits the communities in which these corporations operate. In this way we can harvest resources to create the highest universal standards of care for all American children. Ideally, this would be offered on a complimentary or reduced-fee basis for low-income or welfare-supported families. Participating corporations in return could receive greater tax breaks and brand exposure.

I have spent a decade observing, analyzing, and experiencing the child care industry in New York City, but I've also connected with professional nannies from all over the country. The consensus about where child care as an industry is heading is pretty uniform. Marni Kent, a professional nanny in California, puts it this way:

The industry as a whole is lacking in providing a defined long-term future with respect to the retirement and upward mobility opportunities. Specifically, the stigma of "a babysitter" that is sometimes associated with the nanny profession can diminish the aforementioned opportunities due to misinformation and underrepresentation by employers and the industry alike. While the nanny profession has made significant progress in term of salary and health care issues, I believe that unless wage and health care compensation continues to grow at its currents rate, nannies from all levels could experience financial hardship and career instability.[19]

Many parents now work full-time, but that doesn't mean that they are not actively parenting. Millions of working moms and dads help their children with their homework and take their children to the doctor or to school in the morning. Such parents understand that they can be a presence in their own home all week long despite employing a nanny. Most kids intrinsically sense that their parents are doing the best for them. We can build on this sentiment.

But no matter how much new parents try to make their time at home enriching, most worry about leaving their babies in the care of strangers. In turn, new parents must navigate the world of employment. The constant pressure of paying bills, inflated mortgages or rent, taxes, and even basic living expenses renders the average parent powerless to assert her or his right to a more flexible workweek.

Working families living in the postindustrial West exist in the void of two tax systems: one that has clearly passed, based on the traditional family unit where a father worked full-time and a mother raised the children, and the model yet to emerge whereby both parents work hours that are spread over a flexi-time schedule and both share the joy of child rearing with the aid of a good child care provider, either a nanny or a day care facility. New corporate approaches to child care such as flextime and on-site crèches are evolving, but clearly more needs to be done to support working parents across the board.

The question remains: What will today's parents do to improve their child's right to a happy child care experience? The most vital change you can make right now is how you view a potential nanny. Is she your family's greatest asset or simply someone who shuttles your children from school to classes for a low hourly rate?

The search for a good nanny will prove to be one of the best endeavors that you—as new parents—will ever undertake. Parents who work alongside a good nanny in a team effort help to ensure the provision of consistent care for their children throughout their formative years. If your nanny is apathetic or perfunctory, there are ways to enhance her performance.

Outside of the home, you can vote for political candidates who support definitive child care reform. Ask your congressional representative when the federal government is going to change tax laws that hurt modern families. Parents can lobby in their workplace for better practices such as flexitime and working from home. Last but not least, in a general election, parents should vote for a candidate who shares their vision of comprehensive child care reform.

In the "Resources" section, I provide useful website addresses of organizations that are concerned with creating public awareness around these issues. There is power in numbers.

Until extensive child care reform occurs, working parents will continue to juggle their commitments *on their own*. They will fall asleep on their children's beds after reading a bedtime story out of sheer exhaustion, or perhaps they will be forced to miss their child's bedtime routine altogether. Parents will prematurely age because they attend every school show, help in every school fête, and support community events on weekends while working a full-time job. Children will believe that being chronically stressed out as a parent is the status quo for a middle-class life. It needn't be.

Until extensive child care reform occurs in America, some of our children will continue to be neglected, ignored, stuck in front of a TV or a screen, or strapped in their strollers and fed fast food. Until reform, overworked, emotionally exhausted, or mentally ill nannies will continue to show up to the job and do the bare minimum *or far worse*. And they will bring with them their economic fatigue, their resentments, and their misery to us all.

I wrote this book to expose the practice of bad child care across the board by caregivers and employers alike. *The Nanny Time Bomb* wasn't written to scare or shame working parents. It wasn't written to scapegoat nannies. It was created with the intention of raising awareness. While it is true that the great majority of emotionally repressed children survive without being severely damaged, how many of them carry deep scars into adulthood? Attachment issues, addictions, and lifelong depression caused by a lack of appropriate care in infancy need not be a child care legacy.

The time has come for us to respect the emotional rights of our children. The time has come for us to respect and support working parents. The time has come to take a good hard look at the nation's child care providers. After all, as William Ross Wallace wrote, *the hand that rocks the cradle is the hand that rules the world.*

It's time to enact child care reform.

Notes

INTRODUCTION

1. Names and identities of persons have been changed.

CHAPTER 1

1. Daniel Goleman, *Emotional Intelligence: Why It Can Matter More Than IQ* (New York: Bantam, 1995).

2. T. Berry Brazelton and Stanley I. Greenspan, *The Irreducible Needs of Children: What Every Child Must Have to Grow, Learn, and Flourish* (Cambridge, MA: A Merloyd Lawrence Book, Da Capo Press, Perseus Books Group, 2000), 39.

3. Pat Wingert and Martha Brant, "Your Baby's Brain: New Research; From Jealousy to Joy: How Science Is Unlocking the Inner Lives of Infants," *Newsweek*, August 15, 2005, 36.

4. Ibid., 39.

5. Ibid., 38.

6. Sue Gerhardt, *Why Love Matters: How Affection Shapes a Baby's Brain* (London: Routledge, 2004), 217.

7. "Child Neglect," American Humane Association, http://www.americanhumane.org/children/stop-child-abuse/fact-sheets/child-neglect.html.

8. Gerhardt, *Why Love Matters*, 41.

9. Karen Kaufman, PhD, LCSW, interview with the author, 2013.

10. Gerhardt, *Why Love Matters*, 211.

11. "Occupational Outlook Handbook: Childcare Workers," Bureau of Labor Statistics, http://www.bls.gov/ooh/personal-care-and-service/childcare-workers.htm.

12. "Mission statement," International Nanny Association, http://www.nanny.org/about-us/mission/.

13. Ibid.

14. Linda Burnham, Nik Theodore, and Barbara Ehrenreich, "Home Economics: The Invisible and Unregulated World of Domestic Work," National Domestic Workers Alliance, 2012, http://www.domesticworkers.org/sites/default/files/HomeEconomicsEnglish.pdf.

15. Hillary Rodham Clinton, *It Takes a Village: And Other Lessons Children Teach Us* (New York: Simon and Schuster, 1995, 2006), 210.

16. "US Licensure Organizations: The Importance of a Professional License in the US," University Language Services, http://www.universitylanguage.com/guides/getting-a-professional-license-through-us-licensure-organizations/.

17. Clinton, *It Takes a Village,* 216.

18. "Occupations Licensed or Certified by New York State," New York State Department of Labor, Labor Statistics, http://labor.ny.gov/stats/lstrain.shtm.

19. Sue Gerhardt, *The Selfish Society: How We All Forgot to Love One Another and Made Money Instead* (London: Simon and Schuster, 2010), 209.

20. "Employment Characteristics of Families Summary 2013," United States Department of Labor, Bureau of Labor Statistics, http://www.bls.gov/news.release/famee.nr0.htm.

21. "Public Opinion", Pew Research Social and Demographic Trends, http://www.pewsocialtrends.org/2014/04/08/after-decades-of-decline-a-rise-in-stay-at-home-mothers/#public-opinion.

22. Ibid.

23. Sarah Coles, "Nicola Horlick 'Superwoman': You Can't Have It All," AOL UK, October 25, 2014, http://money.aol.co.uk/2014/10/25/nicola-horlick-superwoman-you-can-t-have-it-all/.

24. Karen Kaufman, PhD, LCSW, interview with the author, 2013.

CHAPTER 2

1. Arlie Russell Hochschild, *So How's the Family? And Other Essays* (Oakland: University of California Press, 2013), 25.

2. Michelle LaRowe, interview with the author, 2014.

3. Marni Kent, interview with the author, 2014.

4. Sarah Schweitzer, "Much to Check before Entrusting a Child's Care," *Boston Globe,* January 23, 2013, http://www.bostonglobe.com/metro/2013/01/23/navigating-path-nanny-fraught-process-for-parents/skyiEb4IBPffG3sbaYbpIJ/story.html.

5. Jennifer Quaggin, *The Other Secret: How to Recover from Emotional Abuse and Live the Life You've Always Wanted* (Bloomington, IN: IUniverse Books, 2012), 56.

6. "Brenda" is an anonymous nanny known to the author.

7. Material adapted from the blog I Saw Your Nanny, http://isawyournanny .blogspot.com.

8. Kenneth Lau, Kathryn Krase, and Richard H. Morse, *Mandated Reporting of Child Abuse and Neglect: A Practical Guide for Social Workers* (New York: Springer, 2009), 33.

9. Quaggin, *The Other Secret,* 55–56.

10. Name and nationality changed. Celeste's nationality does not indicate that this is typical of foreign nannies.

11. *Page Six* weekend magazine, *New York Post* (February 24, 2008).

12. Ibid.

13. Not her real name. Marjorie is a fictional character created from anecdotes and observations gathered by the author.

14. Abigail Pogrebin, "Nanny Scam," *New York Magazine,* http://nymag.com /nymetro/urban/family/features/9527/.

15. Ibid.

16. Darren Perron, "Accused Nanny: Pedophile Activist?," WCAX-TV, Burlington, June 18, 2009, http://www.wcax.com/story/10557718/accused-nanny -pedophile-activist.

17. "Signs of a Bad Nanny," January 2012, Baby Center, http://www.babycenter .com/0_signs-of-a-bad-nanny_5945.bc.

CHAPTER 3

1. Not their real names.

2. Anonymous nanny known to the author, 2014.

3. Anonymous nanny known to the author, 2014.

4. Ai-jen Poo, NDWA director, interview with the author, 2014.

5. Not her real name.

6. An anonymous person known to the author, 2014.

7. T. Berry Brazleton and Stanley I. Greenspan, *The Irreducible Needs of Children: What Every Child Must Have to Grow, Learn, and Flourish* (Cambridge, MA: A Merloyd Lawrence Book, Da Capo Press, Perseus Books Group, 2000), xiii.

8. Not their real names.

9. Anonymous nanny known to the author, 2014.

10. Anonymous nanny known to the author, 2014.

11. Emma McLaughlin and Nicola Kraus, *The Nanny Diaries* (New York: St. Martin's Griffin, 2002), 12.

12. Anonymous nanny known to author, 2014.

13. Karen Kaufman, PhD, LCSW, interview with the author, 2014.

14. Annabelle Corke, interview with the author, 2014.

15. Anonymous nanny known to author, 2014.

16. Not her real name.

17. Anonymous nanny known to author, 2014.

18. Not her real name.

19. Anonymous nanny known to author, 2014.

CHAPTER 4

1. Annabelle Corke, interview with the author, 2014.

2. Geraldine Youcha, *Minding the Children: Child Care in America from Colonial Times to the Present* (Cambridge, MA: Perseus, 2005), 45–66.

3. Sarah Griffiths, "Want Your Child's Attention? Speak with an Accent: Children Listen Harder to the Queen's English Than an American Drawl," *The Daily Mail*, November 20, 2014, http://www.dailymail.co.uk/sciencetech/article-2842376/Want-child-s-attention-Speak-British-accent-Children-listen-harder-Queen-s-English-American-drawl.html.

4. Not her real name.

5. Anonymous nanny known to the author, 2014.

6. Anonymous nanny known to the author, 2014.

7. Nandi Keyi, *The True Nanny Diaries* (Brooklyn, NY: Bread for Brick, 2009), 52.

8. Nandi Keyi, interview with the author, 2014.

9. Susan L. Blake, review of Micki McElya's *Clinging to Mammy: The Faithful Slave in Twentieth-Century America*, in *African American Review* 43 (2–3) (Summer–Fall 2009): 537–539, http://muse.jhu.edu/journals/afa/summary/v043/43.2-3.blake.html.

10. "More Slavery at the South, by a Negro Nurse," *The Independent* [New York], January 25, 1912, University of North Carolina at Chapel Hill, Documenting the American South, http://docsouth.unc.edu/fpn/negnurse/negnurse.html.

11. Vanessa May and Rebecca Sharpless, "Historians on 'The Help': Respond," University of North Carolina Press Blog, August 24, 2011, http://uncpressblog.com/2011/08/24/historians-on-the-help-vanessa-may-and-rebecca-sharpless-respond/.

12. Roxane Gay, *Bad Feminist Essays* (New York: HarperCollins, 2014), 208.

13. Keyi, *The True Nanny Diaries*, 52.

14. Not her real name.

15. Anonymous nanny known to the author, 2014.

16. Po Bronson and Ashley Merryman, *NurtureShock: New Thinking about Children* (New York: Twelve, 2009).

17. The Petra Foundation, http://petrafoundation.org/fellows/nahar-alam/.

18. Nahar Alam, interview with the author, 2014.

19. Not her real name.

20. Anonymous nanny known to the author.

21. Karen Kaufman, PhD, LCSW, interview with the author, 2014.

22. Anonymous nanny known to the author, 2014.

CHAPTER 5

1. Jacalyn S. Burke, The Nanny Time Bomb, October 29, 2012, http:// thenannytimebomb.blogspot.com.

2. "Elzbieta Plackowska, Naperville Babysitter, Charged in 'Demonic' Stabbing Death of 2 Children," *Huffington Post*, November 1, 2012, http://www .huffingtonpost.com/2012/11/01/elzbieta-plackowska-naperville-babysitter_n _2056303.html.

3. "Jury Makes Unprecedented Request to Hug Parents of Dead Baby after His 'Manipulative' Nanny, 25, Is Found Guilty of Shaking Him to Death," *Daily Mail*, March 15, 2014, http://www.dailymail.co.uk/news/article-2581941 /Sarah-Cullen-trial-Jury-makes-unprecedented-request-hug-parents-dead-baby -manipulative-nanny-25-guilty-shaking-death.html.

4. Karen Miles, "Abusive Head Trauma (Shaken Baby Syndrome)," Baby Center LLC, May 2013, http://www.babycenter.com/0_abusive-head-trauma-shaken -baby-syndrome_1501729.bc.

5. Sara Rimer, "British Nanny Found Guilty of Murder in Baby's Death," *New York Times,* October 31, 1997, http://www.nytimes.com/1997/10/31/us/british -nanny-found-guilty-of-murder-in-baby-s-death.html.

6. Not her real name.

7. Not her real name.

8. Interview with anonymous parent known to the author, 2014.

9. Emma McLaughlin and Nicola Kraus, *The Nanny Diaries* (New York: St. Martin's Griffin, 2002), 241.

10. Not her real name.

11. Anonymous nanny known to author, 2014.

12. Anonymous nanny known to author, 2014.

13. "John Bowlby (1907–1990)," Good Therapy, http://www.goodtherapy.org /famous-psychologists/john-bowlby.html.

14. "Adult Attachment Disorder & Treatment," Evergreen Consultants in Human Behavior, http://attachmenttherapy.com/adult.htm.

CHAPTER 6

1. Julia Quinn-Szcesuil, "How to Set Up Health Insurance for a Nanny," Care.com, https://www.care.com/homepay/how-to-set-up-health-insurance-for -a-nanny-1307121554.

2. Lisa Belkin, "Knowing Noreen," *New York Times Magazine,* January 7.

3. Ibid.

4. Jennifer Johnston, "Nanny Cam Tells the Story That a Baby Could Not," *Daniel Island News*, April 1, 2014, http://www.thedanielislandnews.com/artman2/publish /Top_Stories_69/Nanny_cam_tells_the_story_that_a_baby_could_not.php.

5. "Nanny Cameras," Spytech, http://www.spytecinc.com/nanny-cam-guide/.

6. Brooke Chateauneuf, "Nanny Cam: Yes or No?," Care.com, https://www
.care.com/a/nanny-cam-yes-or-no-1209271139.

7. "Nanny Cams Protect What Matters Most," BrickHouse Security, http://
www.brickhousesecurity.com/category/hidden+cameras/nanny+cams.do?gclid
=CjwKEAiAh7WkBRCQj.

8. Ibid.

9. Ibid.; "Baby Shakers Beware: Video Surveillance Not Just for the Government,"
BrichHouse Security, http://blog.brickhousesecurity.com/baby-shakers-beware
-video-surveillance-not-just-for-the-government/.

10. Chris Golis, "Brief History of Emotional Intelligence," 2013, Practical
Emotional Intelligence, http://www.emotionalintelligencecourse.com/eq-history.

11. Stanley I. Greenspan and Jacqueline Salmon, The Four-Thirds Solution
(Cambridge, MA: Perseus, 2001), 33–36, 73, 163–165, 181–202, 212–213.

12. Greenspan and Salmon, The Four-Thirds Solution.

13. Allan C. Carlson, "The Fractured Dream of Social Parenting," November 3,
2003, The Howard Center, http://profam.org/docs/acc/thc_acc_frc_dream.htm.

14. Ann Douglas, Choosing Childcare for Dummies (New York: Simon and
Schuster Macmillan, 1998).

15. Allan C. Carlson, "The Fractured Dream of Social Parenting: A 'Short
Version' for the Family Research Council Symposium on Child Care," The Howard
Center for Family, Religion & Society, November 3, 2003, http://profam.org/docs
/acc/thc_acc_frc_dream.htm.

16. Douglas, Choosing Childcare for Dummies.

17. Explore + Discover, interview with cofounder Daniel Koffler, 2014.

CHAPTER 7

1. Home Economics: The Invisible and Unregulated World of Domestic Work
(Chicago: National Domestic Workers Alliance, Center for Urban Economic
Development, University of Illinois at Chicago, 2012), http://www.domesticworkers
.org/sites/default/files/HomeEconomicsEnglish.pdf.

2. Stanley I. Greenspan and Jacqueline Salmon, The Four-Thirds Solution
(Cambridge, MA: Perseus, 2001) (my emphasis).

3. Ibid. (my emphasis).

4. "How Much do I Pay a Nanny?," Nannies 4 Hire, http://www.nannies4hire
.com/tips/1045-how-much-do-i-pay-a-nanny.htm.

5. John C. Goodman, "Statement on Modern Families; Outdated Laws," January
31, 2007, National Center for Policy Analysis, http://www.ncpa.org/speech
/statement-on-modern-families-outdated-laws.

6. Kimberley A. Strassel, Celeste Colgan, and John C. Goodman, Leaving
Women Behind (Lanham, MD: Rowman and Littlefield, 2006), 22.

7. Wendy Wang, Kim Parker, and Paul Taylor, "Breadwinner Moms," Pew Research Center, May 29, 2013, http://www.pewsocialtrends.org/2013/05/29/breadwinner-moms/.

8. "Tax Relief for Child Care Should Be Maintained," National Center for Policy Analysis, March 6, 2013, http://www.ncpa.org/sub/dpd/index.php?Article_ID=22915.

9. Kathleen Webb, HomeWork Solutions, interview with the author, 2014.

10. Ai-jen Poo, interview with the author, 2014.

11. Dan Berger, Curran & Berger LLP, interview with the author, 2014.

12. Alena Shautsova, Alena Shautsova Law Office, interview with the author, 2014.

13. Ibid.

14. Ibid.

15. Dan Berger, Curran & Berger LLP, interview with the author, 2014.

16. Geraldine Youcha, *Minding the Children: Child Care in America from Colonial Times to the Present* (Cambridge, MA: Perseus, 2005), 17–44, 211–264, 307–335.

17. Ibid., 335.

18. William Martin, *What Liberals Believe* (New York: Skyhorse Publishing, 2008), 321; "Celina R. De Leon: The State of the American Mom," Feministing, September 14, 2006, http://www.feministing.com./; Kristen Rowe-Finkbeiner and Joan Blades, *The Motherhood Manifesto* (New York: Nation Books, 2006).

19. Marni Kent, interview with the author, 2014.

Bibliography

Auerbach, Jessika. *And Nanny Makes Three: Mothers and Nannies Tell the Truth about Work, Love, Money, and Each Other.* New York: St. Martin's, 2007.

Bapat, Sheila. *Part of the Family: Nannies, Housekeepers, Caregivers, and the Battle of Domestic Workers' Rights.* Brooklyn: IG Publishing, 2014.

Big Apple Parent, May 2006, 67.

Blades, Joan, and Kristen Rowe-Finkbeiner. *The Motherhood Manifesto: What America's Moms Want—And What to Do about it.* New York: Nation Books, 2006.

Blaine, Tasha. *Just Like Family: Inside the Lives of Nannies, the Parents They Work For, and the Children They Love.* Boston: Houghton Mifflin Harcourt, 2009.

Brazelton, T. Berry, and Stanley I. Greenspan. *The Irreducible Needs of Children: What Every Child Must Have to Grow, Learn, and Flourish.* Cambridge, MA: Perseus, 2000.

Cancelmo, Joseph A., and Carol Bandini. *Child Care for Love or Money? A Guide to Navigating the Parent-Caregiver Relationship.* New York: Jason Aronson, 1999.

Carlton, Susan, and Coco Myers. *The Nanny Book: The Smart Parent's Guide to Hiring, Firing, and Every Sticky Situation in Between.* New York: St. Martin's Griffin, 1999.

Carroll, Deborah, and Stella Reid. *Nanny 911: Expert Advice for All Your Parenting Emergencies.* New York: HarperCollins, 2005.

"Childcare Workers." Bureau of Labor Statistics, January 8, 2014, http://www.bls.gov/ooh/Personal-Care-and-Service/Childcare-workers.htm.

Chomsky, Noam. *Power Systems.* New York: Metropolitan Books, Henry Holt, 2013.

Clinton, Hillary. *It Takes a Village: And Other Lessons Children Teach Us.* New York: Simon and Schuster, 1995.

Douglas, Ann. *Choosing Childcare for Dummies.* Hoboken, NJ: Wiley, 2004.

Douglas, Ann. *The Unofficial Guide to Childcare.* New York: Simon and Schuster Macmillan, 1998.

Frost, Jo. *Jo Frost's Confident Baby Care: What You Need to Know for the First Year from America's Most Trusted Nanny.* New York: Hyperion, 2008.

Gerhardt, Sue. *The Selfish Society: How We Forgot to Love One Another and Made Money Instead.* London: Simon and Schuster, 2010.

Gerhardt, Sue. *Why Love Matters: How Affection Shapes a Baby's Brain.* London: Routledge, 2004.

Greenspan, Stanley I., and Jacqueline Salmon. *The Four-Thirds Solution: Solving the Childcare Crisis in America Today.* Cambridge, MA: Perseus, 2001.

Goleman, Daniel. *Emotional Intelligence: Why It Can Matter More Than IQ.* New York: Bantam, 1995.

International Herald Tribune, April 11, 2007, 22.

Kaylin, Lucy. *The Perfect Stranger: The Truth about Mothers and Nannies.* New York: Bloomsbury, 2007.

Keyi, Nandi. *The True Nanny Diaries.* Brooklyn, NY: Bread for Brick, 2009.

Lau, Kenneth J., Kathryn Krase, and Richard Morse. *Mandated Reporting of Child Abuse and Neglect: A Practical Guide for Social Workers.* New York: Springer, 2009.

Lindner, Melanie. "The Most Important Hire You'll Ever Make." Forbes, July 2014, http://www.forbes.com/2008/03/20/child-care-nanny-ent-hr-cx_ml _0320hirenanny.html.

McLaughlin, Emma, and Nicola Kraus. *The Nanny Diaries.* New York: St. Martin's Griffin, 2002.

Merchant, A. M. *The Nanny Textbook: The Professional Nanny Guide to Child Care 2003.* Lincoln, NE: Writer's Showcase, 2003.

New York Times Magazine, January 7, 2007, 39.

New York Sun, February 27, 2007, 3.

"Page Six Magazine." *New York Post,* February 24, 2008, 18.

Pippert, Julie. "New Study Reveals Importance of Comprehensive Maternity Leave, Brings up Questions about Tie between Leave and Fair Pay." Momocrats, January 9, 2009, http://momocrats.typepad.com/momocrats/2009/01/new -study-revea.html.

Quaggin, Jennifer. *The Other Secret: How to Recover from Emotional Abuse and Live the Life You've Always Wanted.* Bloomington, IN: IUniverse Books, 2012.

The Record [UK], October 14, 2006, cover story.

Russell Hochschild, Arlie. *So How's the Family? (And Other Essays).* Berkeley: University of California Press, 2013.

Russell Hochschild, Arlie, and Barbara Ehrenreich. *Global Woman, Nannies, Maids, and Sex Workers in the New Economy.* New York: Holt Paperbacks, 2004.

Russianoff, Penelope. *When Am I Going to Be Happy? How to Break the Emotional Bad Habits That Make You Miserable.* New York: Bantam, 1989.

Strassel, Kimberley A., Celeste Colgan, and John C. Goodman. *Leaving Women Behind: Modern Families, Outdated Laws.* Lanham, MD: Rowman and Littlefield, 2007.

Sunday Telegraph, November 27, 2005, 13.

Thompson, Rosemary. *Nurturing Future Generations: Promoting Resilience in Children and Adolescents through Social, Emotional, and Cognitive Skills.* New York: Routledge, 2006.

Wall Street Journal, October 24, 2006, D3.

Wiggans, Helburn, Suzanne, and Barbara R. Bergmann. *America's Child Care Problem: The Way Out.* New York: Palgrave Macmillan, 2003.

Wingert Pat, and Martha Brant. "Your Baby's Brain: New Research; From Jealousy to Joy: How Science Is Unlocking the Inner Lives of Infants." *Newsweek,* August 15, 2005, 36.

Youcha, Geraldine. *Minding the Children: Childcare in America from Colonial Times to the Present.* Cambridge, MA: Perseus, 2005.

Resources

Nanny Advocacy Organizations and Professional Associations

NDWA

The National Domestic Workers Alliance (NDWA), http://www.domestic-workers.org/, is the nation's leading voice for dignity and fairness for the millions of domestic workers in the United States, most of whom are women.

DWU

The Domestic Workers United (DWU), http://www.domesticworker-sunited.org, is an organization of Caribbean, Latina, and African nannies, housekeepers, and elderly caregivers in New York organizing for power, respect, and fair labor standards and to help build a movement to end exploitation and oppression for all.

Sakhi

Sakhi for South Asian Women, http://www.sakhi.org, exists to end violence against women. Sakhi unites survivors, communities, and institutions to eradicate domestic violence as it works to create strong and healthy communities. Sakhi uses an integrated approach that combines support and empowerment through service delivery, community engagement, advocacy, and policy initiatives.

International Nanny Association

The International Nanny Association (INA), http://www.nanny.org, serves as the umbrella association for the in-home child care industry by providing information, education, and guidance to the public and to industry professionals.

Nanny Van

Nanny Van, http://www.nannyvan.org, created by REV (lead artist Marisa Jahn) in collaboration with the National Domestic Workers Alliance, is a bright orange mobile design lab and sound studio that "accelerates the movement for domestic workers' rights nationwide."

Studio REV, www.studiorev.org, is a nonprofit studio whose public art projects combine creativity, bold ideas, and sound research to address critical issues. The studio's women- and minority-led team of artists, techies, media makers, low-wage workers, immigrants, and teens produce work to impact the issues we face.

IDWF

International Domestic Workers Federation (IDWF), http://www.idwfed.org/en, is a membership-based global organization of domestic and household workers. A domestic or household worker is any person engaged in domestic work within an employment relationship. The IDWF believes that domestic work is work and that all domestic and household workers deserve to enjoy the same rights as all other workers.

Hand in Hand

Hand in Hand, http://domesticemployers.org, is a national network of employers of nannies, house cleaners, and home attendants, our families and allies, who are grounded in the conviction that dignified and respectful working conditions benefit worker and employer alike. Hand in Hand envisions a future where people live in caring communities that recognize all of our interdependence, supports employers to improve their employment practices, and collaborates with workers to change cultural norms and public policies that bring dignity and respect to domestic workers and all of our communities.

Employer Payroll and Tax Services

HomeWork Solutions

HomeWork Solutions, http://www.homeworksolutions.com, is where family turn to for outsourcing nanny tax compliance when they privately hire a nanny or caregiver.

Nanny Agencies

Hey Day Nannies

Hey Day Nannies, http://www.heydaynannies.com, was founded in 2007 out of the glaring need for one-on-one help with the process. Heyday's president, Annabelle Corke, makes it her mission to conduct targeted searches based not only on logistics but also on corresponding child-rearing styles and values. Heyday has recruiters identify outstanding individuals from a variety of ever-changing sources, including our own busy website.

Immigration Offices

Curran & Berger LLP

Curran & Berger LLP, http://curranberger.com.

The Law Office of Alena Shautsova

The Law Office of Alena Shautsova, http://www.shautsova.com.

Parent Advocacy Groups

Moms Rising

Moms Rising, http://www.momsrising.org. First a handful of women came together, that handful became hundreds and then thousands, and then through friends telling friends Moms Rising is now more than 1 million members strong and growing. Moms Rising take on the most critical issues facing women, mothers, and families by educating the public and mobilizing massive grassroots actions.

Nanny Cams

Brick House Security

Brick House Security, http://www.brickhousesecurity.com.

Spy Tech

Spy Tech, http://www.spytecinc.com.

Experts Interviewed for This Book

Psychology

Karen Kaufman

Karen Kaufman, PhD, LCSW, has worked in the field of mental health for more than 30 years. She works in private practice with adults and children in Manhattan and Westchester and was on the faculty of Fordham University Graduate School of Social Service/Westchester Division for 16 years until 2014. She has had her work published in the Clinical Social Work Journal, *Big Apple Parent* and *Westchester Parent*.

Domestic Workers

Ai-jen Poo

Ai-jen Poo is a labor organizer whose compelling vision of the value of home-based care work is transforming the landscape of working conditions and labor standards for domestic and private-household workers. She is the director of the National Domestic Workers Alliance (NDWA) and codirector of the Caring Across Generations campaign and has been organizing immigrant women workers since 1996. In 2000 she cofounded Domestic Workers United, the New York organization that spearheaded the successful passage of the state's historic Domestic Workers Bill of Rights in 2010. She is also a fellow of the MacArthur Foundation.

Payroll and Tax

Kathleen Webb

Kathleen Webb cofounded HomeWork Solutions, http://www.home-worksolutions.com, in 1993 to provide payroll and tax services to families employing household workers. Webb has extensive experience preparing nanny tax payroll taxes. She is the author of numerous articles on this topic and has been featured in the *Wall Street Journal, Kiplinger's Personal Finance,* and the *Congressional Quarterly.* She also consulted with Senate staffers in the drafting of the 1994 Nanny Tax Law. Webb is a magna cum laude graduate of Boston College. She currently serves as copresident of the International Nanny Association, the leading professional association in the in-home child care industry.

Professional Child Care/Nannies

Michelle LaRowe

Michelle LaRowe, www.MichelleLaRowe.com, was the 2004 International Nanny Association's Nanny of the Year. She is the author of *Nanny to the Rescue!* and *Working Mom's 411.* LaRowe is also the editor in chief of eNannySource.com and the executive director of Morningside Nannies.

Marni Kent

Marni Kent, Marni@thenannymentor.expert, is a career nanny with over 28 years of service. She currently resides in San Francisco, California. She has held jobs as a household nanny and a baby nurse. She currently travels frequently with her executive employer and infant charge. Kent is the 2002 International Nanny Association's Nanny of the Year and authored the INA Mentor/Protege program. She is active in the nanny community and has spoken at the Denver Area Nanny Conference, the INA conference, and Nannypalooza.

Immigration Law

Dan Berger

Dan Berger, http://curranberger.com.

Alena Shautsova

Alena Shautsova, http://www.shautsova.com.

Index

ABC, 131

abuse, 2, 15–16, 30, 87; day care, 100; emotional, 34–35; evidence of, 133–134; help with, 134; how to deal with, 133–134; of nannies, 13–16, 85, 92–93, 111; outside the home, 131; physical abuse, 42–43, 95–100, 129; preventing, 43–46; psychological damage caused by, 134–135; reporting, 134; revenge for, 135; risk factors, 44–46; signs of, 42–43, 128–129, 132–133; suspecting, 133; therapy for, 134–135; verbal, 133

abusive head trauma (AHT), 98–99; preventing, 100

activities, 4, 23; reviewing, 137–138; scheduling, 136–137. *See also* creativity

affection, 5, 7

Affordable Care Act (Obamacare), 126

Alam, Nahar, 85–87, 163, 167

Alena Shautsova Law Office, 165

altruism, 5

Andolan, 85–88, 163

anger, 57, 64, 99

apathetic nannies, 4, 31–32; daily checklist for, 135–137

Ashland, Barbara, 26

assisted living, 52

attachment disorders, 110–114

attachment theory, 113, 150

au pairs, 9, 26, 37, 99, 116; getting the best from, 138–139

authority, resisting caregiver's, 18–21

awkward moments with family, 63–64

Baby Center LLC, 98–99

babysitters, 25–27, 30, 52, 89, 96, 107, 115; college, 138–139; getting the best from, 138–139; immature, 36–38; short-term, 138–139

background checks, 15–16, 39, 43–44; conducting your own, 100, 168; forgoing, 118; hidden dangers, 99–100

behavior, reinforcing positive, 4–5

Belkins, Lisa, 128–135

Bell, Cash, 98–99

Berger, Dan, 165, 167

Big Apple Parent, 6

Blake, Susan L., 78

body image, 141–142

body language, 122
bonding, 61, 63–64, 108–110, 112
bonuses, 10
boundaries, 65–66; professional, 55,
    56–57; setting for children, 19–20
Bowlby, Edward John Mostyn, 113
Bramdean Asset Management, 18
Brazelton, T. Berry, 3, 54
breast-feeding, 16, 26, 115, 146, 149
Bronson, Po, 82
Bureau of Educational and Cultural
    Affairs of the Department of
    State, 9
Bureau of Labor Statistics, 9
burned-out nannies, 32–34, 58–60

Caring Across Generations, 165
Certified Nurse's Aide certification,
    51–52
The Challenging Child, 143
child abuse registry, 132
child care; caste system, 67–74; Civil
    War, 170–171; federal support of,
    18, 100, 170–171; Gilded Age, 69–71,
    170; Great Depression, 170; history
    of, 69–71, 169–170; reform, 100, 144,
    151–176; regulation of, 8–11
Child Development Associate
    credentials, 14
child labor, 93
childhood development, 28
Civil Rights Act, 80
Civil War, 170–171
clean-up games, 142
Clinging to Mammy, 78
Clinical Social Work Journal, 6
Clinton, Hillary, 14
coercion, 100–107
collective nurseries, 143–144
communication, nanny-parent,
    27, 61
confidence, 61
confinement, 7
conflicted parents, 16–17
consistency, 6–7, 66

contracts, 11, 106; agreed upon
    responsibilities, 124; confidentiality
    clause, 124; creating, 123–124;
    dismissal and resignation, 125;
    household rules and personal
    standards, 124; standard
    employment agreements, 13;
    termination of employment, 124
Corke, Annabelle, 61, 68
Cornell University, 4
corruption, 6
CPR Certification, 9, 99, 138. See also
    nanny(ies), licenses
creativity, 61, 139, 150
crèche, 143–144
credit history, 43–44. See also
    background checks
criminal, 132–135; history, 119–120;
    nannies, 2, 38–46, 132–133
Croombs, Kevin, 71
Cullen, Sarah, 98–100
Curan & Berger LLP, 165

Daniel Island News, 129
day care, 100, 135, 143–150, 174;
    affordable, 172; child-to-adult
    ratio, 145, 147, 149; discipline
    methods used, 148; environment,
    144, 147; hygiene issues, 144, 146,
    149; location, 145; nutrition, 147,
    150; privacy, 144; schedule,
    149–150; security, 145–146;
    staff training, 146–147, 150;
    staff turnover, 147; taxes and,
    158
defiance, children's, 19
denial, 53
Department of Homeland Security, 8
Department of Justice National Sex
    Offender Database, 41
Department of Labor, 8, 161
depression, 4, 7, 96; children's, 19
diplomatic immunity, 88, 166
disengaged nannies, 3
disrespect in the workplaces, 13–16

domestic workers, 12–13, 51–52,
    87–88; H1D visa, 166–167; visa
    interviews, 165
double standards, 59
duties, 155; bait-and-switch, 55;
    leaving out information about, 55
dysfunctional relating, 5–6

Eappen, Mathew, 99–100
early childhood development
    degrees, 8. *See also* nanny(ies),
    licenses
emotional intelligence (EQ), 3, 139;
    definition of, 139–140; teaching,
    140–150, 145
empathy, showing, 5, 112
European cultural superiority,
    69–71. *See also* white
    privilege
expectations, 106; clear, 27, 126–127;
    unclear, 27
exploitation, 6, 80, 87
Explore + Discover, 148–149

Fair Labor Standards Act, 157–158
fathers, roles and activities of,
    17, 172
Ferber method, 122, 146
financial hardship, 12, 96
flexibility, 28, 172
flextime, 158
floor time, 142–143
fool's errands, 55, 59. *See also*
    micromanaging
The Four-Third's Solution, 143, 154
Fox, James Alan, 30
frustration, 99; children, 19–20

Gay, Roxanne, 80–81
Gerhardt, Sue, 5–7, 16
gifts, 156
Goldstein, Michael, 4
Goleman, Daniel, 2
Goodman, John C., 157
gossip, 106

Great Depression, 157, 170
green card, 52, 91; fast-track,
    166–168
Greenspan, Stanley I., xix, 3–4, 54,
    142–143, 154
guilt, 57, 100–107

Hashmi, Razia, 86–87
health insurance, 91, 125–126, 156.
    See also nanny(ies), benefits
The Help, 79–81
Hey Day Nannies, 61, 68
holidays, 23–24
Horlick, Nicola, 17–18
Hoschild, Arlie Russell, 17, 25
Housekeepers, 12, 26, 80, 89,
    137–138
human rights, 93
Hurricane Sandy, 96
hustling, 47–53

ignoring, 5
immigrants: Caribbean nannies,
    xviii–xix, 76–83; Filipina, Thai, and
    Tibetan nannies, 84–88; Hispanic
    nannies, 91–93; Sri Lankan nannies,
    88–91
immigration reform, 83, 88, 93,
    162–168, 173
impulsive nannies, 3
incentives, 154–155
independence, building, 28
infants: anxiety, 6; brains, 2–4;
    development, 4–5; emotional
    vulnerability, 2; facial interaction,
    4, 6; gaze-following, 4; intrinsic
    needs of, 2–8; language skills, 4;
    newborn, 2; stress, 6; institutional
    slavery, 79
Internal Revenue Service, 156, 158,
    161–162
International Nanny Association
    (INA), 8–9, 11, 13, 26; Annual
    Conference, 27; Basic Skills Exam, 9;
    Nanny of the Year, 26–30

interviews, nanny, 103, 116–117,
    120–129; questions to ask during,
    120–122
The Irreducible Needs of Children, 3
isolation, 5. *See also* abuse
It Takes a Village, 14

jealousy, 60–61
job creep, 27, 47–53, 57, 74
job security, 30
Johnston, Jennifer, 129
journaling, 136

Kaufman, Karen, 6–7, 20, 60
Kent, Marni, 28–30, 174–175
Keyi, Nandi, 76–77
Koffler, Daniel, 148–149
Krim, Kevin and Marina, xxii,
    96–97, 101
Kuhl, Patricia, 4
Kytle, Elizabeth, 80

Lanham Act, 170
Lanham Centers, 170–171
LaRowe, Michelle, 26–28
Loss, sense of (children's), 19
low performance nannies, 16

maids, 70–71
mammies, 77–82
management, 135–150
mannies, 26, 115–116
Mary Poppins, 68–70, 72
maternity leave, 18, 172
Matney, Whitney, 131–132
McElya, Micki, 78
Medema, Melissa, 131–132
Meltzoff, Andrew, 4
mental illness, 2, 96–98, 128–129
Merryman, Ashley, 82
micromanaging, 54, 74, 108
Miles, Karen, 98–99
milestones, developmental 4,
    127–128, 140–142
Minding the Children, 69, 171

mommy blogs, 97
Morgan Grenfell Asset Management, 18
mothers, public opinion about
    working, 17-18
murder, 30, 95–100. *See also* abuse

Nanny Credential Exam, 9. *See also*
    nanny(ies), licenses
nanny(ies): agencies, 99, 116, 155;
    archetypes, 25–46; aspects of
    job, 10–11; benefits, 10, 12–13,
    125–126; career, 11, 28, 30, 74;
    class, 72–76, 81–82; daily schedule,
    152–153; definition of, 25, 115–116;
    educated, 67, 71, 107; elite, 75–76;
    firing, 13, 105–106, 108; full-time,
    100–101; meeting with, 116–117;
    hierarchies of, xxi, 81–82; hours,
    115; identification, 120; information
    packs for, 127; interaction with
    child, 117; licenses, 14–15, 83–84;
    live-in, 62–63, 108–110, 155;
    long-term, 100; not-so-good,
    30–38; pensions, 52; performance
    enhancement, 139; performance,
    transforming, 135–150; profile of,
    9–10, 117; relationships with family,
    27, 29, 106–107; replacing, 126–127;
    resources, 29, 85–87; screening,
    43–44; stereotypes, 68–69; tips,
    29–30; training, 135–150; vacations,
    33, 104; where to find, 116; white,
    xxi, 74–75
nanny cams, 40–41, 100, 128–135;
    disclosing, 129–130; horror
    stories, 131–133; legal issues, 131;
    troubleshooting, 131; types of, 130;
    where to put, 130
The Nanny Diaries, 58, 67, 71–72, 107,
    110
Nanny 911, 71
National Center for Policy Analysis,
    157
National Domestic Workers Alliance
    (NDWA), 12–13, 53, 152, 163–164

National Institute of Child Health and Development, 144
negativity, 3
neglect, 1–12, 57, 133, 138. *See also* abuse
New York Magazine, 38
New York Post, Page Six, 36–37
New York Times, xxii, 128
newborn care specialists, 26, 30, 100, 115
Newsweek, 3–4
nitpicking, 55, 58–60, 108. *See also* abuse, of nannies
Northeastern University, 30
NutureShock, 82

Obama, Barack, 163, 167
Ortega, Yoselyn, 96–98
The Other Secret: How to Recover from Emotional Abuse and Live the Life You've Always Wanted, 32
overattachment, 65–66. *See also* bonding
overtime, 10

parent-child relationship, supporting, 27, 29
parent message boards, 97. *See also* nanny(ies), where to find
parenting styles, 7
passive-aggressive behavior, 60, 100–107, 133
patience, 61
perfunctory nannies, 3, 35–36, 137–138
Petra Foundation, 85–87, 163
Pew Institute, 17, 158
pets, xviii, 51–52, 89. *See also* job creep
Pikler, Emmi, 150
Plackowska, Elzieta, 97–98
Plato, 143
play, 31, 140–142; meaningful, 142–143
Poo, Ai-jen, 53, 164
Pogrebin, Abigail, 38–39
potty training, 127–128, 141–142
predators, 40–42

Professional Child Care Graduates, 8
profiling, 44, 115–128
psychotic breakdowns, 97–98

Quaggin, Jennifer, 34–35
Quinn-Szcesuil, Julie, 126
Qureshi, Rana, 86

racism, xx, 72–83; in the home, 82–83
references, 38–39, 49, 52, 92, 102, 104, 128, 129; children, 119; credible, 116; criminal history, 11–120; employer, 118–119; medical, 119–120; motor vehicle, 119–120; personal, 118; requesting, 116–117; what to ask for, 118–120. *See also* background checks
resentful nannies, 7, 34–35, 106
Resources in Infant Educare (RIE), 150
Rockpool, 18
Rosewood, 81

sabotage, 53–61; definition, 54
Sakhi, 86–87
Schore, Allan, 6
Secure Communities, 163
self-worth, 28, 66
The Selfish Society, 16
shadowing, 131, 136
shaken baby syndrome, 98–99
Shautsova, Alena, 165–167
Shepherd, Douglas, 40–42
social inclusion, 82
social media, 42, 116
Socrates, 143
Sonquist, Hanne, 171
The Sound of Music, 68–70
A Spoonful of Sugar, 26
Stanford University, 29
Stockett, Kathryn, 79–80
stress, 7, 97, 104
surrogacy, 61–66, 79, 91, 110–113; definition, 62

taxes, 151–162, 165; back-tax returns, 161–162; child care credit, 158;

declaring and filing, 125, 157–160; employment, 161–162; forms, 159–160; nanny, 159, 172; penalties, 162; social security, 162; structure, 157–158
temper tantrums, 19
terrorizing behaviors, 6
thieves, 38–40
time bomb; aftermath, 97–98; avoiding, 115–150; definition of, 1; hostage takers, 95–114; risk factors, 1–24
tourist visas, 87, 91
transient workers, 12, 70
transition, 126–127
trial runs, 122–123
The True Nanny Diaries, 76–77, 81
tutor caregiver, 115–116

underperformance, factors contributing to, 30–38; undocumented workers, 30, 47–55, 77–82, 83–89, 111–112, 163–164; criminal background checks, 164; deportation, 163–164; helping, 166–167; visa interviews, 165
U.S. Citizenship and Immigration Services, 8

U.S. House Committee on Ways and Means, 157
U.S. State Department, 155
University Language Service, 14
University of California, Berkeley, 17
University of Washington, 4

wages, 9–12, 30, 74, 151–162; calculating, 154–155; gross versus net pay, 160; negotiating, 162; off the books, 160–162
Wallace, William Ross, 176
weaning, 127–128
weekends, 23–24, 109
Westchester Parent, 6
white privilege, 74–75, 81
Why Love Matters, 6
women's liberation movement, 17, 171
Woodward, Louise, 95, 99
work agreements, 27, 106. *See also* contracts
work visas, 85–87
Works Progress Administration, 170
World War II, 170–171
Wright, Willie Mae, 80

Youcha, Geraldine, 69, 171
Young, Barbara, 163

About the Author

JACALYN S. BURKE is the founder and owner of Baby Does NYC, a website focused on events, products, and services for parents of children 0–24 months old. She has been featured in the *Daily News,* NEWS12, and the Nanny News Network. Burke has worked among Manhattan's nannies since 2004. In 2012, she began consulting as a child enrichment coach. Burke is a graduate of Middlesex University, London.

CPSIA information can be obtained at www.ICGtesting.com
Printed in the USA
BVOW06*1543080816

457818BV00015B/188/P